Orlando Rodríguez Ambrosio

ONE LIFE ON THREE CONTINENTS

The adventures, successes and failures of a child, a student, a businessman and an executive moving through the world of multinational companies in several countries in America, Europe and Asia.

About the author and his published books

Dear reader, if you want to know about the author, or his published books, use the QR code to enter the Amazon.com page.

Disclaimer

This book is for literary entertainment only; readers acknowledge that the author makes no guarantees about the practical usefulness of the content.

The content of this book is inspired by real events, but has been modified for literary reasons, any similarity with companies, institutions, or people is purely coincidental.

Acknowledgments

My most sincere thanks to all those friends who did read the first draft, especially to Becky Ng, Julia Hunt, Choi Chi Shing, Serena Lam, Pierre Chartrand, Luis Guillermo Roca, María Mercedes Navarro, Rubmar González, Angélica Báez and Luisa Rangel.

The readers of the draft made an invaluable contribution, with their comments, ideas and observations, therefore, I am eternally grateful to them, however, any failure or deficiency in the text is the responsibility of the author.

Dedication

To my sister Bárbara, for her invaluable help and support, without which this project and many of the stories told in it would not have been possible.

To my mother and father, for their effort, care and teaching that made possible a life based on learning and the search for a useful and meaningful purpose.

Contents

Introduction

This book tells the life of a person born to learn and move around the world, sometimes because his family decided to do so and other times because he was open to change in a multicultural and globalized world that took him to dozens of countries on three continents.

The stories described in the text are based on real life, although details have been omitted and some names have been changed to respect the privacy of the people and institutions involved.

Each person is a world and a path full of dreams, surprises, successes, and disappointments, as is the case of the protagonist of this story, who intensely lives a long list of adventures, sometimes in the world of corporate politics and other times in the process of personal maturation in the search for his existential purpose.

The book begins with the family history of the protagonist. The second chapter onwards, it focuses on his professional life, narrating the difficulties, challenges, and satisfactions that he encounters on a long path that takes him through a few countries in Latin America, Europe, and Asia.

In the last chapters, the protagonist leaves the corporate world and begins a process of trial and error that leads him to a new paradigm that rejuvenates his energy level in the search for a useful, pleasant, and enriching existence for the last stage of his life's journey.

This book is a message of optimism for all those who want to see life as a learning adventure, traveling a path full of opportunities in each day that gives us its dawn.

THE LIFE OF AN IMMIGRANT BEGINS

4

A MARRIAGE WITH A LOT OF AGE DIFFERENCE

My mother and father met in a textile factory in the industrial zone of Bogotá when my mother was a weaver and president of the workers' union.

At that time, my father was barely 21 years old and worked as a Jacquard loom mechanic. He was a good-looking, nice, funny guy and, according to my mother, very adventurous.

My mother was a very intelligent and attractive 33-year-old woman, struggling to get ahead in a class society, with a teenage daughter from her first relationship.

Despite the age difference, the relationship worked and my parents got married at the beginning of 1947, a few months later my mother became pregnant with a pair of twins, unfortunately one of them died during childbirth.

The other baby survived and became the family's pride, but bad fate once again hit, when the baby was two years old accidentally fell into a water tank and could not be rescued in time.

THE FAMILY UNIT GETS BROKEN

This sad experience emotionally marked my mother for several years and my parent's relationship deteriorated, which prompted my father to accept a job offer in a neighboring country.

At that time, the textile industry was expanding in Venezuela and my father was offered the opportunity to work assembling looms in a new factory in Valencia, an industrial city in the center of the country.

From this contract onwards other followed, and my father saw my mother once or twice a year, but on some of the visits he left her a little gift. This is how my sister Bárbara was born in 1950 and the one who tells you this story in 1956.

At the end of 1956, my father traveled to Bogotá to meet his new offspring, and my mother gave him an ultimatum, telling him that if they didn't live together as a family, he better not come back.

THE FAMILY MOVES TO VENEZUELA

After my first birthday, at the end of 1957 my mother, my two sisters and I landed in the city of Valencia to live with my father in a house that the company had assigned him.

The house was simple but very comfortable, it had a huge patio at the entrance with a gigantic mango tree, which was the source of some of my problems during my childhood.

I don't remember much about my first two years except for one incident where my mother washed me down with cold water at the sink in a restaurant where we went for roast chicken on Sundays, at that time there were no disposable diapers.

From the age of three, I remember sitting in the afternoons next to the mango tree with a dachshund dog named "Canduchas", waiting for my father to come home from work.

When my father opened the gate to the street, he would start to whistle, and Canduchas would run out to meet him, but he would always get entangled with something and roll on the ground. This image was repeated almost every day and I would die laughing.

At that time, the usual family entertainment after dinner was all of us sitting in the living room listening to soap operas on the radio while my father drank a few beers, my mother knitted some articles of clothing, Bárbara made her homework and, I played with the dog next to mother.

MY FATHER BUY OUR FIRST TV

My sister Bárbara and I had a good relationship, she always took care of me and was aware of me, but she was very naughty and always got into trouble, I remember that sometimes she secretly took me to watch the Lone Ranger or Zorro on TV from a Beco Bloom warehouse close to home.

Every time we went, the security guard was a very good person, and he would put two small chairs for us at the entrance of the warehouse and from there we would watch television, but one day my father came by and saw us, and said.

"Let's go home, your mother is waiting for you for dinner".

Bárbara was scared, because she thought they were going to punish us, my father grabbed us by the hand and on the way he didn't say a word.

When we got home he told my mother.

"Tomorrow we are going to buy a television, it makes no sense that I break my back working and my children have to watch television hidden in a warehouse".

My mother was quite surprised by my father's comment, Bárbara couldn't believe it, she had been saved from certain punishment, and I was happy that we were going to have a television at home.

On weekday mornings, my mother almost always prepared a breakfast with coffee and scrambled eggs, we all ate together and when we finished, each one left to start their activities.

My father walked to the factory with a clean, ironed uniform every morning and returned full of grease every afternoon, my sister Bárbara left with her school suitcase on her back that was a little too big for her, and my elder sister María Helena put on lipstick and combed her hair for a long time before going to work in a shoe store. My mother and I stayed at home with the dog and the cat, I watched her wash the dishes.

MY MOTHER TEACHES ME TO READ AND WRITE

After finishing the housework, every afternoon my mother sat with me in the patio where she toughs me letters and numbers.

At first I didn't like it very much but little by little I became encouraged as she bought me an illustrated book with animals that had short stories that she read and used to teach me how to read.

I remember she always told me.

"Orlando, you can't spend all day playing, you have to take advantage of the time and learn something useful every day".

At that time my mother also had the habit of raising chickens and had built a corral in the back of the house where a group of chickens lived together with a rooster and a duck.

In the mornings sometimes I was responsible for collecting the eggs for breakfast, but on more than one occasion I had problems with the rooster that took advantage of my short stature and chased me around the yard while I tried to escape with the basket of eggs.

Some weekends, my mother had the habit of preparing chicken with potatoes and the whole family really liked that dish, although I always avoided seeing the part about killing the chicken.

As the mango tree was very big and strong, one day my father had the idea of hanging a swing from one of the branches so that we could swing on it, which became a very popular activity for my sister Bárbara and me, until one day my sister and I crossed the line and in a very strong push, I went flying and when I fell I lost consciousness, which caused me to end up in the hospital and ended the fun of the mango tree.

MY SCHOOL LIFE BEGINS

When I was five years old, my mother enrolled me in a small school that was very close to home. Initially, they were going to put me with the small children, but since my mother insisted that I knew how to read and write, they gave me a test, and this allowed me to start in the first grade, although I was the smallest in the class.

Every day when I returned from school, my mother would prepare a snack for me, which was usually bread with jam or a fruit salad, and then she would ask me to clean the yard, which I didn't like very much, since collecting the leaves from the tree mango was a long and boring task, so I was distracted by watching the insects and collecting stones.

When I complained, my mother always told me.

"You have to help with the housework, here everyone has to contribute and as far as I know, you don't have a crown".

Another thing that bothered me a lot was making my bed every morning, and I always protested by telling my mother.

"Why do I have to make the bed if I'm going to unmake it at night?"

Then she told me.

"for the same reason you clean your teeth, even though you are going to eat again".

And here the discussion ended, because with the topic of teeth she had already explained to me about cavities and being left without teeth.

A TANTRUM TO LEAVE HOME

I remember that, one of the many times the dog urinated in the living room, my mother ordered me to clean it up and I forgot, when my father came home from work the dog's urine was still in the living room and my mother got upset, she scolded me and told me that next time she would kick the dog out of the house, so I got very upset and told her.

"I'm tired of being bossed around all day, I'm going to leave this house"

Then my mother told me.

"That's your decision, if you want to go, go".

Her answer annoyed me even more, and crying I went to my room, put some clothes in a backpack and left the house. When I was on the street I realized that I had nowhere to go and I sat down crying on the sidewalk in front of our home.

A while later, my mother appeared and said.

"If the tantrum has passed, come on and I'll give you bread and jam"

I wiped my eyes and with a broken voice, I told her.

"Okay, but I'd like it better with condensed milk".

MY RELATIONSHIP WITH MOTHER WAS VERY SPECIAL

Despite the tantrums, my relationship with my mother was always very special, I was lucky to be born when she was a very mature woman and her life was not as hard as it had been in the years when my older sister María Helena was born.

My mother did not have the opportunity to have a good formal education, but she acquired a lot of wisdom from long conversations with my grandfather and everything she had to go through, which added to her persistence, responsibility, creativity, and optimism made her a very special person.

I remember that she often told me stimulating and motivating phrases that I did not understand in the early years, but over time I discovered their true meaning.

1. Men are the size of the problem they decide to solve.

2. When the student is ready, the master shows up.

3. A man is worth what he knows and what he has.

4. The important thing is not what happens, it is how you handle it.

Over time, my sister María Helena became independent, Bárbara and I grew up and we began to make friends in the neighborhood, but we also began to discover some of the disadvantages of being foreigners.

MY FIRST EXPERIENCE WITH DISCRIMINATION

In the 60s, Colombia was much poorer than Venezuela and there was a wave of migration between the two countries driven by the better living conditions in Venezuela.

My first close experience with discrimination was an incident that happened to my sister Bárbara at her school. One day when she returned home, she had a scratch on her cheek and told my mother that she had had a fight with a classmate, and that the next day mother had to go with her to talk to the director.

My mother asked her what had happened, and Bárbara told her that a classmate had told her that our father was a Colombian thief and pushed her against the wall and thus scratched her cheek, so Bárbara defended herself by punching the girl, who then ran out to accuse Bárbara with the director.

After hearing the story, my mother said to Bárbara.

"Daughter, it's okay for you to defend yourself if someone attacks you, and also be very clear that your father is an honest and hard-working man, tomorrow we'll both go to talk to the director".

The next day my mother went with Bárbara to school, clarified what had happened with the director, and insisted on having a meeting with the parents of the girl who had assaulted Bárbara, the director agreed and two days later it took place a meeting at the school.

Bárbara told me that my mother handled the situation very diplomatically, and the problem ended with an apology from the girl and her parents to Bárbara.

AN UNEXPECTED BEATING

Bárbara's story stuck with me and I often imagined that something similar would happen to me, since in my school there were two brothers whose fun it was to hit the little ones when the teachers were not looking and I was their favorite target.

They hit me on the head or yanked my hair and they threatened me saying that if I accused them it would be worse.

One Saturday morning, Bárbara and I were coming back from buying bread at a bakery near our house, and the aggressive children were walking on the other side of the street, so it occurred to me to say.

"Bárbara, those are the brothers who always hit me".

Then Bárbara called them and said.

"So you are the ones who hit my little brother, why don't you dare to do it in front of me".

When Bárbara finished her sentence, Domenico, the older of the two brothers, looked at me, punched me, and said to my sister.

"We hit him and so what"

I fell sitting down from the blow and began to cry while Bárbara plucked up her courage and grabbed the two children by the ears, so they began to cry, then Bárbara release them and they just ran away, while Bárbara yelled at them.

"If you hit my little brother again, I'll rip your ears off".

It was a violent and painful experience, but the ear-pulling had a long-term effect, since then the two brothers did not hit me again.

THE FAMILY MOVES TO CARACAS

Time continued its course, Bárbara started high school, I went to second grade, and in 1962, when I was six years old, I heard my father telling my mother that he got an offer of a better job in a textile company in the capital.

My parents discussed this issue for a while and finally decided that we would move to the city of Caracas, my father would go first, and the rest of the family at the end of the school year.

When the day of the move arrived, my father came with a friend who had an old truck and we spent half a day putting all the furniture and family things in the back of the truck, it was so loaded that it seemed that things were falling from the sides of the truck.

Around five in the afternoon we said goodbye to the neighbors and to that house that had seen us grow for almost five years.

We set out on the road to Caracas, my mother, my father, and the friend in the front of the truck, and since there was no space, Bárbara and I were tied to some chairs in the back.

The trip lasted more than three hours and we arrived dead tired around 9 at night in an area of Caracas called the Cemetery where my father had rented an apartment since the company did not provide him with housing for this job.

AN UGLY AND DANGEROUS HOME

Our new home was actually the terrace of a house that had been converted into an apartment and was basically a single space with a kitchen in the back and a bathroom, the roof was made of a metallic material that resonated with the rain that was falling just as we arrived.

When my mother realized what awaited us, she said to my father.

"This is the improvement in the quality of life that convinced you to accept the job in Caracas, I knew that you are a bit of a jerk, but I didn't think that you were also stupid, how do you think we can live in this dump, in Valencia we were a thousand times better, tomorrow I go out to look for something decent to live in, and if it is not possible, I will go with my children to Colombia".

My father didn't say a single word, he just listened, I think he knew my mother was absolutely right, this terrace was a dump.

The next morning when we saw the terrace and the surroundings in daylight, the impression was much worse, the house was surrounded by very deteriorated buildings, on a rather ugly street, and we had to use a very narrow metal staircase.

The night before had not been possible to climb most of the family's furniture, so it was stowed away in a parking lot rented by my father in emergency in order to unload the truck.

My mother was super upset, so my father tried to apologize saying that it was the only thing he had found because he was working even on weekends, and that this was only for a few days.

My father went to work, my mother and Bárbara went to look for something better and I was left in charge of taking care of the family's belongings, since the area was not safe at all, according to the owner of the house it was necessary to be careful of thieves.

This routine repeated for several days until on Friday afternoon my mother and sister returned earlier than usual with a satisfied face.

A VERY SPECIAL APARTMENT IN DOWN TOWN

They had found an apartment to rent within the family budget, which had a living room, dining room, kitchen, bathroom, two large bedrooms, and a huge balcony with a spectacular view of the legislative palace.

Our new home was a flat in a five-story office building on Av. Universidad, in front of the National Congress building.

The rent was the equivalent of about $90 a month and I think my father's salary at that time was close to $500, so the house would take a bit less than 20% of the family income.

I have no idea if my parents duly analyzed the structure of the family budget and the differences in the cost of living between Valencia and Caracas, but it seems to me that my father was influenced by an increase in his monthly income and did not consider all aspects of his compensation and benefits package.

In any case, moving to Caracas was the beginning of a new stage with great positive and negative changes for each member of the family that possibly would not have happened if we had stayed in Valencia.

The place of residence creates opportunities for access to services, institutions and interaction with different groups of people.

Living in the capital put the family close to the country's executive, legislative, and judicial power, we were half an hour from the international airport, and we had access to services, study centers, and companies that did not exist in Valencia.

All these, in the long run, represented a significant change in the future potential of each family member.

The apartment we rented to live in was in the Bolsa building, and it was occupied mainly by lawyer's offices.

In the building, there were only 3 families, which made it very quiet, especially on weekends.

After we moved, we began to get familiar with the area and quickly settled in, even though I was the only kid living within a hundred yards.

My mother enrolled me in a public school that was about eight blocks away, very close to the institute where my sister Bárbara studied.

My father was less fortunate since he had to take a bus to go to work making a journey of almost an hour.

A GIFT THAT CHANGED MY LIFE

My sister María Helena had moved to Caracas when she became independent and now she visited us quite frequently, which made me very happy since I missed her, she had a very good character and we got along very well, I remember that when I was eight years old, she gave me a chemistry set and a biology set that included a lot of experiments, I loved everything that had to do with science and nature and those gifts aroused my curiosity and imagination even more.

Every afternoon when I came home from school after doing my homework, I would spend my time doing experiments with the chemistry and biology kits that were gradually growing with new components, flasks, tubes, and whatever old gadgets I found interesting.

EXPERIMENTING WITH THE BRAIN OF A COW

On one occasion, I saw a TV program about the brain and the electrical impulses produced by the neurons, that made me very curious and I thought it would be interesting to have a cow brain and stimulate it with electricity to see what would happen, so in the first opportunity I had, I went to the butcher shop, and with what I saved from my allowance, I bought a brain, the butcher asked me what I wanted it for and I told him it was for a school job.

With my chemistry and biology set, I stimulated the brain with 9-volt shocks and injections of different liquids.

Since nothing interesting happened, after exhausting all the test ideas I could think of, I put the brain in the fridge and forgot about it.

Two days later my mother prepared scrambled eggs for breakfast, but they tasted different and they had something that looked like very soft meat. My father said, these brains taste very good, then I asked what brains, and my mother said, some that my father brought.

Then my father said "I didn't bring any brains", I immediately intervened saying "mom you have used the cow brain that I put in the fridge".

At that point my father, my mother and my sister looked at me with an incredulous face and before they said more I explained my experiment.

Fortunately, we had eaten very little and no one got sick or had any consequences from eating the remains of my experiment.

But this served me as a lesson and I learned that there are risks and that I had to be more careful.

MY FATHER LEAVES HOME

Although at first everything was going well in the apartment in the Bolsa building, over time my parents began to fight and things went from bad to worse.

Before I was nine years' old, my parents had a very strong fight and my father left home, at first they did not want to tell me what had happened, but little by little I found out that my father had a lover and my mother discovered it, so the thing ended in separation.

My relationship with my father hadn't been good or bad, I loved him as his son, but he was a person of few words who was generally nice to me, but we didn't have much to talk about.

The separation, in a certain way, made me happy for the whole family, since it is easier to live in the remains of a battle than to be in the middle of a battle every day of your life.

OVERCOMING AN ECONOMIC CRISIS

Since things ended so quickly, they didn't get divorced, they didn't make any kind of economic arrangement and overnight my mother, my sister and I were left without any source of income.

My mother and my father had built a house in Colombia that was rented and that income could help since mother controlled that money, additionally my mother decided that she, my sister and she would sleep in one bedroom, divide the living room in two, thus creating a new room and in this way the apartment had two rooms for let. Fortunately, this worked quickly and became a stable source of income.

Besides, my mother also organized a food service at lunchtime that she offered to the building's lawyers and that also helped to keep the boat afloat, we didn't have extra money, but it was enough to survive and pay the rent.

Although we never talked about this topic, I think my mother wanted to show my father that he wasn't necessary and that she could get ahead on her own.

The first year after the separation, my mother had a hard time, not so much because of the financial difficulties, but because of the emotional implications regarding her self-esteem, often when I came home from school I would find her with red eyes and more than once when I asked her what was wrong, she would go off topic saying that she had been cutting some onions.

But as an old saying goes, time fixes everything, little by little, my mother's mood improved, my sister María Helena gave us a hand, and a brother of my mother's named Zoilo moved to live with us and contributed to the family economy.

Bárbara began to study commercial high school at night and worked by day as a secretary at the Simon Bolívar Center.

We went back to having a relatively normal life and I was again interested in doing experiments with my chemistry and biology kits.

EXPERIMENTING WITH THE MEMORY OF A CAT

I don't remember where the idea came from, but I had read somewhere that memory is affected by magnetic fields and I decided to do an experiment with the house cat to test if it was true.

I put the cat in a cage and kept it for a day without eating to make sure it was very hungry, at the end of the fasting period I would take it out of the cage and show it a bowl of food in my room instead of the usual eating place, then I brought the cat to the kitchen and set him free.

My theory was that the cat should run to my room remembering that the food was there.

I did the experiment and the cat ran to my room to eat, this proved that it remembered where the food was. The next day, I would repeat the experiment after having the cat fasting for another 12 hours, but this time after showing him the food and taking him to the kitchen, I would stick its head in a magnetic field that I had created with three coils energized by a car's battery.

When I released the cat, it stayed in the kitchen meowing as it always did when it wanted to eat, so I assumed that the experiment had proven that the cat's short-term memory was erased by the magnetic field.

After the experiment, I fed the cat and from what I could see it was still a very normal cat, fortunately, this experiment had no side effects.

EXPERIMENTING WITH MY BRAIN

The next step in my brain study was an experiment to look at how a sequence of low-frequency electrical pulses can affect mood.

This idea occurred to me after watching a documentary about electroencephalography and the electrical activity of the brain, where they talked about the relationship between alpha waves of 12 cycles per second and meditative states.

To carry out the experiment, I had to be the guinea rabbit, for which I decided to build a pulse generator using a reduction mechanism from an electric toy car connected to a 12-position switch.

By changing the voltage that fed the motor of the electric cart with a variable resistor I could generate pulses between 6 to 60 cycles per second while applying 12 volts to the electrodes that stimulated my frontal lobe.

The electrodes were two thick screws that I had put in the front area of an old motorcycle helmet that I found in the trash.

I repeated the experiment many times, testing different frequencies for periods of 5 minutes, but I could not observe any significant change in my mood, I only detected a small luminescence that appeared above my eyes when I received the electrical pulse.

I finally decided to end the experiment one day when my mother found me with the helmet on connected to the pulse generator and she was scared thinking that I could get electrocuted.

AN ELECTRICAL BUSINESS AT CHRISTMAS

Christmas was approaching and the mayor's office allowed street vendors to set up small tarantines to sell Christmas items, until the end of the year.

All the streets around my home's building were filled with this type of vendors and I would go around the area to browse everything they sold.

One day I found out that most of them had lighting problems since they couldn't have an electric generator and some had to close the sale as soon as it got dark, so it occurred to me that I could lower a cable from our apartment and sell them electricity so that every point of sale had one or two light bulbs.

At that time, I was starting high school at the North Technical Institute (NTI), and I knew something about electricity, but just in case I explained the idea to a teacher and he helped me do the calculations to know how much I should charge for each point of light, what type of cable to use and how much power could be drawn from my home.

According to the calculations, I could put two light circuits each of 15 amps, and if the thing worked, with 1-dollar day per point of light I could recover the cost of the cable, pay the electricity bill, and have a profit to help with the expenses at home on Christmas.

When I proposed the idea to my mother, she didn't like it very much at first, but when I explained that I had reviewed the plan with an NTI professor, she reluctantly agreed.

Fortunately, the plan worked very well, I sold a point of light from 6pm to 10pm to everyone that I could cover with the two circuits and it was an experience to win multiplied by three, since I learned a lot of things, I earned a little money for Christmas gifts, I helped the vendors and helped my mother with some of the household expenses in addition to paying the electricity bill for the month of December.

RISK OF LOSING THE SCHOOL YEAR

At that time, the year was 1967, I was 11 years old, every day I took a bus on Av. Baralt, one street from where I lived, to go to the NTI, it was a journey of about 20 minutes, but sometimes it was extended due to traffic accidents on the road.

The NTI was a public institute that combined high school with a technical dree in electronics, which was what interested me at that time, since I could do high school and simultaneously obtain a technical degree that would allow me to work to help at home and continue my university studies at night.

The problem was that at the NTI there were frequent demonstrations in support of students from public universities who at that time were demanding the restitution of university autonomy.

I didn't really know what was happening, but every week classes were suspended once or twice, as soon as the students of the higher years began to burn tires at the entrance of the institute.

This situation was repeated quite frequently and sometimes I wondered if we wouldn't lose the school year due to so many suspensions from academic activities, so my mother began to explore the possibility of transferring me to another institute with fewer problems.

At NTI, I had made a new good friend who shared many interests with me, his name was Arturo, a boy of Portuguese origin who studied in the same classroom as me, if classes were suspended we went home, and always try to do a new experiment.

A BLACK EYE FOR A FRIEND

One of the many days that classes were suspended at the ETIN, I was returning home with my friend Arturo walking along Av Baralt.

Suddenly we saw a beautiful young woman with a little dog and Arturo told her "How I would like to be your little dog to walk with you every day", the girl smiled and we continued walking.

When we got to the corner, there was a tall, muscular guy who grabbed my friend by the neck, and lifted him into the air while telling him, "I'm going to teach you not to mess with my girlfriend".

Then it occurred to me to tell him: "You're a bully, my friend didn't say anything bad, why don't you pick on someone your size?"

Then the big guy let go of my friend and hit me in the face while saying, "Shut up or I'm going to hit you too".

Fortunately, at that moment a police officer passed by and approached saying, "What's going on here?".

The big guy pretended nothing was happening and walked to the other side of the street, while I recovered from the shock and rubbed my eye.

When I got home my mother saw me with a black eye and then I told her the story, she told me. "My son, sometimes in life one goes to play the Redeemer and ends up crucified, the next time you try to defend someone, take precautions before opening your mouth".

A ROCKET IN THE WRONG DIRECTION

On one occasion, we had read how to prepare gunpowder to make a rocket and we were very curious to see if we could make one and launch it from the roof of the building and then have it fall with a parachute.

We spent several weeks to get all the materials and ingredients we needed and finally we built a rocket about 50 centimeters high and about five centimeters in diameter, it looked spectacular painted red with three yellow fins that kept it standing and were going to stabilize it. In flight, the parachute would deploy by a spring mechanism that would be activated when gunpowder burned the anchor point at the top end of the tube.

When we had everything ready we went up to the terrace of the building, looked for a clear place and placed the rocket on the ground resting on the fins, but enthusiasm and inexperience were about to give us a big scare.

We lit the ignition fuse, but just before the fire reached the base of the rocket, a strong wind blew and the rocket fell on its side and was ejected towards the Legislative Palace.

Fortunately, it didn't do any damage, but it caused a huge commotion in the legislative palace as it entered through a window and they imagined it was a terrorist attack.

The palace security guards ran back and forth trying to identify the source of the projectile, but they found no clues.

Arturo and I were about to have a heart attack from the scare we got and we crawled out of the roof of the building, that was the first and last experiment with rockets that we carried out.

We learned a lot that day about the risks we didn't anticipate and the good luck we had had.

Enthusiasm, curiosity and ignorance are dangerous combinations, so we refocused our projects and experiments on those that appeared in a magazine called Popular Electronics, which were generally low risk and only required a few electronic components to assemble, radios, amplifiers, oscillators, etc.

UNEXPECTED REUNION WITH MY FATHER

The weekend after the rocket experiment, while I was doing my homework, my mother said to me. "Son, come out to the balcony, I think your father has been standing on the corner in front of the building for a while, and I imagine he wants to see you".

It had been a long time since I had seen my father, and I was surprised that my mother knew that he was standing at the corner, so I peeked out of the balcony and he was really standing looking up. I went down to the street and approached to greet him, he hugged me and told me.

"Son, for a long time I wanted to see you and your sister, but it has not been possible, one day when you grow up, you will better understand the situation and the problems of the adults".

I listened to him without asking questions, I took him by the hand and suggested that we go for a drink on the other street. When we sat in the coffee shop, I asked him how he was doing, and where he lived, he told me that he was fine, that he worked in another textile factory and that he lived in a small hotel near of "Plaza Miranda", about ten blocks from where we were.

So I told him about my studies at NTI, about my experiments, and that my sister Bárbara was studying economics at the Venezuela Central University (UCV) at night and worked at the Simón Bolívar Center during the day.

He was very pleased with my sister's progress and then asked me how my mother was doing, I told him "just fine" without going into details or further explanations, and then I pushed the conversation towards the possibility of seeing each other from time to time and he reacted positively. From that day on, we began to see each other every Sunday for breakfast. This routine lasted for many years, and was only interrupted when I left the country. We never touched on the issue of separation, I knew from my mother that my father did give us a monthly pension and that it was interrupted at my request when I started working since it was not necessary.

Over the years, Bárbara also got closer to my father and there came a time when my mother accepted that we invited him to the Christmas and New Year gatherings, but kept her distance with a polite but impersonal treatment.

My father and I had a respectful relationship, with the affection of father and son, but without much conversation, he listened carefully to what I was saying, but he did not get hooked on the subject, however, he made me feel that he cared to be there with me.

His family had a large extension of agricultural land in Colombia, but when his parents died, he never had an interest in claiming anything, he said that he had not worked it and therefore it did not belong to him.

This attitude seemed noble to me on his part, and was an example of consistency with a principle that he repeated frequently.

"You have to earn things honestly with your effort and your work".

23

FROM MY FIRST JOB TO MY FIRST COMPANY

24

PROGRAMMING COMPUTERS

I started working at a very young age, having finished my technical degree in computer science when I was 15 years old, after that, I was hired as a computer programmer in the Personnel Directorate of the Ministry of Public Works in Venezuela.

In the early 1970s, computing was very new and most people had no idea what it meant to program a computer, although there was a general perception that it was something complicated and related to mathematical calculations.

I studied computing a bit by accident since my mother took me to a Jesuit high school institute to enroll in an electronics program, which was what I liked, but we arrived late and there were no places.

When I put on a disappointed face, the priest who attended us told me "we have a place in computing, which is a new specialty and since computers are electronic, may be you like it".

Something inside me made me feel that it was a good idea and I said to my mother, this could be interesting, as we are here sign me up for this, it has something to do with electronics. Besides the NTI is always in trouble.

Thus passed two years of high school combined with computer sciences which included subjects such as binary logic, hardware architecture, flowcharts, algorithms, Fortran, Cobol, PL/1, systems analysis, and systems design.

The practices were carried out using perforated cards on the IBM360 computer of the Ministry of Public Works (MOP) and on a Digital PDP-11 minicomputer that the institute had.

Studying computing was a blessing and a heaven-sent opportunity, as it was a career with extraordinary potential that was just beginning and was going to change the way of life around the world for decades to come.

In order to work, due to my young age my mother had to get a special permit which fortunately was not very complicated, I was willing to work and we really needed the money.

My first salary in 1972 was about 600 dollars a month, that wasn't great, but it wasn't bad at all, it was enough to pay the 95 dollars rent for the apartment, support myself and my mother, since in recent years we had dependent on a small pension that my father gave us, renting rooms and the help of my older sisters who had already become independent.

Studying at night at the university and working during the day was not ideal, but the family economy did not allow anything else, also statistical science had a night shift and had a certain synergy with computing, so I went down that path and began to combine my work in the ministry during the day with the subjects of the basic cycle of statistics during the night.

My job was to maintain the jobs position budget system and act as liaison officer with the ministry's Computer Center, which left me a lot of free time that I used to do my university homework and learn everything I could. about the functioning of the different departments of the Personnel Directorate, this allowed me to develop a very complete vision of all the functions covered by human resources administration and imagine how a long list of processes could be automated.

MY FIRST CAR AND A SCARE ON THE HIGHWAY

Since I was a child I have always liked cars and I was very frustrated that my father was never interested in owning one, so when I started working, I set the goal that when I turned 18 I would buy my first car.

I started saving, got my driver's license on my first test, and bought my first car in September 1974. It was a second-hand '68 Javelin made by American Motors.

Having my own car, in addition to fulfilling a dream of many years, allowed me to move with much more freedom and improved my quality of life.

With my car I could go to and from the university without depending on public transportation schedules, on Sundays I could go pick up my father from the hotel where he lived and take him to breakfast at a restaurant on the outskirts of the city.

Some weekends I convinced my mother to go to the beach and eat fried fish, but having my car also had its drawbacks. I remember that on one occasion when I was returning from the beach with my mother, my sister María Helena, and my two nephews, my car was about to catch fire since I had installed an ammeter and one of the cables came loose causing a short circuit.

In a few seconds the interior of the car filled with smoke and we were very scared, but thank God I was able to stop the car, open the hood, and disconnect the battery in time.

A SCHOLARSHIP IN THE EMPIRE OF THE RISING SUN

When I was finishing the basic cycle of statistics, one day a notice appeared on the Personnel Directorate's news bulletin board about an opportunity to do a specialization program in systems engineering in Tokyo with a scholarship from the Japanese government.

The program was super interesting, the scholarship covered all expenses in Japan and the Ministry of Public Works would continue to pay my salary in Venezuela if they gave me paid leave.

I did the paperwork to apply for the scholarship thinking that I didn't have much hope since I imagined there would be many applicants, and to my surprise I was selected and the Ministry gave its approval.

When I told it to my mother she loved the idea, she always said, a man is worth what he knows and what he has, and insisted that I should not miss this opportunity.

During my absence, she would be authorized to collect my salary and would not have financial problems, but she would have to overcome the emotional difficulties of having her son on the other side of the planet and not being able to see him for a time that would seem endless.

At that time my level of English was quite poor, since I only had what high school gives you and some courses that my sister María Helena had paid for me at the American Institute during school vacations, but what I lacked in vocabulary I made up for it with a huge desire to learn and take advantage of the adventure that was about to begin.

FLYING TO JAPAN OVER THE NORTH POLE

The flight from Caracas to Tokyo was very long and exhausting, including two stops, one in New York and another in Anchorage in

Alaska before crossing the North Pole to finally land at Haneda Airport near Tokyo.

Flying over the pole was an unforgettable experience, contemplating an immensity of ice and northern lights. Unfortunately, I did not have a good camera to record the spectacle, so I had to settle for recording that wonderful landscape in my memory.

When I landed in Japan, the program coordinator was waiting for me at the Haneda airport, a young Japanese woman named Sachiko whom I identified thanks to a sign that said Mr. Orlando - Venezuela.

Sachiko was around 30 years old, she was very kind and tried her best to make the students who had arrived that morning feel welcome, one was Dae-Seong from Korea and the other was Mauricio from the Philippines.

At the airport, we took the train to go to Tokyo and there we changed to the subway to get to Shibuya station from where we walked a few streets to get to the Sunroute hotel where all the students of the program were staying.

When I entered my room I was impressed by how small it was, there was barely enough space for a single bed against the wall, a small table and a chair in front of a window that overlooked the street, but the worst thing was entering the bathroom, since It was almost like the one on airplanes, only it had a plastic capsule where the shower was.

Space was a very valuable resource in Tokyo, and this was one of the many aspects that I would have to get used to if I wanted to successfully overcome all the challenges that awaited me.

UNSALT RICE AND RAW FISH

Another problem area was the food, as I didn't like most of the dishes, the rice was completely tasteless and unsalted, many of the soups were served cold, a chicken egg was often added, but it was frequently raw.

To top it all off, I didn't like raw fish and sushi wasn't to my taste either. I remember that when I was new, I used to stop at the entrance of restaurants to look at the sample of dishes they were offering to see if there was anything that looked appetizing, and on one occasion I saw a pizza that looked very good and at a very good price, the problem was how to tell the innkeeper what I wanted since I didn't know how to say it in Japanese and at that time it was not easy to find people who spoke English. So I decided to write very carefully the characters that were next to the pizza on a piece of paper and entered the restaurant. When the waiter came I showed it to him and he said "pizza". This lifted my spirits and I ate many pizzas at that restaurant.

Over time I improved my Japanese repertoire, and I got used to eating what was available, although I always had a small jar of salt with me to give some flavor to the rice.

TIGHT ON THE SUBWAY FROM MONDAY TO FRIDAY

Academic activities were in English from Monday to Friday at the Fujitsu Institute of Computer Sciences (FICS) study center, which was about 40 minutes by subway from the hotel. The journey was quite uncomfortable due to the jostling involved in moving in the middle of an ocean of people who used the subway, especially at rush hour.

When I became familiar with the schedules and variations in passenger volume, I started leaving very early and returning late with my colleague from Korea so we could travel more comfortably on the subway, eat quietly at FICS, and read some of the academic content before and after classes. However, I had to adapt my routine to take into account the temperature changes of the seasons.

GETTING TO KNOW JAPAN AND ITS CULTURE

Tokyo has a climate with very marked variations depending on the time of year and I had lived all my life in a climate where the entire year was more or less the same.

I frequently had to work on the development of a project and on some occasions I had the opportunity to visit companies or educational institutions in other cities such as Kyoto, Hiroshima, Nagoya and Osaka.

These trips were greatly appreciated by everyone and we always tried to get the most out of them to see temples, parks, shopping centers and museums.

The natural landscapes in Japan are very beautiful and reflect a spectacular color of the vegetation that changes with the seasons.

The travel and accommodation expenses related to the projects were covered and in general they were enriching experiences that allowed me to use the high-speed train many times and observe customs in several cities that were very different from what I was used to in Venezuela, for example:

- If someone has the flu, they should wear a mask to cover their mouth and nose to reduce the risk of infecting other people.
- If a couple goes to a self-service restaurant, the usual thing is for the woman to buy the food while the man stays at the table.
- If a couple is walking down the street, it is usual for the woman to walk behind the man.
- If there is a business dinner with the wives, it is usual for the men to be at one table and the women at another.

The mask thing seemed very good to me, but the other customs did not fit with the image of the developed and prosperous country that was seen everywhere, but they were customs of traditional Japanese culture, which should be observed and not criticized.

THE JAPANESE ECONOMIC MIRACLE

During my time in Japan between 1976 and 1977, the Japanese economy was experiencing accelerated growth, with a high level of productivity and innovation that indicated that it could become the first world economy if it maintained the trend that began in the 1960s, unfortunately. Things went wrong in the following two decades and although it remains an admirable country, it currently has major demographic and financial problems.

The Japanese development model, based on a high level of efficiency, innovation and productivity, was a widely studied example in the Western world, for this reason almost all of my fellow students continually expressed admiration and respect for everything we were seeing and learning, although some aspects of the culture were difficult to understand.

A WELL-DESIGNED ACADEMIC PROGRAM

The academic program of my specialization consisted of 16 subjects distributed in four periods that included topics such as database design, network design, physical security, logical security, logistics systems, administrative systems, manufacturing systems, management information systems, organization of computer centers, project management, and systems planning.

Each subject included theoretical sessions, case analysis, visits to companies and the development of some team work that always ended in presentations evaluated by the instructors and the rest of the class.

Fortunately, I made good friends with most of the classmates, especially with the Korean, the Filipino and the Iranian with whom we organized a study group and when possible we were on the same team for project development.

During the development of projects, it was common to visit companies linked to the FICS and attend presentations made by teams of managers and supervisors who shared key information about the case we were developing. This allowed me to observe the Japanese organizational culture and some very interesting customs, for example:

- When they arrived at work everyone took off their shoes and wore open slippers during the work day.

- In the middle of the day in the morning and afternoon, work activity was interrupted for a few minutes to play a sport or do exercises. The interruption is controlled with a bell that marks the beginning and end of the exercise period.

- When you are introduced to someone, the usual thing is to bow, it is not customary to shake hands or other forms of physical contact.

Japan was an incredible experience that transformed my vision of life, since, between cultural differences, communication difficulties, academic demands, and a group of classmates from 20 different countries, my life was not simple, it was a permanent challenge of adaptation, learning and flexibility.

Fortunately, with the help of good classmates, a lot of dedication, and a positive attitude, in addition to passing all the subjects, and improving my level of English, I learned a million things that went far beyond the technical aspects of computer science.

I had the opportunity to appreciate the implications of a multi-cultural world in a country that had achieved a miracle in its recovery and development after the Second World War.

Living with fellow students, who represented cultures as diverse as they were interesting was almost like living on another planet, each one was a different personal story and a valuable source of exposure to the social, economic and political reality of countries as different as Thailand, Korea, Iran, Vietnam, Singapore or Sudan.

ADVISOR AT MINISTRY OF URBAN DEVELOPMENT

When I returned from Japan in 1977, I was 21 years old and the Ministry of Public Works no longer existed, in its place there were three ministries, Urban Development, Environment and Transportation.

With the reorganization they dismantled a mega structure and I landed somewhat by accident as information technology (IT) advisor in the Ministry of Urban Development, an organization without a computer that gave me a job to do the organization project for its own computer center thanks to the recommendations from some former co-workers I had had at the Ministry of Public Works.

At that time, planning a computing center in a government agency was a task that combined technical and political variables, since the scope of automation depended largely on control, security and strategic benefit factors rather than efficiency, productivity and profitability as is the case of a private company.

A VISIT TO CAMBRIDGE IN THE UK

As the development of the project to create the computing center progressed, a high-priority study suddenly appeared.

It involved the evaluation of a hospital design software package that was purchased by the previous government, the ministry didn't know what to do with it, and the supplier had not been paid.

At that time, no one in the ministry knew about the purchase of the package or had any interest in using it, there was only a contract signed in the previous government by a ministry that had disappeared.

Since we did not have a computer and I could not find someone to lend us one locally with the appropriate configuration to install the package and evaluate it, I asked for permission to visit the creators of the system in the United Kingdom, a company called ARC "Applied Research of Cambridge".

When they approved my trip, I contacted my sister Bárbara, who was studying in England, and she managed to take a break from her studies and accompany me on the visit to Cambridge.

It was an unforgettable experience, on the one hand, I had not seen my sister for a long time and on the other, the visit to the creators of the system confronted me with a complex ethical problem to handle.

The package worked perfectly on a Prime 300 computer with a Tektronix 4010 graphics monitor. Conceptually it was based on the use of prefabricated components and it really was a marvel to accelerate the design and reduce the cost of hospital projects, which by the way are works very complex due to the functionality and equipment requirements.

The problem was that a package purchase contract had been signed without considering that in Venezuela there was no supply chain of prefabricated materials to build something like a hospital, the ministry carried out a project of this type every 5 years and we did not have the equipment. to install the system.

In other words, the vendor fulfilled their part of the contract by supplying the software package that worked perfectly, but those who made the decision to purchase did so without considering all the implications.

I returned to Venezuela, presented my report and the ministry paid the outstanding bill, but a bad taste was left in my mouth as I witnessed a decision that had wasted millions of bolivars.

LOOKING FOR NEW HORIZONS

At the beginning of 1978, while I was finishing the project to create the computer center, I was in the process of searching for new horizons, since the episodes of inefficiency and influence peddling that I had witnessed encouraged me to seek my professional future on my own or in the private sector.

Since I returned from Japan, in parallel with my work as an advisor in the ministry, I also taught computer science classes, in the mornings at the Jesús Obrero Technical Institute and in the evenings at the International Computer School.

Although the remuneration as a teacher was almost symbolic, teaching was an activity that I enjoyed a lot, it helped me keep up to date, and I felt that I was doing something useful for the country, I did it almost for the love of art, especially at the Jesús Obrero since it was located in an area of low economic resources, it was run by the Jesuits who did extraordinary social work and I felt emotionally connected since I had studied there.

At that time, I had the habit of buying the newspapers "El Universal" and "El Nacional" on Sunday mornings, and I would sit down and drink coffee while I looked through them, curious about anything that caught my attention. One of those Sundays, while turning the pages of "El Universal" I saw some ads from the "Professional Extension Center of the Central University of Venezuela" that offered short courses in "Computer Science for Executives".

This piqued my curiosity and I began to check the newspaper every day to see what other offers of this type there were.

Then I discovered a whole constellation of public and private institutes that offered courses and seminars of 20 to 40 academic hours and charged tuition ranging between $350 and $500 per participant.

I remember that I made a simple calculation in a notebook, where I imagined this scenario: "If I have 20 participants in a course and I charge $350 per tuition, this generates $7,000 in gross income. If I spend $1,000 on a hotel and $1,000 on advertising, I would have $5,000 left. per course if I am the teacher.

In 1978 my salary as an advisor at the Ministry of Urban Development was around $1,500 a month, which was not bad, but $5,000 for me was a fortune.

My enthusiasm for teaching and the calculations in the notebook gave me the impetus to continue researching.

I needed to know how much it cost to rent a room in a hotel, how much an ad in the newspaper cost, what topics might interest professionals and mid-level executives, what courses I could cover, what people I knew could be instructors.

MANAGEMENT DEVELOPMENT INSTITUTE IS BORN

When I felt I had enough information, I developed a business plan that involved offering two or three seminars a month, promoting them with press notices, having an office with a telephone, a secretary and an administrative coordinator.

With this infrastructure it would be possible to answer telephone queries, transcribe and photocopy support material, keep track of reservations, take care of participants at the hotel, and carry out collection procedures.

It wasn't too much work, but I needed two people and a small office space to cover everything that needed to be done, one person would work daytime in the office and the other would have an hourly schedule with some duties in the day and others in the evening during the execution of the courses.

I had learned many of the details of how to organize and carry out a course of this style when I first worked as a programmer in the Personnel Directorate of the Ministry of Public Works. At that time, I had the opportunity to become familiar with many processes of human resources administration, especially with the training area where I had an excellent friend named Mireya, who facilitated my registration in many internal courses such as management by objectives, time management, management grid, supervision principles, etc.

I registered a company with the help of my friend Olga, who was a lawyer and had experience in these issues. Olga drafted the incorporation document, helped me register the business name "Management Development Institute" (MDI) and guided me regarding the company's paid-in capital, which at that time was an almost symbolic amount. To start with the minimum possible cost, I made an agreement with my sister María Helena to use her landline and her apartment as a reception for the "Management Development Institute".

The idea was to launch each course with several newspaper advertisements, interested people would call by phone for more information and reserve a spot before formalizing registration.

Based on my market study, more than 99% of the participants would come from private companies and government agencies that covered the cost of tuition, individuals were not the basis of this market.

I spent several months choosing and preparing the first courses until at the end of June 1978 I was in a position to launch a first season of courses that included the following titles:

1. Automation of Personnel Administration.
2. Audit of Computerized Systems.
3. Database Design.
4. Forms Design.
5. Design of Administrative Manuals.
6. Design of Administrative Processes.

The first three would be dictated by me and were based on ideas I had developed on topics I found attractive at the time.

The next three were already developed courses taught by a good friend I had met in the former Ministry of Public Works. Professor Luis, who had become an authority on these topics.

In July 1978, I resigned from the position of information technology advisor at the Ministry of Urban Development, I started the rental agreement with my sister María Helena, I hired her as administrative coordinator, hired a secretary, bought two desks, an overhead projector and a typewriter.

The first course was called "Automation of Personnel Administration" and was launched in August over a weekend, with two advertisements in the newspaper "El Universal" and one in "Nacional".

The cost of advertising was about a thousand dollars and represented the only promotion mechanism.

From the time the advertising came out until the start of the course, there was a period of two weeks to receive reservation calls and fill a quota of 20 participants.

The days began to pass and the phone rang from time to time, followed by the voice of Margot, the secretary, and my sister saying:

"Management Development Institute, good morning".

"I already told you not to call at this time".

"Who was".

"A friend of the children".

The first week we did not receive a single reservation, there were only four calls from people who wanted to know if there was space left and if there were other dates planned for the course.

As the days went by, the tension was increasing, and many catastrophic ideas ran through my head. If no one signed up, I would lose the investment in advertising, the hotel reservation, and everyone's job future would be up in the air.

But as if by magic, on Monday of the following week, the phone began to ring with reservation calls, and some application letters also arrived through motorized messengers.

I had overlooked a very important detail to understand the first week, as the course was paid for by the company, those interested had to obtain authorization before making the reservation.

Finally, 21 people signed up and we had to leave out 4 more people for another date that we would announce soon.

The course took place in a room at the Altamira Hotel during 5 evening sessions of 4 academic hours distributed over two weeks, on Monday, Wednesday, Friday, Tuesday and Thursday. In this way, the course content was easier to digest and the impact on attendees' nights was reduced.

The course evaluation form was anonymous to improve the internal validity of the responses and was distributed in the last session. When we tabulated it, my sister María Helena and I were happy, all the responses were between very good and excellent.

My sister María Helena would receive a commission for each participant, I would cover all expenses and begin to accumulate funds to develop the company.

AUTOMATION OF PERSONNEL ADMINISTRATION

This course had occurred to me because of the experience I had had in the Personnel Directorate of the Ministry of Public Works, where almost everything was manual except for the payroll, the budget and the registration of career civil servants, which were automated in a very rudimentary way, based on batch processes that used punched cards and printouts.

In the course I imagined and described the potential of an integrated personnel administration system that worked on a database using screen terminals and covering, in addition to payroll, many other processes such as the registration of eligible people, training, career planning, job structure, performance evaluation, etc.

The course also included an introduction to what online systems were and the basic principles of feasibility analysis for developing a system.

It was nothing extraordinary, but it was novel and made the imagination fly. The attendees of this course were mostly people linked to human resources management.

AUDIT OF COMPUTERIZED SYSTEMS

The second course that we launched on the market was called "Audit of Computerized Systems" and I came up with it from a conversation I had with a student at the International School of Computing.

This was a person who worked as an external auditor and was curious about how a computer system could be audited. During the conversation it occurred to me that the evaluation could be focused in different ways, some focused on the operation and others on the components of the system.

Based on that principle I did some research in the library and designed three audit procedures oriented to components, transactions and procedures. This course was very well received and was taught three or four times a year, the attendees were generally people from the financial audit area who wanted to explore the computer science part.

DATABASE DESIGN

At the end of the 70s there were still many companies with systems based on sequential files on disk and magnetic tape, therefore, the concept and use of database managers was not sufficiently widespread and it occurred to me that an introductory course in this subject would be well received.

The course explained the basic concepts of database design and the different organization models that were used commercially at that time.

Because the content of the course was basically theoretical, it occurred to me to prepare examples with file images using a few records with data that seemed real and this made the course more enjoyable and facilitated the explanations of concepts such as normalization, entities, tables, lists, pointers and relations.

COURSES WITH EXTERNAL TEACHERS

In the first stage, the courses with external teachers were based only on Professor Luis, and they were also successful, but I could not launch them very frequently since he also had other commitments and since his courses had already been on the market for years, they were beginning to show a certain level of saturation.

IMPROVEMENTS IN THE ADVERTISING IMAGE

Before the end of 1978, the manager of an advertising company called "Trading Press" visited the institute one day and made me the following proposal.

- I will charge you the same rate that you currently pay in the Universal and National newspapers.

- I will improve the presentation of your notices by laying out the content with different fonts and including the institute's logo.

- I will advise you on the effectiveness of the days and pages to publish your notices.

- A messenger would come to get the order for the publication of the notices every week.

- You will have thirty days to pay the published notices.

I found the proposal very attractive, since by spending the same amount on advertising, the ads would have a better image, I would have thirty days of credit and María Helena would save the trip she had to make to place the ads.

Trading Press handled the institute's advertising for all the years of its existence and taught me a few useful things about win-win relationships between customer and supplier.

DEPENDING ON A SINGLE PHONE LINE

A very stressful experience was that in November we launched one of Professor Luis's courses, and after publishing the advertising notices we discovered that the only telephone line we had was not working, the telephone company was doing repairs in the area and accidentally cut our line.

For many people, being without a phone for a few days is just a small inconvenience, but for us it was a catastrophic incident since without a phone we would lose advertising, the hotel reservation, and Professor Luis, would not be very happy.

Fortunately, María Helena had several contacts in the telephone company since she had a therapeutic and slimming massage institute in the past and her best clients were female executives from the telephone company.

We lasted three days without a phone in the middle of a course promotion campaign, but some angel in heaven helped us and the course was carried out with 17 participants.

A TEACHER WITH "STAGE FRIGHT"

The activity of the institute continued to teach me, and at the beginning of November a somewhat older, well-dressed man named Hildebrando showed up at my office.

Hildebrando was a public accountant with a lot of professional experience, and he proposed that I launch a course on "Operational Auditing", a topic that, according to him, had a lot of market; he had taught the course in Peru several times with very good results.

He gave me a copy of his resume and supporting material and we agreed that I would study it and give him a response the following week.

When reviewing the material, I found it interesting and thought it was worthwhile since it was something similar to the audit of computerized systems but applied to administrative processes.

We scheduled the course for early December at the Altamira Hotel and the participant's quota was filled, everything indicated that it was going to be a total success.

Hildebrando was very excited as he would receive a good commission, which would possibly be repeated several times a year.

María Helena and I were also happy, since expanding the institute's course inventory with attractive programs was an important goal.

The day the course started arrived and I went to introduce Hildebrando and do the opening dynamics exercise.

I used to start the first session with a small group exercise that consisted of each person exchanging their name, position and company with the person on their left. Once this was done, the circle of attendees went around and each person introduced their partner.

This activity lasted about 10 minutes and had an amazing effect on the atmosphere of the group. When the attendees sat at the work tables in front of the sign with their name, at first there was a lot of silence, the natural tendency of people was to be serious, and wait for the instructor to start talking.

People did not know who they had next to them and saw him or her as a stranger, but upon receiving the instruction that they should introduce themselves to the colleague on the left and exchange information about their name, position and company where they worked, the room erupted in a flurry of conversations that broke the ice and positively transformed the atmosphere of the group.

I had learned this little exercise from my friend Mireya, and it always gave very good results. In this course, it also allowed me to learn about the profile of the attendees.

Once we finished the cross-presentation exercise, I passed the floor to Professor Hildebrando and left the hotel on my way to the office since I was preparing the support material for another course.

When I arrived at the office, I was surprised that María Helena had called me several times to return to the hotel.

I had no idea what had happened, but I felt that whatever it was not good. When I arrived at the hotel, María Helena was waiting for me outside the conference room and immediately gave me the bad news.

Hildebrando had a nervous breakdown that was destroying the course, we had to do something since the attendees were uncomfortable and were getting nervous too. We could have a stampede.

To try to save the situation, I told María Helena to advance the break to talk to Hildebrando and try to find a solution.

Minutes later the plan worked, Hildebrando interrupted the session and I asked him to accompany me to another room in the hotel that was empty and there I asked him if he was aware of what was happening.

He told me yes, that he had had a nervous breakdown since he hadn't taught class in a while and that some participants had a very high level.

Clearly Hildebrando had a self-confidence problem that could not be easily resolved and the way it was going the course would be a disaster, we would possibly have to cancel it amid a barrage of complaints and claims from the participants.

Then it occurred to me that I could replace Hildebrando as instructor, I had read the material, it had some similarity with the methodology that I had developed for the Computerized Systems Audit course and today I only had to cover 20%, on the other hand, I had a lot of experience as an instructor and knew a few tricks to control the attention of the participants.

I explained to Hildebrando what I had decided and we agreed that we would put on a little theater to justify him leaving the course that day.

Upon returning to the classroom, he would drink orange juice and it would go down the wrong side, then he would have a coughing fit and would not be able to continue teaching, we would tell the people that since I had worked with him on developing the course and that I would continue the session.

We put the plan into action, Hildebrando drank the orange juice and I think it really went the other way because the coughing attack was spectacular.

I entered the room as planned, took control of the session and by a ray of energy from my guardian angel, I developed the content of the first session, stimulating the participation of the attendees with questions that verified their understanding of the content and gave them the opportunity to comment on the topic in question.

The next day I met with Hildebrando in the office, he was very saddened by what had happened, I felt that he was not going to work as an instructor and we agreed that I would continue teaching the course, but he would help me prepare the following sessions.

We told the group of participants that Hildebrando had a throat problem and that I would continue teaching the classes, there were no objections and thank God the course was completed satisfactorily and with an evaluation between good and excellent.

I did not open again the Operational Audit course, but I learned several useful lessons from that experience. I should not hire an instructor without having verified the teaching experience, a failure like Hildebrando's could be catastrophic for the image of the institute.

THE INSTITUTE JUMPS TO THE NEXT STAGE

The results of the courses from August to December had been quite good in economic and academic terms. The quota could not always be filled, but the average had been 18 participants per course.

Experience taught us that we could launch up to four courses in a month, but it was risky and logistically complicated.

Managing advertising, hotel reservations, registrations, support material, availability of instructors and collections for 4 courses, 80 participants, 60 applicant companies was not easy.

All the effort had been worth it and with the experience and benefits accumulated I felt that I could take the next step.

Renting a large apartment with a room to teach courses at night and having the offices operating during the day generated a few advantages.

I wouldn't have to pay for hotels, snacks would be cheaper, we would have more flexibility in planning dates, and we wouldn't have to rush from one place to the other.

I needed an apartment of 150 to 200 square meters in a commercial-residential area that had nearby parking and easy access from the highway since most of the attendees came by car.

I started looking at apartments for rent with María Helena around the Hotel Altamira, until we found one with a huge living room carpeted in dark red, a beautiful view, 4 bedrooms, 3 bathrooms and an equipped kitchen, it cost 1,400 dollars a month, it was located across the street. to Altamira Suites, 100 meters from the Plaza Center in a residential building that looked like a high-end office.

I paid the deposit, signed a one-year contract and we took possession of the apartment the second week of December 1978, I immediately purchased two additional desks, a photocopy machine, a blackboard, 25 visitor chairs, 3 management chairs and 5 modular tables that could form a "U" in the conference room, I had to design the tables to adapt to the dimensions of the room and my uncle Armando, who had a carpentry shop, made them with rosewood-colored laminate tops.

By having this apartment available, I also solved a housing problem for my mother and me, since the building where we had lived since I was a child had been demolished to build a subway station, which forced us to temporarily move to the apartment of my sister Bárbara who was doing a postgraduate degree in the United Kingdom.

Because the phone number was different, we had to do a small public relations exercise and notify clients and suppliers of the change; moving always brings problems and inconveniences.

The advertising for the first course of 1979 came out in the second week of January promoting "Database Design" that would begin two weeks later. This meant that January only covered part of a course and forced me to revise my calculations since it was not possible to have three courses on average per month.

I was learning that, although you pay rent every month, there are months when you cannot have courses, sometimes due to holidays and other times due to the effect of school or end-of-year vacations that I had not anticipated the previous year.

The course scheduling for the first semester began to function smoothly in the institute's conference room and the experience of the previous year was repeated in the average reservations, but there were new fluctuations, the same course could receive 12 reservations in a month and 25 two months later.

Even though it used the same number of ads on weekends that were the busiest days, the results could fluctuate significantly. I had discovered that the number of reservations for a course is a more complex random variable and more difficult to predict than I had initially assumed.

Not being able to take advantage of the 12 months of the year to run courses and the variability in the level of response to advertising, introduced an additional level of complexity in the business model, however, the decision to convert the conference room into a fixed cost was still good, but the profit margin was smaller than I had initially calculated.

Having the apartment in the Miravila building as an operations center, class room and housing for my mother and me had its advantages and disadvantages.

On the positive side we had flexibility in scheduling dates, enough space, a comfortable environment to work. María Helena had her office and I had mine, with the photocopier and the binder we could prepare the support material internally, that gave us flexibility and lowered reproduction costs. Another important aspect was that María Helena returned to normality for her and my two nephews in their family environment, without the limitations imposed by using her apartment as an office.

On the negative side, my mother and I lived in the office, and my mother had to be in her room during the courses since she liked to be in her pajamas and it was not good for her to go out like that to the class room area when the course was taking place.

Other little inconvenient was that some residents of the building were not happy having an office in their residence, although the use of the building allowed it.

Another small inconvenience was that I still taught classes in the mornings at the Jesús Obrero Technical Institute and I had to get up very early to travel almost 30 kilometers to go and another 30 to return since the two places were at opposite ends of the city, and the highway traffic was hellish.

THE FORMATION OF A FAMILY BEGINS

The year 1979 when I was 23 years old, was one of many changes in my personal life as well, since, in the middle of launching the institute, I proposed marriage to a young psychologist I had met at the International School of Computing. We contracted a civil marriage with a small family gathering in the Miravila building party room.

Before marriage, my mother and my wife had a good interpersonal relationship, but unfortunately things changed when I announced the marriage, my mother thought that I was too young to get married and the relationship between her and my wife deteriorated quickly and could never be recovered.

With the rest of the family it was different, my sisters had a cordial relationship with my wife and I always had a good relationship with her parents, aunts and cousins.

MY FIRST DAUGHTER IS BORN

In August 1980, my first daughter was born, a beautiful 3.5 kilo baby girl named Alejandra, I saw her for the first time when the nurse was taking her to the newborn check-up room at the Leopoldo Aguerrevere Clinic while she was giving one of her first crying concerts. Her arrival marked an important change in my perception of the purpose of life, since at 23 years old I began to feel a whole new universe of emotions and responsibilities derived from parenthood.

I remember that the first few weeks I would get up to help prepare the bottle of milk in the early morning and when she fell asleep again I would sometimes touch her because I couldn't see her breathing, which sometimes woke her up and this required half an hour more of lulling her to sleep again.

This is how the first months passed until it was time to spend the night in her room, and the dark circles below my eyes returned to normal.

To facilitate the care of the baby, my cousin Isabel appeared on the family scene, helping my wife in her new duties and paving the way for her to return to her medical studies that she had started at the UCV just before becoming pregnant.

At that time, the Management Development Institute was on the right track, and the family economy was also facilitated by the use of an apartment that my wife had received from her parents as a wedding gift. As the old saying goes, children bring milk for the bottle.

ADVENTURES WITH ORGANIZATIONAL DESIGN

During the break of one of the courses at the institute, Professor Luis told me that he had a friend who was looking for office space to develop his consulting activity and that he could put us in contact since it could be a win-win relationship.

That's how I met Weldon, an American graduate of Syracuse University with a PhD in organizational development.

From the first conversation we had an excellent chemistry and reached a collaboration agreement, I provided him with office space at a very low cost and he advised me to develop courses related to organizational climate and organizational design.

This is how the "Organizational Design" course was born, which was an experience and a source of opportunities in the consulting area.

The purpose of the course was to introduce participants to the formal concepts of organizational structure and functioning and then apply them by analyzing organizations in the real world.

From a structural point of view, an organization is a set of resources that give rise to capabilities to create or change things and this represents power. Organizational capabilities are derived from the exercise of functions, which are the authorized uses of resources, and this leads us to the concept of authority.

Authority is the organizationally granted right to decide on the use of resources, which leads us to the concept of responsibility, which is the obligation to respond for the decisions that are made and their consequences.

Playing with all these concepts, during the course the organizational structure of private companies and official organizations was analyzed through a series of examples.

Most people regularly use the concepts that govern organizational design, but do not stop to think about what they mean, which is why a systematic analysis represented a new and interesting experience that captured the attention of attendees.

When we finished developing the course material we launched it on the market with advertisements where Weldon and I appeared as the instructors, but once the advertising was in the newspaper, Weldon had a family emergency and had to travel to the USA which meant that I would have to decide whether to cancel the course or dictate it myself.

Reservations began to arrive and only 8 people signed up, which barely covered the costs, but I decided to keep it since it was preferable to lose less than to lose everything and at the same time it would serve as a learning experience.

When the opening day of the course arrived I was surprised, two participants were very high-level people, one was the president of the National Securities Commission and the other was the president of the National Pipeline Institute, this initially generated a halo effect that affected my self-confidence to run the course.

Fortunately, everything worked well and the course was developed satisfactorily, to the point that the president of the National Securities Commission (NSC) asked me to visit them in their office at the end of the course to talk about consulting services.

That's how I met the NSC's president, and I developed a small consulting contract that consisted of reviewing with him and his legal advisor the implications of a bill on the capital markets, my participation was to play devil's advocate and look for problems and interpretation flaws in the draft of the bill.

It was a very specific job, but it represented an interesting experience that was possible thanks to the Organizational Design course.

When Weldon returned from his trip, he informed me that he was going to dedicate himself with his family for a year to working in a Bahai community, which was a religious group to which he belonged. This surprised me a little, although I knew about his religious affiliation.

Thus ended the idea exchange experiment that we had started. I never saw him again, but I always kept a good memory of that short and fruitful interaction.

I did not include the Organizational Design course in the program again, since it had a very small market and without Weldon accompanying me in the advertisements my profile was not solid enough on this subject.

INFLATION ACCELERATES IN VENEZUELA

Since the mid-70s, inflation began a growth cycle that reached 21% in 1980. Under this scenario, all economic activities were affected and many people were not familiar with the effects of this phenomenon or how to minimize its impact. For this reason, it occurred to me that some seminars on inflation could be useful and attractive.

The problem was that I needed external instructors and it was not easy to find people with teaching experience who wanted to develop a course, but fortunately through an old university classmate, I contacted a relative of his who was an audit manager at a bank.

That's how I met Carlos, a mature guy with teaching experience who felt attracted to the subject and in this way two new titled courses were born:

"Interpretation of Financial Statements under Inflation".

"Inventory Management under Inflation".

The two courses were launched into the program in the late 1980s and had good results until 1982, when Carlos began to have health problems and had to reduce his activity level.

A SEASON IN CARACAS INSURANCE

In one of the "Database Design" courses there was a group of participants that came from "Seguros Caracas", the largest insurance company in the country at that time. The director of the computer center was one of the attendees to the course, and in the last session he invited me to visit their facilities to talk about a possible consulting contract.

I found the idea interesting and when I went to visit him the following week, we had a long conversation exchanging ideas about system development strategy and methodology, finally, he offered me the position of deputy director of the computer center instead of a consulting contract I was expecting, I told him I had to think about it and I thanked him for his trust and kindness.

At first I had doubts since a permanent job would take a lot of my time away from MDI, but he insisted that I wouldn't lose anything by trying for a while, since the two activities were compatible and took place at different times.

The good side of the offer was that it gave me the opportunity to become familiar with the operations of a large insurance company, the IBM 4341 platform they were using at the time, and they would pay me a good salary that would help compensate for any unexpected fall in MDI revenue.

The downside was that if I strayed too far from the institute it could begin to decline if I didn't develop new course ideas.

After speaking with María Helena, she helped me see that it was worth trying, since the institute already had a stable course schedule that we repeated periodically and she could put more time into controlling the day-to-day life in the office.

GETTING TO KNOW THE COMPUTER CENTER

I accepted Alberto's proposal, and began working at "Computaciones Santiago de León", the legal entity that brought together computer resources to provide services to several companies in the Seguros Caracas group.

The computing center had around 100 people, distributed in an organizational structure that included General Management, Systems Development, Technical Support, Computer Services and Organization & Methods departments.

At that time all systems operated in batch mode, that is, in batches of transactions, there were no online systems which explained the need for a huge data transcription team.

In 1980, Seguros Caracas was presented as a holding company that included various business units dedicated to insurance, reinsurance, financing, advertising, administration and computing.

Seguros Caracas was the largest unit and had more than 100 offices nationwide to manage a network of agents that sold life, health, fire, theft, accidents, civil liability, transportation and automobile insurance.

The company had grown rapidly in recent years and the computer center was receiving an enormous demand for services that was difficult to meet.

From the first day I began to familiarize myself with the center's operations and interview the managers and supervisors of each area, taking notes and cross-referencing information. In a few days I had a first impression of the computer center, which told me that things were not going to be easy.

On the one hand, all the systems were very old, based on batch processes on sequential files controlled by some programs full of patches that exceeded 20 thousand lines of code, which made their maintenance difficult and risky.

The IBM 4341 computer did not have any database manager installed, the most advanced thing available at that time were the master files for issuance, renewal and collection receipts in indexed formats on disk.

Application programming was done in a combination of languages that included Cobol, PL/1 and Assembler.

A VERY UPHILL PATH AT CARACAS INSURANCE

Analysts and programmers still used coding sheets and did not have an individual screen. To create or modify the source code of the programs they sat at a general-purpose table that had a row of screen terminals.

To further complicate matters, relations between the computing center and the business units were not very fluid, due to frequent complaints about the quality of service and the slowness to respond to requests for system improvements.

To top things off, the organizational climate within the computer center was not very friendly and my arrival as deputy director was not viewed very favorably. Some managers felt they were demoted by putting a deputy director in the middle, and others thought the new position was unnecessary.

While I was carrying out my familiarization program, Alberto suggested that we attend a course organized by IBM called BSP "Business Systems Planning" which was an excellent idea.

Although the course was quite theoretical, with some modifications, it was going to give me very good results in the future.

A FAREWELL PROJECT

When I finished my familiarization process I came to the conclusion that it was not a good idea to spend too much time in Seguros Caracas since it would take many years of effort to put things right.

The level of dedication required was very high and would take me far away from the institute, in a difficult organizational environment that did not guarantee a good long-term result.

I would feel bad if I left without leaving some concrete result, so I came up with an idea that could be a win-win.

Since the issuance, renewal and collections master files were in indexed format, a personalized query application could be developed for each branch of business that would allow the users to consult all the available information through a screen terminal.

This only resolved a small percentage of the pending user requests, but if it was done in record time and at a very low cost, no one was going to protest, Alberto could score a few points with the Executive Committee and I could leave with my conscience clean and peaceful.

I presented the idea of the "ERCO" project to Alberto and the managers, the reaction was one of disbelief, they did not think it could be done in a month, it was impossible.

So I told Alberto, if you give me a month with a team made up of Tenorio, Blanca and Flerida, I am committed to delivering the system working.

When I said this, some of the managers' eyes were opened because I was making a commitment that if I didn't fulfill it would leave me in a very bad position in front of the entire team.

Alberto responded positively saying, "for me there is no problem, but if you don't comply you are risking your head". Everyone laughed at the comment, and I told him "deal".

What the management team didn't know was that I had already found a way to accelerate development in a very significant way.

When everyone finished their part, we did an integrated test and everything worked the first time, Tenorio, Blanca and Flerida had done an excellent job and were super enthusiastic, it was the first time they had developed something like this and in such a short time. We set up several test inquiry functions and the next day we gave a demonstration to Alberto and the management team, everyone was impressed.

The Organization and Methods department collaborated by collecting information from users and the following week screen terminals for online inquiry began to be installed for the first time for end users.

I spoke with Alberto and resigned from the position of deputy director of the center, explaining to him that I could not do both jobs and I had decided to return to my Management Development Institute.

We ended on good terms and closed my time at Seguros Caracas, which, although short, was useful on a technical and managerial level.

OPPORTUNITY TO EXPAND THE MDI OFFICE

December 1981 was approaching and one morning when I returned from teaching at Jesús Obrero, I saw an advertisement for an apartment rental in the tower next to my office. Curiosity prompted me to see what the space distribution was like since the other tower had one apartment per floor.

I spoke to the owner who lived two levels up and she showed it to me immediately since it was empty, the apartment was a beauty on the 11th floor, it was bigger than the one where my office was, it had a better view and the rent was 200 dollars less per month, this surprised me and made me think that I had a good opportunity in front of me.

Having the office in a building with only one apartment per floor and more square meters generated several advantages, the conference room would be larger, there would be no neighbor who would be bothered by having the institute next to them, I could put the name of the institute with large letters on the entrance wall, the reception was better located, my mother's room was larger with access to the kitchen and the front door without going through the conference room.

The only drawback was the cost of moving, and some remodeling, but as the expiration date of the other contract was approaching it was the perfect time.

I verified that the termination and start times of the contracts were convenient, I gave the deposit to the owner of the apartment and signed the contract for two years in the new apartment.

The cost of moving was not a big deal and the remodeling was minimal, since I only had to put new carpets to cover the ceramic and parquet floors which, although they were not bad, in my opinion the carpets gave the institute a better image.

My mother and María Helena liked the new apartment and immediately gave it their approval.

THE FAMILY CONTINUES TO GROW

In January 1982, my second daughter, Tatiana, was born, a 4 kilos baby girl who completed the family plan to make a duet with her sister Alejandra.

The idea was that, having a small age difference, they could easily share many of their experiences, especially in childhood and adolescence.

The second baby also slept in the master bedroom for a few months and I helped prepare the bottle milk for her in the early mornings, but I had already learned not to move her when she fell asleep.

When the right time came, we moved her crib to the room where her little sister Alejandra slept, and thus a beautiful lifelong relationship between sisters began to develop. Isabel continued to help take care of the two girls, and my wife was able to return to her studies of medicine at the UCV.

LOOKING FOR NEW PRODUCTS FOR THE MDI

In the new office, the courses continued to operate successfully, although there was a certain downward trend in the number of participants in Professor Luis's courses.

I had the impression that the market was becoming saturated and I had to look for other courses and other service areas with more market potential.

In exploring ideas, it occurred to me that I could try to develop video courses and sell them on VHS cartridges, another possibility was to develop software for the personal computer market that was beginning to appear.

The IBM PC had come out the year before and I was crazy about buying one to explore applications development, so the first chance I got, I traveled to Miami for a weekend and bought the first one I could find. At that time there were very few IBM PCs in Venezuela and seeing one at the institute was a novelty for many of the attendees.

My PC had 64K RAM, two 160K floppy drives, a monochrome display, and could be programmed in Basic, which was impressive at the time, especially considering the $3,000 it cost me.

I tried to develop a small file manager simulating what I had developed in Seguros Caracas, but I had to abandon the project quickly, the capacity of my computer was light years away from what was needed, so I changed direction and started using it as support tool in the courses for a few months, but I sold it at the first opportunity as it would quickly become obsolete and I needed a more powerful machine. The PC XP with a hard drive had already been announced, but it had to wait until 1983.

The idea of video courses did not prosper either, I had bought a VHS recorder and camera to do some testing, but it turned out to be much more complicated and expensive than I had imagined. Recording the classes without editing the recording was practically impossible, there were always things that I would have to eliminate, this meant having video editing equipment that at that time was very expensive, besides, I had also learned that making a quality video required enormous investment of time and effort, so the project of making video courses was also abandoned.

Fortunately, my traditional courses were still working and at the moment I had no financial problems, but I knew that I had to expand my business model with more courses or other activities.

ADVENTURES WITH AN UNEXPECTED PARTNER

In mid-1982, the husband of an old friend appeared at the office one day. He was an industrial psychologist graduated from UCAB who worked in the area of human resources in the oil industry and had seen the ads for my courses in the newspaper.

I invited Hernán to have a coffee and he immediately got to the point, he had in mind the idea of becoming independent and was looking to partner with someone like me who had a management training company, his idea was to take advantage of his contacts in the oil industry to get participants in the courses and thus avoid investing in advertising.

He assured me that this promotion mechanism was very effective and that I could fill the courses easily; the oil industry was very large and had a multimillion-dollar training budget.

I had some participants from the oil industry in my courses, but it was a very small percentage. So imagine that, if Hernán was right, there was a lot of potential.

On the other hand, he had teaching experience and could contribute to the development of new courses.

After a long conversation we reached an agreement that he would be my partner in the institute earning a monthly salary of one thousand dollars per month and a share in the net benefits of the courses that he promoted after reducing all expenses.

It was the first time I had a partner and I thought that between the two of us we could find the solution to the stagnation problem I was experiencing.

He would provide a new distribution channel based on his contacts in the oil industry, his training as an industrial psychologist would help the development of courses.

We agreed to start the partnership the following month with some specific courses that he would promote, which I would not advertise in the press. We also agreed to jointly develop a course on "Design and Evaluation of Research Instruments".

Hernán began to spend his time visiting the training departments of the oil industry and only four participants enrolled in the "Database Design" course. On the other hand, the "Audit of Computerized Systems" course, which was advertised in the press, was carried out with 18 participants.

The following month the low level of registrations generated by Hernán was repeated and this forced me to make the decision to break the agreement. Hernán had overestimated his level of influence in the training departments or there was not enough market in the industry to justify the volume he needed to generate. Additionally, the low level of participants generated by Hernán also affected María Helena and the viability of the institute.

When I spoke with Hernán to terminate the agreement, he seemed reasonable and immediately accepted my decision as inevitable. I got the impression that he was aware that he had overestimated his ability to generate participants and therefore the partnership was not viable. However, years later, one day I saw him by chance in a bank branch, and I tried to greet him, but he did not respond to my greeting and quickly walked away.

This incident left me confused, since from my point of view I had acted honestly, I incurred losses by trying his distribution model, which did not work, I paid him the months of salary that he worked although he did not meet what was expected.

But obviously he saw things differently. If I have learned anything in interpersonal relationships, it is that the perception of what is right and what is wrong is always subjective and relative.

STORMS AND OPPORTUNITIES ON THE HORIZON

The institute had benefited from an economy that had grown rapidly in recent years driven by oil prices and an expansionary public spending policy, but we were about to enter a change of direction in the economic cycle and I had not yet detected it.

In the first week of December 1982, I launched the "Automation of Personnel Administration" course on the market and, as usual, it was well received and we reached 17 participants. On this occasion, two of the attendees came from Bilden, a subsidiary of the multinational British International Tobacco Co. (BIT Co.) in Venezuela. When these attendees introduced themselves, they caught my attention because they were two mature, high-level people. They were the director of human resources and the personnel administration manager.

The course developed as usual, but at the end of the last session, something interesting would happen.

During a small toast that we made at the end of the course, the Bilden representatives told me about the problems they had in their computer center and told me that they were looking for an information technology manager, indicating that if I was interested they could include my resume in the selection process.

The story they told me about the problems with the manager they had just fired reminded me of the experience I had had at Seguros Caracas and I thanked them for the offer, but I was discouraged from entering the selection process.

I closed the year and, as was my custom, I analyzed the results and felt calm to see that, despite my concern, 1982 it had been a good year. My courses had maintained a good level of participants, the courses with external teachers also had an acceptable result, the price adjustments I had made offset the effect of inflation. Although I did not yet have an expansion strategy, I imagined that in 1983 we would also have a good year, so I prepared the schedule for the first quarter and mentally put the label "End of the year holidays".

A BOMB IN THE VENEZUELAN ECONOMY OF 1983

1983 began with my programming of courses and advertising in the second week of January, but something strange was happening, there were many rumors about an imminent economic crisis. On mid-February, the bomb exploded, the government announced a devaluation of the bolivar and exchange control mechanisms. Excess debt and the overheating of the economy began to take their toll. Venezuela was entering a negative cycle for many years, although I didn't know it at the time. What I was clear about, was that with an economy in crisis, training activities were going to fall substantially, and I did not have a strategy to compensate for this problem. Overnight, what had been a long-term concern became an imminent problem. If companies started cutting back on their training programs and some of my courses were cancelled, or I had to operate them at a loss, my cash reserves could be depleted within a year, so I had to do something, and quickly.

AN OPPORTUNITY IN THE PRIVATE SECTOR

Suddenly, I remembered the offer to enter Bilden's information technology manager selection process, although almost two months had passed, I call the human resources director to ask if they were still looking for someone. To my surprise the response was positive, and when I explained why I had changed my mind, he invited me to start the interview process.

The following week the interviews began, the first with the director of finance, the second with the corporate IT manager who came from London, and the last with the director of human resources where the process ended with an offer to be appointed as Information Technology Division manager with a monthly salary equivalent to about four thousand dollars, a good set of employment benefits, and plenty of opportunities for career development at international level.

Working for Bilden would allow me to keep the MDI running, but I decided to suspend operations, dedicate myself 100% to the new job, and maintain the MDI's offices while I developed a new long-term vision, which could be pursuing a career in a multinational or finding another business model to be my own boss again.

REFLECTIONS AT THE END OF A STAGE

Almost five years had passed since I founded the Management Development Institute at the age of 22 in 1978. It was a period of great intensity that left me with a long list of personal contacts, and a wide range of knowledge and experiences on a personal and professional level.

I learned that meeting the right people in an academic and professional environment is a valuable source of opportunities.

I discovered the importance of financial planning and the management of the cost and expense structure to ensure the viability of a company.

I discovered that I could solve problems that I had not even imagined if I dedicated enough time to them and surrounded myself with capable and reliable people.

I discovered that offering an innovative product, adapted to the customer's needs and with good quality, is a way to develop a space in the market, but that this can only be maintained with a continuous process of innovation.

I verified the power of advertising as a promotion mechanism and a fundamental factor in the operation of some business models.

I learned that being my boss was an immense source of personal and professional satisfaction, but it required a permanent effort seven days a week as long as I did not have a self-sustaining economic and financial structure.

On a personal level, the institute allowed me to support my family with a reasonably comfortable life and begin to build an economic foundation for the future.

I also learned that companies are like living organisms, they must continually adapt to the environment to survive, the profits they generate in a period are of little importance, what really counts is the ability to innovate, evolve and survive in the long term.

61

IN A BRITISH MULTINATIONAL IN VENEZUELA

62

THE FIRST DAY AT BILDEN

I joined Bilden in March 1983 when I was 27 years old. My first day began in the Los Ruices building, with an induction interview in the office of Mario, the personnel administration manager.

Mario was a big, strong guy, very nice and with a lot of experience in the area of human resources, he had made a career in the company and since I met him we always had an excellent relationship.

On the day I joined, Mario dedicated almost two hours to familiarizing me with the company's organizational structure while interspersing anecdotes from Bilden's history and explaining the general organizational chart.

Bilden was a subsidiary of British International Tobacco (BIT Co.), a multinational with operations in more than 140 countries and more than 40 factories worldwide.

Bilden was organized into six functional areas or directorates that reported to the presidency in Venezuela and to functional directors in England; it was a very common matrix organization in multinationals. The functional directorates were Agriculture, Production, Marketing, Finance, Human Resources and Corporate Relations.

Once Bilden's general organizational chart was covered, Mario gave me a copy of my induction program, which included a long list of interviews and visits in Caracas and in the interior of the country that in total covered almost a month.

When I realized the length of the induction plan, I was surprised that it was so long, but Mario quickly convinced me that it was an opportunity I shouldn't miss.

The next step was to familiarize myself with the structure and background of the IT Division and the two reporting lines I had over my head, one was to the CFO at Bilden and the other to the corporate IT manager at BIT Co. in London.

When I finished the entry procedures, Magaly, the secretary of the IT Division, came to pick me up to take me to my office, which was in the finance area, far from the computer center. It was quite spacious with a huge window that overlooked the parking lot for visitors.

GETTING TO KNOW THE WORKING TEAM

After getting to know my office, I went with Magaly to the area where the IT Division operated, there I met Isaías, the data processing manager, and Jesús, the systems manager.

Isaías and Jesús introduced me to the rest of the IT staff who were located next to the computer center at the beginning of the factory building in an internal area where there were no windows to the outside and the noise of the cigarette manufacturing machines could be heard in the background.

I asked Isaías if the noise from the factory didn't affect him and he told me that after a while you get used to it and stop noticing it, which was good news since I had intentions of moving my office to be next to the rest. of the team.

Lunch time quickly arrived, and as my induction program indicated, I went to lunch with Isaías and Jesús in a small restaurant near the office where each told something of their personal story before Isaías and Jesús gave me their versions of the recent history of the IT Division.

According to the story, the previous year, based on recommendations from the parent company, a IT Division manager had been hired who was supposed to have started a technological renewal process. This person unfortunately managed to hurt people's feelings and develop a bad relationship, both with users at the management level and with members of the data transcription team.

With users, the problem apparently originated from some cartoons where the new IT manager tried to explain the benefits of computerized systems.

With the transcription staff it was a problem of tactlessness in the work interaction. Finally, the bomb exploded when all the data processing staff below Isaías resigned from their positions on the same day and at the same time.

Under these circumstances, the personnel administration manager, was able to calm things down and stop the collective resignation without promising anything concrete, but over the weekend the IT manager resigned and officially the subject was no longer discussed.

The story I had heard from the human resources director and the personnel administration manager was not as colorful, but it certainly indicated serious problems in interpersonal relationships.

As a new IT manager, all of this meant that I would have to be very careful in managing my relationships with all staff both inside and outside of IT.

Having covered the topic of my predecessor's resignation, I focused on learning something about the personal history of Isaías and Jesús.

Isaías, was a mature man with silver hair, he had been in the company for 22 years at that time, he had started in the administration area and when the opportunity arose he was transferred to data processing, where over the years he became the manager.

Isaías was a capable, responsible, reliable, analytical and dedicated person to his work. I thought that if he had been given the opportunity he would have been able to lead the technological renewal, but his lack of command of English possibly closed the doors for him.

Jesús was a different profile, he was quite young, he had been hired recently, graduated from a university college in computing, he did not have much managerial experience, but he could handle himself well with his level of English.

After lunch we returned to the IT area to get to know the staff and facilities a little more.

We started with the data transcription section, which had a group of ten people supervised by Adelaida, who, like her team, had many years in the company.

Then we went to the machine room where there was an old IBM S/3 computer and next to it was an IBM S/38.

The IBM S/3 was considered a small-scale computer that certainly did not fit the image of a company with 2000 workers with two plants equipped with the latest technology in cigarette manufacturing.

The IBM S/38 was an intermediate level computer that represented a huge technological leap with respect to the IBM S/3.

The IBM S/38 had been acquired at the suggestion of the parent company, but it had been waiting for more than a year to be programmed to do something useful.

José-O, was the head of operations and Isaías's right-hand man, he was a very intelligent and ingenious young man always willing to learn and to cooperate with the other members of the team.

Manolo, was the only programmer on the staff, he was a very alert young man and a good connoisseur of IBM S/3 who helped Isaías keep the systems in operation.

In summary, at that time the IT Division had a staff of 16 people that included 10 data transcribers, an operator, a programmer, a secretary, a data processing manager, a systems manager and now an IT Division manager that wasn't quite sure what he had gotten himself into.

Despite the IBM S/3's reputation as a dinosaur, Isaías had been able to set up a series of systems capable of processing sales reported by 20 branches, maintaining an accounting system, processing employee payroll and workers, which by the way is the most complex payroll I have ever seen in my entire life.

REFLECTIONS OF THE FIRST DAY AT BILDEN

At the end of the afternoon I was able to sit down in my office to reflect on the day's experiences and suddenly Magaly appeared with a cup of coffee as an excuse to give me some instructions on the use of the telephone system and familiarize me with some logistical details that had been omitted, such as the location of the cafeteria, the schedules of the 3 factory shift and the organization of the different parking areas.

Magaly offered to help me with whatever I needed and took the initiative to suggest a filing system that included several sections dedicated to suppliers, division staff, projects, and personal matters.

I still didn't know practically anything about the company, but I knew that there were many expectations of technological renewal and I had doubts that an IBM S/38 would have enough capacity to support the requirements of a company of Bilden's caliber, but I didn't know much about it, so as a summary of first day I established three lines of work.

- Continue taking advantage of the induction to meet people and become familiar with the operation and business model.

- Begin preparations to propose the development of a BSP "Business Systems Planning" exercise involving Isaías and Jesús.

- Familiarize myself with the architecture, operation, cost and capabilities of the IBM S/38 platform.

THE INDUCTION PROCESS BEGINS

The first induction interview was with the finance director Roger, I had met him in the selection process, he was an Englishman close to forty years old and represented one of my reporting lines.

In the interview, he first described the organization of the Finance Directorate and then focused on talking about the different reporting processes to London that were divided into monthly, quarterly and an annual "Business Plan".

The preparation of these reports was supported by a series of standard formats developed at the headquarters, however, the key part beyond the numbers was the entire process of analysis, discussion and design of the business strategy that the management team should conceive to produce a viable and high quality "Business Plan".

When Roger finished the explanation of the "Business Plan" I was impressed by the level of development in the management processes that this type of reporting implied.

GETTING TO KNOW THE FINANCE MANAGER

The next interview was with Alejandro, finance manager and Roger's right-hand man. Alejandro was an Argentinian responsible for coordinating the Departments of Treasury, Accounting, Planning and Control of Branches.

Alejandro was a nice guy, with extensive experience in finance and a lover of the sea, which was quickly captured by the decorations and photos he had in his office.

The induction interview was quick; he didn't go into many details as the reporting had been covered with Roger.

We focused more on getting to know each other personally, talking about our origins and exchanging opinions about multinationals since he had worked in a few before joining Bilden.

Alejandro gave me some indications about Bilden's organizational culture and paved the way for me to get to know his team.

When I asked him what was the most priority in his area regarding systems, he thought for a few moments and told me.

"If you could make me a system that at the touch of a button would generate the Business Plan, that would be fantastic, but I don't think that will be viable for a while, so I'll settle for a good set of systems for accounting, budgeting, treasury, costing and branch control".

At this point he laughed and said, I think I've asked enough of you.

THE WORLD IS A HANDKERCHIEF

The next interview was with the accounting manager and I got a surprise, it was Jeffrey, someone I had met in a "Business Systems Planning" (BSP) course at IBM some time ago and through coincidences of life that. At that moment I could not imagine, destiny would take us along the same path on three continents.

When we talked about the "Business Systems Planning" course, he asked me if I thought it was a good idea to do a BSP at Bilden and I told him that I thought so, and that in fact I wanted to propose it when I finished my induction process.

Then we started talking about the IBM PC he had on his desk, it was the first one he had seen at Bilden until that moment.

Jeffrey was a computer enthusiast and had a small accounting system on his machine made with spreadsheets.

On the other hand, he had a fairly critical opinion of the company's systems and I believe that he had contributed to promoting the idea of a technological renewal plan but things had not gone as he expected until that moment.

Jeffrey had started as an internal auditor at BIT Co. and knew how things worked in many subsidiaries, especially in Latin America and Africa.

I asked him about systems priorities and he gave me an answer similar to Alejandro Russel's with a little more detail.

It is his opinion, there was a need to have a strategy that took advantage of the IBM S/38 and the potential of the IBM PC. To remake all the company's systems and automate many manual processes.

When we finished the induction interview he told me "good luck man, you have a lot of work for several years".

BILDEN NEEDS A SYSTEMS PLAN

Before the end of the day I met with Isaías and Jesús to talk to them about my idea of proposing the development of a BSP. Since none of them knew this methodology, I explained to them in general terms what it consisted of and asked them to prepare a list of processes for each functional area of Bilden to use as a guide in organizing the exercise.

Isaías and Jesús were very interested in the topic and agreed to work together to prepare the list of processes.

Involving them in the preparation and development of the BSP would allow me to kill several birds with one stone, on the one hand, I could use their knowledge of the organization, on the other it gave them the opportunity to participate in the technological renewal process and show their potential.

A FUTURE OF OPPORTUNITIES AND THREATS

At the end of the day I sat down to review my notes from the interviews, it had been a high-density day and I had a labyrinth of ideas and sensations that ranged from enthusiasm for the development potential that I saw ahead to the concern of not being able to satisfy the expectations of all users.

The development of new systems was going to require a team of programmer analysts that I did not have yet, on a machine that I did not know and on a time scale and priorities that were totally nebulous at that time.

But on the other hand, I was faced with a huge opportunity to do something totally new, in a complex, sophisticated organization willing to invest in technological renewal.

I left the office late as usual and went to visit my mother as I did almost every night before getting on the highway to travel 30 kilometers to the "Las Fuentes del Paraíso" urbanization where I lived at that time with my wife, my two daughters, cousin Isabel and her son Manyi.

The next morning, I had to teach computer classes at Jesús Obrero at 7:00am and I decided to take a break from the programming class I was covering at that time to talk to my students about the systems and complexities that I had seen that at Bilden.

ISAIAS AND JESÚS IDENTIFY PROCESSES FOR THE BSP

It was Friday and my first week of work at Bilden was ending, mid-morning I met with Isaías and Jesús to review their progress in defining processes for the BSP.

When they explained to me what they had prepared, I felt very excited, since it was good quality work and represented a deep level of knowledge of the entire company, especially on the part of Isaías, whose seniority and knowledge of the organization was reflected everywhere. Jesús had also contributed his good grain of sand.

They had prepared an exhaustive list of the processes carried out by each functional area in Bilden, they could explain what each process consisted of, who was responsible and in which organizational unit it was carried out.

I asked them to try to make a diagram with all the processes they had identified, where each block represented a process and each line the flow of information or product elements between them.

Finally, I suggested that they use the wall of my office to tape up several sheets of flipchart since the diagram would be huge.

INDUCTION PROCESS IN MARKETING

My second week focused on induction interviews in the Marketing Directorate, through which I met the entire management team and began to familiarize myself with the processes and some particularities of the cigarette market.

Venezuela was one of the few markets in the world where activated carbon filters had become popular as part of the specifications of a brand with a high level of penetration.

The market was almost bipolar in the sense that two brands dominated more than 80% of sales, one from Bilden and the other from the competition.

Having a market with a small number of brands has important advantages in terms of efficiency, economies of scale, advertising logistics, production, distribution and storage.

But it also has its drawbacks, if a star brand loses its shine the company can see its sales and market share drastically reduced overnight.

The advertising and image of the brands required a multimillion-dollar budget that at that time covered television, cinema, billboards, newspapers, magazines, sponsorship, events, promotional and merchandising materials.

The connection between tobacco and health was a sensitive topic at that time, and due to my addiction to cigarettes at that time, I did not pay much attention to it.

I think all of us smokers knew that smoking is harmful to your health, but it was easy to go off on a tangent.

There was progress in the trend of reducing advertising freedom in the cigarette market worldwide and how this complicated and made the launch of new brands more expensive.

As there were more restrictions, it was more difficult and expensive to create a new brand, this drove the need to promote regional and international brands.

Bilden's competition in Venezuela was Philips Morris and they had the most important international brand "Marlboro", which was the one I smoked in my teenage years.

JOURNEY ON A SALES ROUTE

The last phase of my induction into marketing management was a long journey accompanying a salesperson in the sequence of visits he had scheduled that day.

My experience began by observing the truck being loaded with packages of cigarettes of different brands according to what was specified in a special form.

Cigarettes are products that attract the interest of criminals since they can be easily resold. This adds a certain level of risk and stress in the operation of the routes since robberies materialized with certain frequency.

While I watched how the salesperson and his assistant took orders, prepared the invoice, delivered the product, inspected the advertising elements, reviewed the status of the shelves and updated the point of sale file, I imagined everything that could be automated with a mini computer and a portable, lightweight and low-cost printer that as far as I knew unfortunately did not yet exist.

After my experience traveling the sales route, when I returned to the office, I learned something additional exchanging impressions with Isaías, it turns out that in some cities like Caracas, there are wholesalers and Bilden sells the packages of cigarettes to them.

The wholesalers distribute the cigarettes combining with other products. Additionally, not all routes can use the same size truck. For example, there are routes in the interior of the country that have long distances and use larger trucks.

The additional details that Isaías explained to me expanded my understanding of the complexity and diversity of situations that the distribution system should contemplate.

We live in a civilization where we are used to finding everything we need around us and most people are not aware of all the processes that are carried out to make that possible.

INDUCTION IN PRODUCTION DIRECTORATE

My third week began with an interview with the production director, a thickly built Englishman named Alan.

Alan, who was over 60 years old and was close to retirement, had had a long career in different countries in Africa, Europe, Asia and Latin America, with which he had accumulated extraordinary experience, not only at a technical and managerial level, but also in the social, economic and cultural aspects of having traveled half the world.

Alan was a tough guy, a chain smoker with nicotine stains on his fingers, typical of someone who lights a cigarette with the butt of the one that runs out.

During the interview he told me about the organization of the factory, the 24-hour operation, six days a week, and how the different types of technology that coexisted added complexity to the production process.

Every downtime of a machine costs money, every machine has parts that wear out, we need to maintain spare parts and trained personnel to repair them and make them work.

Maintaining a high level of quality, efficiency and productivity in a factory that employs more than 1,200 workers in three shifts requires good planning and management control systems.

Every time we change the programming of a machine, waste is generated, errors can be made, and it all involves time, materials, and money.

Cigarettes are not very complex products to manufacture, but if you make more than 50 million every day, you have to have good quality control systems. Imagine what would happen if we put poorly formed packs or defective cigarettes on sale.

I asked Alan about the speed of the cigarette making machines and his answer impressed me, the most modern ones at that time could produce 16 thousand cigarettes per minute, which implied an astronomical leap, if you consider that the first one built in 1880, It could only produce 200 per minute.

As for information systems, Alan was clear that, in the production area, the list was long, although he had reasonable doubts that IT could solve his needs in the short term.

When we explored the topic he told me, "Orlando, we already do everything that needs to be done manually with a calculator, but obviously it can be improved, if we could do it faster, with fewer errors and at a lower cost I would be happier.

In production we have to keep track of the use and stocks of packaging materials, filter materials, tobacco, essence materials, spare parts, tools and finished products.

In the manufacturing process we must control the production level, efficiency and quality of the product at each stage, in each machine and in each shift.

To respond efficiently and at low cost to the sales forecasts prepared by marketing, we have to take into account the stocks in the fiscal warehouse, the current production schedule and the installed capacity in such a way that we make the minimum number of specification changes in the machinery.

Additionally, remember that finance uses much of that information to determine standard costs and make the variable cost calculations that feed into accounting.

INDUCTION IN AGRICULTURE DIRECTORATE

A company driver picked me up at home at 7 in the morning to take me to the Valencia plant. It was a highway trip of almost two hours that flew by thanks to the stories that Mr. Pacheco shared with me during the tour.

Pacheco had been a driver for the company for many years and was very familiar with the management team since he took this and other tours quite frequently.

During the trip he gave me a pre-induction about what I was going to find at the Valencia plant and about the characters who in his opinion were friendlier and more interesting, especially in relation to the pork barbecues that were organized on the weekends.

My visit occurred on an ideal day since the tobacco purchasing process was in full development and that gave me the opportunity to see how the trucks that brought the bales of tobacco were unloaded onto a conveyor belt that took them to the inspection point.

At the inspection point, a purchasing technician stopped the belt when the bale was on the weighing unit, reviewed the contents of the bale, and assigned a purchase grade.

The degree of purchase determines the price per kilo, which is related to the shape and size of the tobacco leaf since there are significant variations in the levels of aroma, nicotine, sugars and proportion of sheet vs vein.

After the inspection point, another conveyor belt began that took the bale to the interior of a huge warehouse where there was a row of metal baskets identified with the different grades of tobacco.

The tobacco stored in the baskets had to go through a deveining process where the tobacco leaves were cut into small pieces that could be separated by gravity in wind tunnels that sent the sheet to the upper level and the vein to the lower level.

During the development of the harvest, farmers were visited by Bilden agronomists who advised them on the fertilizers and herbicides they could use to guarantee the quality and productivity of the harvest.

Each farmer was hired to grow a certain amount of kilos of tobacco using the seeds supplied by Bilden, in this way the quality and genetic variety of the tobacco was controlled.

Upon learning about the process, I was once again impressed by the organization and efficiency with which everything was done while thinking that it was a shame that this level of organization was not met for all food crops.

When I had the opportunity to talk to the purchasing manager, he went straight to the point and told me.

"Orlando, I have been waiting for you, I want you to help me develop a purchasing system that will be the pride of Latin America, you have already seen the process, now imagine that the purchasing technician has a special keyboard with a button for each grade and when the bale is weighed, the data is transmitted to the computer, then the buyer presses the grade button and this causes a ticket to be printed with the weight, grade and the farmer's code. When the purchase is finished, another button is pressed to print the settlement at the administration office and issue the check at once. What do you think of my idea?"

I told him, with your enthusiasm and creativity, I assure you that one of the first systems we will put into operation will be the purchase of tobacco, he smiled and told me, "I think I'm going to buy you a cup of coffee in the office".

During the rest of the visit I met a group of extraordinary people who, like the purchasing manager, had an incredible work mystique.

From the director of agriculture, to the plant engineer, the agronomy manager, the head of administration and the head of the laboratory, everyone had very clear and practical ideas of their requirements in terms of information systems.

Their information requirements included the tobacco purchasing system, control of the deveining process, inventory of dried tobacco, inventory of spare parts, control of orders to the Caracas plant, and control of the expenses budget.

THE BSP METHODOLOGY

During the induction process, I had learned that there was enormous potential for automation, which made my imagination fly and filled me with enthusiasm, but also generated a lot of stress when I thought about the resources required and the risks derived from managing too many projects at the same time. To calm myself down, I often repeated to myself something my sister said.

"You have to cross bridges when you are in front of them, not when you see them in the distance".

Guided by the list of processes carried out in each directorate, I updated with Isaías and Jesús the macro diagram that they had prepared on the wall of my office where the flow of information and products reflected the operations across the whole company.

The BSP methodology that I had in mind was relatively simple, if a process is efficient, reliable, productive at a reasonable cost and the customer is satisfied, it is marked green and not much attention is paid to it, but if any of the five indicators are considered a problem, it is marked red and assigned priority.

During the evaluation of the processes, their owners must analyze them one by one and transfer requests to previous processes that represented the origin of a problem and must request opinions on the degree of satisfaction of their clients.

The transfer of problems and the request for satisfaction opinions are carried out using forms that are filled out and passed to the appropriate person. This gives rise to a chain of interaction between the people participating in the BSP.

In theory, if all processes have the five indicators of efficiency, reliability, productivity, cost and customer satisfaction in good condition, the BSP ends very quickly with an evaluation of excellent for everyone, but in practice this never happens, since there is always a dissatisfied customer, a process manager who is not satisfied with any of the indicators, or simply does not have a way to measure them and this forces him to define the existence of problems and propose a solution strategy.

If the solution strategy depends on an information system, the process in question is considered a candidate for automation or reengineering and is added to the list of projects to be evaluated for consideration in the systems plan.

By developing this exercise with the participation of the users responsible for the processes, several important objectives are achieved.

First, the information needs are identified to solve concrete problems using a perspective that encompasses the entire company and originates from the vision of those responsible.

Second, the different management areas are nourished by the analysis of possible solutions proposed by their colleagues from other functions.

Third, a perspective is created that crosses the barriers of the formal organization and facilitates the visualization of the needs for coordination or integration of information between different functions.

Fourth, the macro process diagram becomes a guide for planning the development and integration of systems throughout the organization.

BILDEN'S BSP DEVELOPMENT

When everything was ready, I presented the BSP development proposal to Roger and suggested that if we made a presentation to the Board of Directors and they approved the idea, the BSP would have a better chance of success.

The proposal was approved and the BSP was held in the conference room of the Bilden administrative building with the participation of 22 representatives of the 6 functional directorates.

It was an unforgettable, fun, interesting and super useful experience that exceeded all my expectations.

The conference room had been set up with a huge diagram of the entire company's processes on one of the walls and each participant was given a folder with their name containing a list of all the processes they would need to evaluate and blank forms to fill out the evaluation, and prepare problem transfers and satisfaction requests from clients.

When I explained the methodology and the sequence of activities we should develop, many began to joke with the idea of sending problem transfers if they did not receive a good satisfaction evaluation from their customers.

Once the methodology was explained, each participant began evaluating their processes and sending transfers of problems and requests for the level of satisfaction of their clients, and as we expected, no one was saved from receiving transfers or requests for evaluating the level of satisfaction.

During the evaluation, there were telephone calls and visits to people from the functional areas to clarify any issue that the representative did not know in depth.

I don't know if it was because of Bilden's organizational culture or the Venezuelan idiosyncrasy, but the process was fun and at the same time serious and constructive, everyone assumed a positive and responsible attitude when receiving problem transfers.

I heard several times comments like:

"Had not thought of that".

"Thanks for the information".

"Let's see how we can solve it".

"I have to delve deeper into the topic".

"Let me consult with the experts on this topic".

To make the process a little more interesting, we had developed a small application in the IBM S/38 where each participant would record through a screen terminal the evaluation of the processes they had carried out, the problem transfers they had received, the ones they had had sent and the statement of the solution strategies in mind.

From all this material, the IT Division would extract the part that had to do with information systems and each participant would receive a printed copy of what they had recorded in the system and what was related to their transfers of problems to other people.

At lunchtime we all went to eat at a grilled meat and chicken restaurant that was next to the factory, where the warm and participatory atmosphere of the morning session continued.

In the afternoon session, each person would give a short presentation summarizing what they had evaluated, the transfers they had received, and the solution strategies.

When the presentations were over, I thanked everyone for their participation and promised them a copy of the BSP general report that would be prepared in the coming days.

Isaías, Jesús, Magaly and I were left alone in the conference room to collect all the material that had been left and then Jesús told me.

"Orlando, I have the impression that you already knew what people were going to ask for in the induction interviews, if that was the case, why did we have to do this whole process".

So I told him.

"Very good question, Jesús, but let me ask Isaías to see how he sees it, before I give you my answer".

Isaías said.

"If users ask for things in their own words and relate it to the solution of specific problems that themselves have raised, I think it will be easier for Board of Directors to give us the resources that we will need to develop the systems plan"

Then I added.

"I completely agree, Isaías, that is the central reason, things have weight not necessarily because they are adequate or correct, the weight is given by the people who propose the ideas. On the other hand, this process allowed everyone to have an overview and realize that there is a lot to do in all areas"

FORMULATION OF BILDEN'S SYSTEMS PLAN

The following Monday, Isaías, Jesús and I spent the entire day meeting in my office, organizing and analyzing all the material collected in the BSP.

We had to propose a viable systems plan, with a reasonable scale of cost and development time, that was also politically acceptable to the Board of Directors.

This involved establishing priorities for the development of the systems, and establishing a time scale limit for developing the project.

To manage priorities, we established three categories called: critical, important and secondary.

Critical meant that the system should be developed in the first wave, due to its impact on the day-to-day life of the company, or that it already existed in IBM S/3, for example, payroll, accounting, registration of sales, budget control.

Important meant that it was a new system that affected the reliability of the measurement of the company's operating results or would allow a significant reduction in expenses, costs or operational risks. For example, inventory control systems, production control systems, and sales statistics fall into this category.

Secondary was the default classification, when the system did not meet the requirements of the previous two categories, for example, the eligible registry, the performance evaluation records.

Finally, we made an estimate of time and resources to develop the systems plan, which after long discussions with Isaías and Jesús ended in the formulation of a plan to develop 46 applications in 3 years with 10 programmer analysts.

Ten programmer analysts represent 330 working months of analysis and programming, assuming that each developer has 11 working months per year for three years.

If we divide 330 months of "MAN POWER" between 46 applications, we have 7.1 months per application. In my experience this was enough and had a certain margin of safety, but there were risks and although I was confident that it could be done, I could not guarantee it 100%.

Many things could go wrong, for example, a programmer analyst could resign or be fired in the middle of the project, a user could be especially difficult and not provide clear and reliable specifications, the expected functionality in the applications could be more extensive and complex than expected, IBM could change strategy and not continue expanding the capacity of the IBM S/38 platform, etc.

But good things could also happen, for example: Development on the IBM S/38 would be faster than expected, the analyst-programmer approach would double productivity, users would be reasonable in their expectations and collaborate 100%.

When we analyzed all these aspects, Isaías and Jesús calmed down a little, but neither of them would have bet their heads if they had been asked, on the other hand, Jesús was not very optimistic that the Board of Directors would approve the hiring of 10 programming analysts in one fell swoop.

I also had my reservations about the 10 programmer analysts, but if they cut it, the time would be longer and ultimately that would be an advantage for IT since it would reduce the level of risk and make the work easier in the short term.

Managing 10 projects is not the same as managing 5.

Hiring 10 programming analysts sounded like a tough nut to crack to some, but if you put it in the right context, things looked different. Bilden had around 2,000 workers at that time, therefore, 10 people represented only 0.05% of the workforce.

All functional areas had a long list of applications to develop and the 10 people would be assigned by directorate, this implied that each directorate had resources permanently assigned to the development of their applications and would not have to compete with the other areas.

On the other hand, the cost of the 10 programmer analysts to carry out the technological renewal of the information systems represented an immaterial amount when compared with other company strategies, for example, the annual advertising campaign or a new Protos machine for the cigarette manufacturing.

APPROVAL OF THE BILDEN'S SYSTEMS PLAN

Once I had analyzed the systems plan and the proposal to hire 10 analysts from every angle I could imagine, I prepared a presentation, explained it to Roger and suggested that he ask for a turn to present it to the Board of Directors.

Roger suggested that I print out all the materials and prepare a copy for each director, so they would have a chance to see it before the presentation and it would be easier to get approval.

I prepared the material and gave it to Roger before the meeting that would take place that week and I assumed that the following week I would have my turn to make the presentation and that possibly in another week or two I would have an answer.

In the meantime, I would dedicate myself to experimenting with the IBM S/38 to become a little more familiar with the management of the database and its programming language.

After the Board of Directors meeting, Roger appeared in my office and I assumed it was to talk to me about when the systems plan presentation would be, but instead he told me.

"Orlando, the systems plan is already approved, you can hire the 10 programming analysts"

I was pleasantly surprised and asked Roger.

"What happened, how come there is no need to present the plan?"

Then Roger told me.

"Yesterday at the meeting, I distributed the material and proposed making the presentation next week, but everyone was curious and began to look at the content and the request for approval, then someone said, why are we going to give this topic more thought? , the BSP has already been done, we have had the machine stopped for more than a year and the presentation is to approve 10 heads, which is less than 2 per functional area, for me I sign it today and thus we advance faster, so we all agreed and the proposal was approved".

In my heart I thought that the material of the presentation was quite clear and that since all the directors were involved in the BSP that had prepared the ground, however it never ceases to surprise me, if I had been one of them I would have asked a few additional questions For example, what would happen to the 10 analysts when the systems plan was finished, or how much it would cost to expand the IBM S/38 and all the screen terminals, printers and personal computers that would have to be purchased to implement the systems.

But sometimes it is preferable not to think too much about things since there is a risk of getting lost in excessive analyzes that do not necessarily eliminate uncertainty or improve decisions.

When I told Isaías and Jesús the good news, they couldn't believe it. They were surprised that the proposal had been approved without even making the presentation or setting conditions.

We prepared a profile for the programmer analyst position to discuss with the recruitment and selection department and began to plan a remodeling of space in the IT area to locate the development.

I also thought it was a good time to move my office and be closer to the team.

Isaías was in charge of the remodeling and Jesús was in charge of speaking with the Recruitment and Selection Department.

The Recruitment and Selection Department published a series of press notices for the recruitment of the analyst programmers mentioning the IBM S/38 platform with PC and that the work included all phases of the development of new applications.

In less than two months we had the team selected, and as they were incorporated they went through a good induction program at the end of which there was a period of familiarization with the IBM S/38, the systems plan and the methodology.

The 10 hired people were assigned to the different functional areas according to the following scheme:

- Frank. Finance.
- Blanca. Finance & RC.
- Zaida. Human Resources.
- Fred. Human Resources.
- Amira. Production.
- José Luis. Production.
- Judith. Agriculture.
- Antonio. Agriculture.
- Mari. Marketing.
- Fernando. Marketing.

All those selected were young people eager to participate in systems development, but Amira and Frank had more experience and were initially named team leaders, and later system managers.

Although each member of the team was a world different in their personality traits, they all had an excellent human and professional caliber that was key to the success of the development of the plan.

Despite the large number of projects that were developed, there were no cancellations, significant failures or extraordinary delays.

The entire team did a very professional job and I don't remember having to ask anyone to make more efforts. Everyone was clear about their responsibility and strived to do things well and maintain a good relationship with users and their colleagues.

I don't know if it was luck, or the idiosyncrasy of the Venezuelan, or the organizational culture of Bilden, but the human and professional quality of this team of people was a key factor in the success of the development of the system plan formulated in 1983.

Personally, for me it was a pride and a blessing to be able to count on this team in my professional life.

DEVELOPMENT OF THE SYSTEMS BEGINS

At the end of July 1983, the first wave of systems plan applications was in full swing and then we received a visit from Gordon, BIT Co.'s corporate IT manager.

Gordon knew about the development of the BSP, the hiring of the 10 analyst programmers and that things were going according to plan, since I kept him informed, but he had some ideas in mind that almost interrupted my career at Bilden.

His visit lasted three days and during that time he met with several directors and managers from the functional areas, with all the analysts in a group meeting, and with me to review the plan and the progress achieved up to that point.

Near the end of the visit, he told me that he was very pleasantly impressed by what was being done, since until that moment a BSP had not been successfully carried out in the other companies of BIT Co.

MY MOTIVATION COLLAPSES

When I thought we had already exhausted the visit agenda, Gordon told me something totally unexpected.

"Orlando, I have thought about using Venezuela as the regional IT headquarters for Latin America, and this means that a regional IT manager will be transferred to Bilden to whom you report, as well as the other countries in the region".

As he explained his plan, the idea didn't sit well with me and I told him.

"Gordon, I imagine you have your reasons to justify this change in the organization, but in my opinion that is going to complicate things for me locally and at the same time it changes my contracting conditions, therefore, I cannot accept it, so it is better to start looking for someone to replace me".

Then Gordon told me.

"But what's the problem, I don't see how a regional manager is going to complicate things for you".

I thought for a few seconds and told him.

"Gordon, I am used to working based on general objectives, strategic guidelines and high-level policies. If you put a regional manager in Venezuela to intervene in the day-to-day running of the IT Division, I will not feel comfortable in the organization, that changes the conditions under which I was hired".

"Don't worry about me, if I resigned now I still have time to reactivate my management training company, Bilden already has a systems plan and a development team working that can surely be led by the regional manager and whoever replaces me".

Gordon looked at me with surprise and said.

"Orlando, you really surprised me, I didn't expect you to see the reorganization this way, let me reflect on the matter and please don't make an impulsive decision".

Gordon left my office with a somewhat confused expression and went to Roger's office. I have no idea what they talked about and I didn't see him again that day.

His idea of reorganization with a regional manager really didn't sit well with me, since in a way it represented a demotion and certainly changed my hiring conditions, so I thought about it for a while and ended up writing my resignation from the IT Division, I put it in an envelope and left it on my desk.

I thought, if I don't feel comfortable in this job, it's better to return to my "Management Development Institute", no matter how complicated the country's economic situation is, there are always opportunities, whether in training or consulting.

The next day Gordon appeared early in my office and told me.

"Orlando I am very sorry for the misunderstanding yesterday, I honestly did not think that the change in reporting line would affect you so much, we are going to leave the organization as it is when it comes to Venezuela"

"The regional manager will be located in another country and will not have influence over Bilden, you are doing a good job, you have the trust of the Bilden management team and for my part I also support you".

"The change I told you about actually originates from the fact that there is someone who has done a good job in Chile and in order not to lose him, we have to create space in the organization to take advantage of his potential, but not at the cost of damaging something that already works".

By the way, there is another topic I wanted to talk to you about, in November there is a two-week MDP "Management Development Program" in the United Kingdom and Bilden has nominated you to participate, this program is only offered to people with high potential and I think "It will be a good opportunity for you".

After the meeting with Gordon, my spirits returned and I understood that the organizational change he had in mind, although it did not benefit me, was not a negative indication towards my level of performance, but in any case I felt satisfied with myself for having won this little battle of corporate politics.

Years later, when I was recapitulating my work life, I remembered this incident and was convinced that my rejection of change significantly lengthened my professional life at BIT Co.

In my personal experience, success depends largely on the passion you feel towards what you do, but this implies that you must feel very motivated to pursue your goals.

When I lose motivation, that vital energy that allows me to continually strive disappears, and that is what I felt would happen if I accepted the change in the organization. In short, people like me are flexible and adapt to change, but have limits and this was one of them.

A NEW ACCOUNTING MANAGER AT BILDEN

Reviewing the "Reading File" that Magaly put in my inbox, I learned that Jeffrey would soon be transferred to an operating company of BIT Co. in Zaire as director of finance and that Oscar would be the new accounting manager. from Bilden.

When I saw the news I was happy for Jeffrey as I assumed it was a good promotion for him, and I thought I will soon meet the new accounting manager through the induction program.

Oscar was a tall, mature, very nice guy and we had very good chemistry from the first moment. He was very interested in the development of systems in his area and his enthusiasm encouraged me to get involved in what would be a very special accounting system.

Oscar quickly became familiar with the account system used by Bilden and with the organization of cost centers and the concepts of fixed and semi-variable expenses used by BIT Co.

A VERY SPECIAL ACCOUNTING SYSTEM

At that time the idea of feeding accounting in an interactive system was not very popular, the majority perceived accounting as something routine, that had to be done to comply with regulations and have the information base to make financial statements, but not much. further.

Oscar opened my eyes to see accounting as a source of useful information in management control if organized and presented quickly and properly.

When Oscar completed his familiarization with the accounting area at Bilden, he told me something very interesting.

"Orlando, the Bilden account code is very well thought out, and if used properly I think you can kill several birds with one stone, since you can make a good accounting system and a good budget formulation and control system almost at the same time".

His comment piqued my interest and we began to imagine how the system could be structured, so little by little during several informal meetings we conceptualized a database that could support accounting, expense budgeting, and any auxiliaries that were necessary.

With the database designed, Oscar encouraged me to make a prototype program to create accounting entries interactively so he could discuss it with his people.

The use of prototypes to test the conceptual design of applications was something that in my experience had very good results, I was curious to get my hands on the IBM S/38 and this was an opportunity to deepen my knowledge in something that could be of practical use immediately.

I told Oscar that I would follow his suggestion if we did it in the afternoons after office hours, and he agreed so we got to work and in a week we had a working prototype of a program that allowed us to create, modify and approve accounting journals through a screen terminal.

The idea was relatively simple, an accounting journal is a set of charges and credits that derived from an event in the real world that is covered by physical documents such as invoices, receipts, debit notes, contracts, etc.

Oscar's idea was that each receipt be adequately described to easily understand the event that it recorded in accounting and was supported by the attached documents, thus leaving a clear and complete trail of audit and internal control.

On the other hand, the details at the level of charges and credits combined with a certain type of transaction associated with auxiliaries would allow the automatic generation of entries pending reconciliation.

When we demonstrated the prototype to the group of users in the accounting department, everyone was delighted with the design and work methodology that Oscar proposed.

At this point I transferred the prototype to Blanca and Frank and they continued the development of the accounting system and the budget for fixed and semi-variable expenses.

While Blanca and Frank finished the development, Oscar and I continued working in the afternoons, but now focused on making some online management enquiries.

THE MANAGEMENT INFORMATION SYSTEM IS BORN

The idea was that each user at a managerial level could analyze their expenses and budget execution in their cost center, moving from the general to the specific without having to remember any account code.

As the access control system for the IBM S/38 worked with a personalized menu per user, when activating the option to consult expenses versus budget, the system would show a list of the cost centers authorized to the user and from there it would be possible to navigate by month, by cost center, by expense concept and then by account until you the details of the accounting receipt if necessary.

I found this navigation design from general to particular very useful to facilitate the use and access of information and I incorporated it as a reference model for analysts to use in all applications where it had practical use.

In this way, the seed of the management information system began to germinate, which over time grew to cover all functional areas.

The accounting system and the budget formulation and control system were implemented in record time and the IBM S/38 began to be used by end users at the end of 1983.

TWO WEEKS IN THE UK

In mid-November 1983 I made my first trip to the BIT Co. headquarters in London. It was a trip with two objectives, the first was to participate in the MDP "Management Development Program" and the second was to become familiar with the organization, especially with the team that worked with Gordon in Corporate IT Division.

The flight from Caracas lasted just over 9 hours and was quite comfortable thanks to the space and the facilities of a "Business" ticket paid for by the company.

Arriving at Heathrow Airport, I cleared immigration, picked up my suitcase and took a taxi to the St. Ermins Hotel, in Westminster near Millbank where the BIT Co headquarters were located at the time.

The hotel disappointed me a little as it was very old with quite small rooms, although it was well equipped, very clean and tidy.

I later found out that it wasn't cheap, but they used it because it was a few minutes from the BIT Co. offices in central London and they had a good corporate rate.

That night I had dinner in the room and watched television until dawn since my schedule had changed and I couldn't sleep.

The next day was Sunday and I had it free until 5 in the afternoon since at that time a transport would arrive to take me to the training center at Chelwood.

After having breakfast at the hotel, the typical English menu of scrambled eggs, bacon, coffee beans and orange juice, I set out to explore the area and spent several hours walking around Buckingham Palace, Big Ben, Parliament and Trafalgar. Square.

During the tour, I browsed through several toy and souvenir stores and ended up buying a Christmas gift for each member of the family.

In the afternoon, I checked out and sat at the reception to wait for the arrival of the transport. Then I began to recognize other characters who gave the impression of being waiting for the same thing as me, so I introduced myself to those I could identify.

At 5pm a bus well identified with the BIT logo arrived on time, and almost two hours later we arrived at an old building with the appearance of a medieval castle located in the middle of a forest, it was the training center used by BIT Co. around Chelwood.

Everything was perfectly organized and in a few minutes each of the newcomers had been assigned a room, a sticker with their name, and a folder containing a diagram of the facilities and the program of activities for each day.

My room was comfortable, simple with a single bed, a work table, a chair and a cabinet to store clothes. The view was beautiful, overlooking the interior gardens and a forest in the distance that I could see well the next morning.

The program covered some master sessions led by experts on the topics and a good dose of work in groups that rotated in their composition to give the opportunity to interact with different participants.

In total we were a group of 25 people aged approximately 25 to 40 years old, most of whom were members of the management team of operating companies of BIT Co. and a few were local staff working at the headquarters.

There were people from Australia, USA, Canada, Hong Kong, Argentina, Mexico, Venezuela, Zaire, Kenya, South Africa, Chile, Costa Rica, Belgium, Panama, Germany and Spain.

The first day there was a small presentation excise where each one shared some personal and professional information with the group, which made it clear that we were a representative sample of planet Earth and all the functional areas of the operating companies and the headquarters.

There were people from Agriculture, Production, Finance, IT, Marketing, Corporate Relations, Human Resources, Legal and Audit.

The group exercises were designed to demonstrate and encourage the importance of key aspects of an effective organizational culture such as teamwork, negotiation, communication, helicopter vision, cooperation, flexibility, uncertainty management, feedback and objectivity.

Most of the exercises looked like games where we competed for points by working in coordination with other teams or competing against them.

Some exercises provided the opportunity to make decisions in situations of uncertainty or to invest in acquiring information to reduce risk.

Other exercises set an objective and allowed to decide whether to work independently or seek to partner with another team and share results.

All exercises involved external facilitators who monitored the group's activities and occasionally intervened to give advice if the group dynamics had become complicated by the intensity of the interpersonal interactions.

Another very useful and interesting part of the MDP were the keynote sessions, especially those dedicated to finance, marketing and IT.

In the area of Finance, the sessions were developed around a small book published by BIT called "How much profit is enough". Where key concepts such as profit, costs, expenses, contribution, taxes, profitability, return on capital, risk, inflation, financial cost and cash flow were developed in a simple and very didactic way.

In the Marketing sessions, topics such as brand image, brand recognition, the "Above the line" and "Below the line" communication strategy, the importance of market share, and restrictive trends in cigarette advertising were covered.

In the IT area, cases from several countries were presented, including the BSP carried out in Venezuela, and teamwork was carried out that consisted of making a prediction of the technology that would be available in a horizon of 5 to 10 years.

I remember that in my team we proposed the widespread use of mobile telephony, wireless printers and handheld computers, which sounded like a good idea to more than one person.

In the evenings after dinner, we generally met in a Pub that was next to one of the buildings in the complex where the speakers who had participated in the day's sessions and sometimes members of the BIT Board appeared every night to talk informally with the MDP participants. Thus I had the opportunity to personally meet the Chairman and Deputy Chairman of BIT Industries.

KNOWING THE ENVIRONMENT OF HEADQUARTERS

When the MDP ended, I returned to London on the same bus and to the same hotel to continue with the second part of the visit, which was basically meeting people and talking about what we were doing in IT in Venezuela.

My itinerary of activities included induction interviews with key IT people, a visit to the computing center and a brief interview with the corporate finance director.

Eddie, was Gordon's second in command, he was concentrating at that time on coordinating the IVPA "International Volume Procurement Agreement" with IBM, and promoting technology transfer between the group's companies.

Eddie, explained to me how there was enormous difference between companies in terms of resources and level of development. He was organizing exchange seminars by region, one in Africa, another in Asia and another in Latin America to which I would be invited in 1984.

Tony had just arrived from New Zealand and was in charge of the application development area, which at that time included a series of very sophisticated spreadsheets to facilitate the preparation and transmission of the business plan, monthly and quarterly reports from operating companies.

One day, Gordon invited me to have lunch with him and Eddie in an executive dining room that had a few well-spaced tables and a menu with several options. I got the impression that there were several of these restaurants in the building and they were used to reinforce the corporate image with visitors from the operating units.

The last day I had lunch at the general restaurant, which was a kind of self-service with quite a variety of dishes and a cozy atmosphere that included a bar where you could have a drink after finishing eating.

During the interviews with the different people I was able to observe that the organizational culture of the headquarters was very different from what I experienced at Bilden at Venezuela.

There was no constant pressure to meet deadlines or finish projects, visitors from the operating companies were part of the day-to-day life and some even spent long periods of training or working in functional areas. There was a flexible schedule, many arrived a little late and it was very rare to work at night or on weekends, some went to work by bicycle, the vast majority used public transportation and only the directors had a driver and assigned parking space. In central London it was difficult and very expensive to have a personal carpark.

Connecting together several comments made to me during informal conversations about career development at BIT Co., I came to the conclusion that to advance to the highest levels I had to leave Venezuela and spend some time as an expatriate, possibly in the headquarters and in other operating company.

At the end of the visit to Millbank, I took a taxi to the airport and began my return to Venezuela with an updated idea of what the headquarters was like and the cultural variety that a multinational like BIT implied.

During the MDP I had learned many useful things and the interaction with people from so many latitudes was very enriching.

I felt a little more confident in my communication skills in English and how this language was a vital tool to facilitate interaction between countries with so much linguistic diversity. A German, a Frenchman, a Chinese and a Venezuelan could work as a team if they spoke a common language and in BIT it was English.

THE STEERING COMMITTEE OF THE SYSTEMS PLAN

To supervise the development of the systems, plan and the appropriate use of resources, the "Systems Plan Steering Committee" was created in January 1984.

This committee began to meet every three months and was made up of high-level representatives from each functional area and the IT manager who acted as coordinator.

The directors of Finance, Production, Marketing and Corporate Relations decided to participate themselves as permanent members of the committee, this increased the relevance of the meetings.

The meetings followed a standard agenda that, among other things, included reviewing an updated diagram with the development status of the applications covered in the plan and reporting on the progress of each project.

If a new application had been implemented since the last meeting, a short summary of the expected benefits, cost and development time was made.

In some cases, demonstrations of the new systems were made and images of illustrative reports or queries were distributed.

The use of the systems was shown with the queries of usage statistics that were kept available in the IBM S/38, this created more than one controversy on a complex issue that was the balance between user privacy and the need to measure the use of the systems.

To maintain the formality of the meetings, minutes were always prepared detailing each intervention, presentation or demonstration.

When internal auditors came from headquarters, one thing they always asked for were meeting minutes and copies of the information packet that was handed out at each meeting.

At first this seemed a little exaggerated to me, but as time went by I began to justify it and was even glad that it was so, since the materials we prepared for the meetings allowed objectively monitor progress and this was politically very valuable if it were endorsed by the auditors.

CHANGES CONTINUE IN THE MANAGEMENT TEAM

In the first quarter of 1984, just as I was beginning to feel like I knew the entire management team well, two major changes to the organization were announced. Johnny came as the new Production Director and Raúl as the new Marketing Director.

These changes meant that I had to re-sow the seed of the systems plan in two members of the Executive Committee, which was relatively easy since in both cases they were people with an interest in IT.

The two new directors decided to be part of the Systems Plan Steering Committee, which was very good news.

GOOD CHEMISTRY WITH THE MARKETING DIRECTOR

Raúl was an easy person to deal with, he had a lot of management experience, and when I spoke to him about the BSP and the systems plan he became interested in the subject.

Over time we developed a very good relationship, and as the systems in the Marketing Directorate generated a lot of relevant information, every time a new application was implemented I looked for a way to extract managerial information and showed it to Raúl.

If Raúl saw something in the management information system that seemed interesting to him, he generally commented on it and this caused his team members to strive to stay up to date on everything that was available in the system.

Bilden's management information system at that time was not a marvel, but it contained a lot of useful and easy-to-view information, from sales statistics by market, brand and branch to figures extracted from the market audit that included share estimates for own brands and competing brands. I remember that, on one occasion, I ran into Raúl in the office one Sunday while I was working with my team on developing a presentation, and since he was interested in the topic, we showed him what we had prepared. It was a presentation for a visitor to headquarters in an early version of PowerPoint that took advantage of many of the animation features that were available. When Raúl saw the presentation, he was impressed and congratulated the team, but he called me to part of the group and told me.

"Orlando, the presentation is very good, it really impresses, but be careful with the problem of the dog and the tail"

So I asked him what's that thing about the dog and the tail, and he answered.

"If you have a dog, the dog wags its tail, not the other way around. If the presentation uses too many graphic elements, you can create the feeling that it is the tail that is wagging the dog.

If I were you, I would try to moderate the amount of special effects they are using a little, ask yourself what you want the audience who will see the presentation to take away in their minds".

I thanked him for the comment and spent a while reflecting on the implications of the dog and the tail example.

Raúl was right, sometimes we get carried away too much by the form and put the content in second place.

The example of the dog and the tail was also useful to me in the analysis of priorities to differentiate what is fundamental from what is secondary.

A SWARM OF INVENTORY SYSTEMS

In an industrial company, inventory control systems play a very important role in terms of logistics and all have accounting implications.

Taking a tour of the different types of assets to control in Bilden, the full list covered over 20 categories, including raw materials, products in process, finished products, vehicles, machinery, spare parts, promotional items, and many etc.

The systems plan should cover all categories, in some cases with purpose-built systems and in others with a general application with functionality to cover several categories.

Among the special and most complex cases to automate were the inventories of raw materials and finished products, where it was required to control inputs, outputs and stocks with precision, in addition to calculating the accounting valuation and in some cases the replacement levels.

All this variety of cases was studied by analysts in combination with users from finance and the other functional areas involved and gave rise to a series of inventory control applications that satisfied the needs of accounting valuation and supported logistical processes of production, sales and marketing.

Inventory systems were developed and implemented progressively, beginning with spare parts inventory at the end of 1983, followed by packaging materials, finished product, tobacco, fixed assets, and finally promotional items and merchandising.

THE BRANCH CONTROL SYSTEM

When the packages of cigarettes left the fiscal warehouse, they were immediately loaded onto trucks according to a dispatch plan that took them to Bilden branches throughout the country.

The cigarettes represented an enormous amount of money, not only because of the production cost since it had added the value of the cigarette tax, which was at that time 50% of the retail price, and had been paid to remove the product from the warehouse.

This meant that product inventory had a significant financial cost for Bilden, therefore, the Marketing and Production directorates strove to maintain the most optimal inventory level possible.

Additionally, the cost of transportation from Caracas to the branches and the risk of theft, represented two more cost factors that should be managed with a high level of efficiency.

Due to security problems in some areas of the country, the trucks were escorted by armed guards and radio contact was maintained until the truck arrived at the branch. Unfortunately, cigarettes are an easy product to resell and highly coveted by criminals.

When the cigarettes arrived at the branches, they went to a warehouse and from there, they were loaded again into small trucks and other transportation vehicles to distribute them to thousands of points of sale in cities, towns and highway businesses.

This entire process was tracked and controlled by a chain of transactions that recorded the physical movement and conversion of cigarettes into money or accounts receivable from retailers or wholesalers.

The automation of processes in the branch and on the routes was carried out with the help of personal computers, since at that time the IBM S/38 had connectivity problems in the interior of the country due to poor reliability and high cost of the telephone lines necessary to operate an online system.

All this information was entered into the branch's PC, the corresponding balances were made each day, demonstration reports were printed and diskettes were generated with the information to be sent along with the originals of the invoices and receipts to the office. headquarters in Caracas where the data from the diskettes was transferred to the IBM S/38.

In this way, a distributed system was structured that maintained control over stocks, sales, collections and all necessary transactions to feed accounting, bank reconciliation and sales statistics at the national level.

As telecommunication mechanisms improved, floppy disks were replaced by data transmission interfaces to the computer center and a weekly closure was moved to a daily closure.

Once the distributed branch control system was fully implemented and integrated into the IBM S/38, experiments began with minicomputers and portable printers to automate routes, but for security and cost reasons, this technology was not extended to all routes in the 80s.

AUTOMATION IN AGRICULTURE

The tobacco purchasing system was the first application that was implemented in the systems plan for the Agriculture Directorate for the 1984 harvest.

With the help of a local electronic engineering company, we built a small computer with a tailor-made keyboard specially designed to withstand the harshness of the tobacco shopping environment full of noise, dust and electromagnetic disturbances due to conveyor belt motors.

The system eliminated the need to make manual calculations and gave a certain degree of agility to the purchasing process. It was the pride of the purchasing manager, since it was an idea that he fought for several years until it was put into practice.

Like any new system, it also had its drawbacks and we had to make a significant effort to resolve them, creating emergency and recovery procedures in case of hardware or power failure.

As time went by, some improvements were made, such as using a magnetic character screen to display the weight and degree of purchase that was printed on the ticket, and displaying the farmer's code that was going to be processed.

Another important area of systematization at the Valencia plant was the control of the deveining process and the control of the sheet and vein inventory. The inventory system controlled the transfer of tobacco between the plants in Valencia and Caracas and allowed control of the loss that occurred due to the change in humidity.

The control of expenses and the budget of fixed and semi-variable expenses was implemented using the same system developed for Caracas since it only required the definition of accounting areas and cost center codes.

A NEW FINANCE DIRECTOR

At the end of 1984, it was announced that Roger, the finance director would return to work at the headquarters and would be replaced by another expatriate, an Englishman named, David.

This implied a possible change in the modus operandi of my local reporting line, and initially generated some stress for me, since in my experience changing bosses is sometimes equivalent to changing jobs.

My relationship with Roger had been good, we had little personal interaction, but when we spoke there was always a kind and considerate manner. We operated according to general guidelines and objectives that were evaluated periodically and we both felt comfortable working that way.

Roger was a thoughtful, respectful person, who thought carefully before acting, and made an effort to maintain good relationships with all the people around him, I was definitely going to miss him.

David, the new director of finance, arrived in a country that was beginning a negative economic cycle, with the rise of inflation, instability in currency exchange control and a deterioration in the political and social panorama.

Bilden had experienced a long period of profitability, growth and dividend facilities that had placed it in a good position in the ranking of BIT Co. operating companies, but all that was beginning to change direction. At that time no one knew it, but Venezuela was entering a negative cycle from which it would not recover for more than four decades, the difficulties were just beginning.

David did not know the country, nor did he speak Spanish, but he learned quickly, he made an effort to do a good job and fit in with the management team, which was not entirely easy.

There was a certain level of territoriality among some of the directors and the progressive increase in macroeconomic challenges did not make it easier for him to navigate the terrain.

On my side things went in a good direction, David and I quickly developed a good relationship, he maintained the same style as Roger, I think he used a very useful management principle that he says. "If it is working, don't fix it".

David participated in the meetings of the Systems Plan Steering Committee, and was involved in aspects of interest to the headquarters such as systems audits, the development of the contingency plan and the approval of the annual budget.

On the business side, inflation, price increase negotiations, exchange control, treasury, import and export controls and a diversification project promoted by the parent company generated enough challenges and difficulties to keep him very busy.

PRODUCTION CONTROL SYSTEMS

Waste, losses, machine stoppages and deficiencies occur throughout the cigarette manufacturing process and must be systematically detected, corrected and monitored to control production costs, ensure quality and optimize the management of the manufacturing process, taking measurement at each stage of the process is the basis of production control systems.

The measurements made are recorded and entered into the production control system to feed a database that allows calculating efficiency, utilization and productivity per machine, module, shift and day.

Quality control tests are also continually performed in different parts of the process to verify that machine settings reflect expected conditions.

Production and quality control systems began to be automated starting in 1984 and allowed a wide variety of statistical information to be displayed through screen query functions and printed reports.

BUYING A FLAT FOR MY MOTHER

In June 1984, after more than a year working at Bilden, my work schedule absorbed more than 12 hours a day from Monday to Friday and a good part of the weekends, which made it clear that it made no sense to maintain the offices of the Management Development Institute, so I decided to buy a second-hand apartment, for my mother's residence, which would enable to stop renting the Miravila building.

Looking through the classified ads in the newspaper and found a very good apartment at a good price in the Macaracuay urbanization that was 10 minutes from my office. It was a 120 square meter apartment with 3 bedrooms, living room, dining room, kitchen, two bathrooms and two parking spaces, on the 19th floor, with a spectacular view.

I could pay it with a mortgage in easy installments that barely represented 25% of what it cost me to rent the Miravila building.

I did the purchasing procedures and when the apartment was delivered, I took my mother to see it, but something happened that I did not expect, unfortunately that day one of the two elevators broke down and when my mother entered the apartment she told me.

"My son, you think I can live on the 19th floor in a building where the elevators frequently fail".

 This left me disarmed and the only thing I could think of to say was.

"My chubby girl, you are right, but I already bought it, let me think about how we can solve it".

Since I had already sent the letter terminating the rental contract for the Miravila building, I had to find a temporary solution for my mother's residence, which fortunately was easy since one of my mother's sisters had a small apartment that we could rent temporarily, it was a terrace on the 5th floor, which was not ideal, but it had the advantage of being next to my aunt's apartment.

I moved my mother to my aunt's terrace apartment, I handed over the apartment in the Miravila building and began to think about how to find a long-term solution for my mother's home. A few days later I took my wife and daughters to see the apartment in Macaracuay, and curiously they all liked it more than where we lived and then we decided to move the family to this apartment since it was bigger than where we lived, it had two parking places, it was closer to my work, it was closer to the university and we could decorate it to everyone's taste.

Two months later we moved to Macaracuay, and to resolve the failure of the elevators, I made a proposal at the first condominium meeting that ended in my election as president of the community.

By taking charge of the condominium board, I was able to help solve the elevator maintenance problem and convince the community to improve the general level of maintenance of the residential complex, with which we all benefited.

BREAKFAST AT THE FAIR WITH THE WHOLE FAMILY

After the family move to the flat at Macaracuay, some Sundays we got up late and instead of having breakfast at home, we had the habit of going to the Ciudad Tamanaco Shopping Center to a fast food area called La Feria that had more than 15 types of restaurants around an area with tables for the public.

The whole family liked us going there and each one asked for something different. I used to go around the area paying the bill at each place after each person placed the order.

In the end, we sat together but each one had what he or she wanted which generally included German sausages, arepas, fried chicken, hamburgers, Chinese rice, and chocolate cookies.

What we ate were small weekend indulgences that we enjoyed but we couldn't repeat them much since it wasn't very healthy.

EAT DINNER TWICE WHEN VISITING MOM

When I worked at Bilden, almost every day I visited my mother at noon or in the evening before going home.

My mother spent a lot of time alone and my visits were a way of accompanying her and showing her affection.

During my visits, my mother always insisted on preparing something to eat for me, and even though I said no, I always ended up eating what she prepared, which was always very appetizing.

The problem was that I also ate often at home so as not to break the family routine, so I ended up weighing 74 kilos, which I didn't like very much but I didn't give it much importance at that time.

THE IBM S/3 IS DISINCORPORATED

By mid-1985, the development of the systems plan had advanced to allow the decommissioning of IBM S/3 and the elimination of the data transcription department, which was already gradually reduced.

I remember that when I reported on this event at the Systems Plan Steering Committee meeting, several of the committee members suggested that we should celebrate it, so we organized a lunch with the committee members and the systems development team.

During lunch, David surprised us with a commemorative gift for the IT Division, it was a framed cartoon in which four versions of reality were drawn that said:

- This is what the user requested.
- This is how the analyst designed it.
- This is how the auditors imagined it.
- This is how it was finally implemented.

Due to the level of progress achieved in the development of the systems plan, it was time to start putting more effort into the documentation and formal user training, for which I presented a proposal to create an Organization and Methods department with a small team composed of a manager and two O&M analysts.

When the proposal was approved, I offered the management of the department to a young industrial engineer named Jorge, who also had solid knowledge of IT and in this way could have a versatile resource that could handle O&M projects and IT projects.

Jorge did an excellent job and formed a team with two O&M analysts who added a lot of value in the development of administrative procedures, user manuals and training courses for end users.

I remember that I was always impressed by the work mystique of Jorge and his O&M team, especially María Isabel, whom I frequently found on Saturday mornings, teaching a course for end users in the conference room attached to my office.

ANOTHER APARTMENT FOR MY MOTHER

Although my mother lived well in my aunt's terrace apartment, the idea of her having her own apartment never left my mind and I frequently checked the classified ads looking for opportunities in the Macaracuay area, and one day a very good one appeared.

It was a beautiful 100 square meter apartment at a very good price on the 3rd floor, with a living room, dining room, kitchen, two bedrooms, two bathrooms and a parking space.

I could buy it with a mortgage and I could pay the monthly instalments without a problem, since my salary had recently increased.

I carried out the purchase procedures, did a small renovation, and bought all the furniture to surprise my mother who had no idea of what I was doing since she had assumed that would continue living on my aunt's terrace.

When everything was ready, one day I asked my mother to accompany me to visit a friend who lived near my house and I took her by surprise to the apartment that was already fully furnished.

When we entered the apartment she was surprised that I had the keys and put on a serious face for a few moments, I think he thought I had gotten divorced, but then I told her.

"What do you think of this apartment for the prettiest chubby girl in my heart to live in?"

My mother hugged me and we cried for a while holding each other.

The following week we organized the move and my mother lived in that apartment for the rest of her life. I visited her almost every day, sometimes at noon and sometimes at night since it was only five minutes from my family apartment and ten minutes away from my office.

TWO TRIPS TO SOUTH AMERICA

At Gordon's suggestion, in 1986, I had scheduled a visit to BIT Chile and another to BIT Brazil to get a closer look at two portable minicomputer systems that were being implemented to automate sales routes.

At Bilden we were very interested in this topic and Gordon thought that seeing these systems in operation could be very useful in clarifying a long list of doubts and questions that we had at that time.

As it was not possible to organize the visit in a single tour due to availability problems of the people involved, I had to divide it into two trips, the first trip would be to Santiago de Chile and the second to Rio de Janeiro.

The trip to Santiago de Chile had a stopover in Lima and lasted about 12 hours, which took me by surprise, it had not occurred to me that the journey would be so long, it was practically like a trip to Europe.

At the Santiago airport, a driver from the company was waiting for me and took me to the hotel located in the city center near the Palacio de la Moneda.

At that time, Chile was a country of about 12 million inhabitants and had been under the dictatorship of Augusto Pinochet since 1973. It was the first time I visited it and the image I had in my mind had been formed by what I saw on the news, and my interaction with some Chileans residing in Venezuela.

The news in Venezuela about Chile was generally not good, since it frequently touched on topics such as human rights violations, the disappearance of people, repression and the imprisonment of thousands of political prisoners. On the other hand, the Chileans I had met in Venezuela had mostly emigrated due to the problems created by the dictatorship and were generally hard-working people with a good level of education.

I spent Sunday night at the hotel, imagining what the lifestyle of the people would be like under the restrictions imposed by the dictatorship, but at the same time I was struck by the apparent normality of what I had seen since my arrival, I also wondered how was it possible that in such a difficult social and political situation they were testing such a sophisticated system for that time.

On Monday morning I had breakfast in the hotel restaurant and dared to take a short walk around until the time came for the company driver to come pick me up. Everything I saw seemed normal to me, very clean, with ordinary people doing their daily activities, until that moment the only special thing I had experienced was the curfew the night before.

VISIT TO BIT CHILE OFFICE

At 9am the company driver picked me up and after a short ride we arrived at an office building where the BIT Chile headquarters operated. There I met Cristian, the IT manager and some members of his team who had prepared an excellent presentation that covered key aspects of the company and then focused on the IT area and ended by describing the sales route automation system.

Everyone was super friendly and the quality of the presentation made clear a high level of professionalism. They did not talk about the company's IT budget, but it was evident that the company had the resources and the level of development necessary to handle complex projects.

The system used a portable minicomputer and a thermal printer manufactured in the USA, the printer was powered by the battery of the vehicle on the route and the minicomputer had a battery pack with enough autonomy for an 8-hour day and could be recharged if necessary in the vehicle. The cost of the minicomputer and the printer was around 2,500 US dollars, which was not a negligible figure, especially in an inflationary environment.

The software had been developed in-house in assembly language and allowed for stock control on the truck, invoicing, collections, and some point-of-sale information, but memory limitations imposed significant restrictions.

At the end of the day, the salesperson returns to the branch and there he places the minicomputer on a special cradle to download the day's information, recharge the battery and receive the next day's information.

At that time the system was still in the pilot phase in the city of Santiago and they were evaluating the feasibility of implementing it at national level, but this was not yet clear.

Based on the accumulated experience, the system allowed billing to be kept square with the inventory and eliminated calculation errors that the seller could make. Additionally, it allowed the seller's journey to be analyzed minute by minute.

On the drawback side, the little memory available in the minicomputer limited functionality and there had been cases of equipment theft and hardware failures that did not allow 100% reliability and lengthened the time to recover the investment.

With the information available up to that point, the project could be classified as successful, but the economic justification was still pending a longer period of evaluation.

In this type of system, it is necessary to have a sufficiently large operating sample to be able to accurately estimate how much the average useful life of the equipment will be, what the average frequency of failures will be and ultimately how much the operation of the system will cost, including the maintenance and replacement of equipment due to theft and hardware failure.

The system produced concrete efficiency and productivity benefits, but until then there was no evidence of a transformative or revolutionary effect on the productivity or cost of operating sales routes.

A QUICK IMMERSION INTO CHILEAN CULTURE

At the end of the day we went to eat at a steak restaurant near the office, the idea was to have an early dinner, chat for a while and return to the hotel before curfew.

Since the beginning of the military regime in 1973, Pinochet had established an 8pm curfew that everyone took very seriously.

During dinner we put work matters aside and began to talk about the differences between Chilean and Venezuelan Spanish, which were very marked both in the accent and in the use of many words.

It never ceased to surprise me how the idiosyncrasies of each country or even each region made important differences in the language.

To summarize some of the words they taught me, I constructed two sentences to remember the good atmosphere of cordiality at that dinner in Santiago, Chile.

"The black-legged rooster left with the mine and the guagua" this means that the young man and his young lover left with the baby.

"If these roosters don't leave soon, the guanaco will come". This phrase is equivalent to saying that, if the young people do not leave soon, the truck with the water cannon will make them go.

The next day I had several interviews with the staff who designed and developed the system where I could once again appreciate that they had done a good job. To conclude the visit, I had a courtesy interview with the director of finance, a young and very friendly Englishman called Keith, who curiously I would see again over 15 years later in the United Kingdom. I left the BIT Chile offices bound for the airport, ending my visit, but fate had prepared a little farewell scare for me.

A LITTLE SCARE LEAVING CHILE

When I handed in my passport at immigration control, they couldn't find a small entry form that I was supposed to have, so they held me while they investigated the case, I didn't remember being given any papers and that bothered the immigration agents, since it was part of the official procedure.

Time passed and I looked at the clock thinking that I was going to miss the flight, that I didn't have Chilean money and that if it got late it would be curfew and I would possibly have to sleep at the airport.

Suddenly, it occurred to me to take everything out of the suitcase and check everything thoroughly, suddenly I saw the form in an inside pocket of the suitcase, at some point it came out of the passport and I had not seen it.

I called the immigration officer and asked him if that was what was needed and he said with a dirty look.

 "Yes, next time be more careful".

Fortunately, I didn't miss the plane and I learned a new lesson, from that day on I always pay close attention in case they put a form inside my passport.

RIO DE JANEIRO WITH AN UNFORGETTABLE STOP

I returned to my normal activity at Bilden and two weeks later, I undertook the second stage of my traveling schedule, this time heading to Rio de Janeiro with a VARIG flight that had a stopover in Bogotá.

The Caracas-Bogotá flight was a short stopover to take passengers, but after landing they detected some type of problem on the plane that forced them to suspend the continuation flight until the next day and send the passengers and crew to the Bogotá Hilton to pass the night.

The delay broke my arrival itinerary and there was the possibility that when I arrived in Rio de Janeiro no one would be waiting for me, but I decided not to worry since it was Saturday and there was not much I could do from Bogotá.

I was learning another lesson, it's always good to have useful addresses and phone numbers on hand in case your flight is canceled.

Upon arriving at the Bogotá Hilton, after checking in I went up to the room to rest, but it occurred to me to look in the phone book for a relative who lived in Bogotá and whom I had not seen for many years, so I found the number of a cousin named Carlos and I left him a message that his cousin Orlando was in town for a day and was inviting him for coffee.

After leaving the message, I started watching television thinking that it was very difficult to see this cousin, since it would not be easy for him to have time available to see a distant cousin who appeared without warning on a Saturday at noon.

But to my surprise, an hour later he called me at the hotel and suggested that instead of having coffee, we have dinner together with another cousin who, like him, lived in Bogotá and was available that day.

At 6 in the afternoon my cousin Carlos stopped by the hotel with my cousin José and we went to dinner at a typical Colombian food restaurant that he frequented.

Dinner was a very pleasant and special experience where we remembered the adventures of adolescence, when I accompanied my mother to Bogotá on school holidays and went out with them to party on Saturday nights, an activity that my mother did not approve of since these cousins were much older than me.

Carlos was a businessman, he was a very enterprising guy with a lot of business acumen who had amassed a considerable fortune in real estate and several service companies.

José was a lawyer, he practiced the profession, taught at the university and led a very active intellectual and academic life.

During dinner, we toasted so many times and to so many things that the three of us went too far with the drink and ended up with much more alcohol than we should have in our heads.

When we left the restaurant I suggested to my cousin that we take a taxi, but he jokingly told me, don't worry cousin, my car knows the way and is used to me having a few too many drinks.

The next day we spoke on the phone to say goodbye and we asked life that we would have another chance to see each other again, but unfortunately this has not happened, fate did not put us in the same city again in the next 40 years, but I always remember unexpected dinner due to a technical failure in Bogotá.

The next day the flight left to Rio de Janeiro and it was worth not worrying, since, when I left immigration, a driver from the company was waiting for me to take me to the hotel.

The driver told me that delays occurred from time to time and the airlines always gave them information on the new arrival time.

TOURING IPANEMA AND COPACABANA

On Monday morning, Joao-S, the coordinator of the sales route automation project in Rio de Janeiro, came to pick me up at the hotel and took me on a tour of the Ipanema and Copacabana area, accompanying a salesperson who used the system to bill, collect and record some merchandising data.

The conceptual design of the system was similar to the one I had seen in Chile, it recorded sales, collections and controlled the truck's inventory, but it had more functionality to collect information on the situation of the points of sale in terms of promotion, merchandising and data of the competition.

The system was giving positive results, but extending it nationally was very complicated, the geographical dimensions of Brazil are enormous and there are difficulties in transporting supplies, equipment and security in many areas.

For example, in Rio de Janeiro in the favela area, there are many distribution points, but there is a high degree of insecurity and walking down the street with a two-thousand-dollar minicomputer in your hand is not a very good idea.

On the other hand, inflation in Brazil makes the importation of technology and equipment more expensive, just as in Chile, it was imported from the United States.

When a country has a high inflation rate that is maintained over time due to structural problems in the economy, a continuous gap occurs between the cost of labor and that of imported technology, since salaries never rise with the speed at which the currency depreciates and imports become more expensive.

BIT Souza Cruz had more than 260 thousand points of sale nationwide, and the system was in the pilot phase only in some areas in Rio de Janeiro; extending it nationwide was a megaproject that was not planned at the moment.

The next day I had a courtesy visit to see Johnny, Souza Cruz's production director, whom I had met in Venezuela when he held a similar position at Bilden.

Johnny was a very experienced guy, very dynamic and always interested in staying up to date. During the meeting he told me about the challenges posed by the size of Brazil, which compared to Venezuela was a monster in size and complexity.

One of its challenges was the optimization of the conversion cost, but it was a very complex problem since in addition to the cost of machinery, labor and raw materials, an important consideration in the case of Brazil were transportation difficulties throughout the country.

The Amazon rainforest has not allowed the construction of a good rail or road transportation network throughout the country, so there are large areas of the country that depend on river and air transportation, which is an important limitation.

At the end of the visit to the Souza Cruz offices I had a few hours free before the flight and I took advantage of them to walk along the famous Ipanema beach, there were a lot of people and the atmosphere was very pleasant, so I sat in a little bar to have a caipirinha while watching the people playing and having a great time.

During the return flight, I dedicated myself to summarizing what I had learned from seeing the two systems in Santiago and Rio, the potential was enormous, but the cost and memory capacity limitations combined with security, geography and inflation factors reduced its viability on a large scale in the short term.

OPPORTUNITY IN THE BANKING SECTOR

In 1986, the development of systems at Bilden reached a level that attracted attention and was used with some frequency by some people at IBM as an interesting reference for the use of the BSP methodology and accelerated application development. Therefore, from time to time I was approached by executive recruitment companies.

I generally did not show much interest since I felt comfortable at Bilden and it was not easy to compete with the size and benefits of a multinational like BIT.

But a head hunter called me on several occasions to talk about the Vice Presidency of IT in a bank and sparked my interest, since, in the banking sector, IT plays a key role in the business model and competitiveness, while in a company like Bilden, computing is important but it is not vital.

When I was about to confirm the first interview to start the selection process, I decided to mention it to David out of courtesy and this triggered a series of events that changed my career development plan at BIT.

That same day, the president of Bilden invited me to lunch and told me that the group valued my work and that an expansion of my responsibilities at the regional level and a transfer period to the headquarters was planned that would open the door to other opportunities.

Additionally, the human resources director proposed adjusting my benefits package to a higher grade starting with the next payroll.

When we finished lunch, the president told me.

"Orlando, the ball is on your side of the court, you are free to choose your path, but we would like you to stay".

The bank was a new path full of possibilities and with better economic benefits than what Bilden offered me at that time, but I felt comfortable in the organization, I had good relationships with David and with my boss at the headquarters, and the idea of expanding my work to the region and working in London was very interesting to me, so I decided to suspend the interview and continue at BIT.

A WAVE OF CHANGES IN THE AREA OF FINANCE

The period from 1985 to 1987 was quite eventful in the organization of Bilden's Finance Directorate, since in less than three years and due to different circumstances, almost all the heads in management positions changed.

Fortunately, all these changes did not disturb the development of the systems plan and the newcomers integrated very well into the organizational culture, with which I was able to experience a period of great camaraderie with the entire management team of the Finance Directorate.

A HOUSE ON THE OUTSIDE OF THE CITY

At the end of 1986, something interesting happened on a personal level, since due to an increase in my salary grade at Bilden, I had been assigned a car in the company, so at home we did not know what to do with 3 cars and two parking spaces. But suddenly an unexpected opportunity appeared, a friend of my mother-in-law had insisted that we had to buy her a house that she was selling on the outskirts of the city for a bargain price.

I already had two mortgages and I didn't really want to get into more debt, but the woman's son had seen that we had 3 cars and fell in love with the one my wife used, which was a 2-door sports car in very good condition, so he offered that, if we left him that car as part of the house payment, the rest could be a personal loan at very low interest without a mortgage guarantee.

My wife liked the idea, since she preferred the new company car that was easier to park and was a model that was in fashion at the time.

It seemed like a good idea to me since I preferred to use my own car instead of the one the company had assigned me.

The house wasn't much, but when I did the math, it was actually a good deal, as it solved the problem of having a car we didn't need by selling it at a very good price and I could convert part of my income into a real estate asset that It could be rented and revalued.

Thus, at the age of 30, I had unintentionally accumulated three loans for real estate assets, which was going to be an excellent financial strategy, although I did not know it at the time.

DEMOCRACY AND DINNERS IN LAS MERCEDES

In the area of Las Mercedes in Caracas, there was a restaurant that prepared spectacular pork ribs that the whole family liked and once or twice a month we went to eat there on Saturday nights, but one day Alejandra and Tatiana said They didn't want ribs, they preferred to eat pizza, so I proposed that we put it to a vote and that the majority would win, the result was four for ribs and two for pizza, but the girls were not satisfied and made long faces, so I said If they didn't mind eating alone, I could leave them at the pizzeria that was in front of the ribs restaurant, so everyone would eat what they liked.

I thought they wouldn't dare since Alejandra was 7 years old and Tatiana was 5, but to my surprise, they told me that there was no problem for them.

They liked the idea and we ended up split between the two restaurants, they ate pizza and the rest of us ate ribs while we watched them from the other side of the street. That day democracy did not work, there was a solution of flexibility for minorities.

BUSINESS SYSTEMS REVIEW IN 1987

At the beginning of 1987, Bilden's systems plan formulated in 1983 was practically completed, but some new processes derived from the company's adaptation to the incessant change of the macro-economic environment had appeared, therefore, it was a good time to review the scope, efficiency and priorities of what we were doing in terms of systems. To achieve this objective, I proposed the development of a "Business Systems Review" (BSR), which followed a methodology similar to the BSP, but started from a different base, since in 1987 Bilden had an extensive online systems platform that They supported operational and managerial processes in all functional areas, and there were also a significant number of applications on personal computers.

At the end of the BSR, the systems development plan was updated with new projects and the IT Division continued with its usual work, but in a much more efficient and sophisticated Bilden after a successful technological leap.

A MOMENT OF REFLECTION ON THE PATH

Nearly four years had passed since I joined Bilden and I felt very satisfied with what had been achieved, learned, and experienced.

I had achieved all the technological renewal objectives that had been set with the management team.

I had the luck and opportunity to form a competent and efficient human team that closely identified with the organization.

I had the opportunity to successfully design and develop a systematization process for one of the most important industrial companies in the country.

I had acquired extensive knowledge of the tobacco industry and the structure and functioning of a multinational company.

I experienced first-hand the importance of cultivating an organizational culture based on good communication, cooperation, responsibility, dedication, and mutual respect.

I had enjoyed my professional activity and had been fortunate to work in a team of extraordinary people.

On a personal level, my family had a reasonably comfortable and happy life. My daughters were healthy and developing their formal education combined with activities such as swimming, ballet, piano and regular interaction with the rest of the family especially aunts and grandparents.

My wife was advancing in her medical studies, my cousin Isabel and Manyi had definitively integrated into the family nucleus, and my parents and sisters were in good health.

At 31 years old, I was definitely a lucky man.

TOURING
CENTRAL AMERICA

118

REGIONAL ADVISOR FOR CENTRAL AMERICA

In 1987, during a visit by Gordon to Venezuela, he told me that he saw potential in Bilden's systems to be used in other companies of the group, especially in Central America. Under this premise, he asked me if I was interested in collaborating with these companies through periodic visits and the organization of workshops.

I found the idea interesting since, on the one hand, companies could benefit from the systems developed by Bilden and on the other, my team and I would have the opportunity to learn up close the operation of other companies in the group.

Additionally, my absences would create management development opportunities for my team since they would have to replace me several times a year and this was an important objective in my career plan.

The countries covered by this regional support program would be Panama, Honduras, Nicaragua, Guatemala, Costa Rica and El Salvador.

Once we agreed on the general objectives, Gordon told me that he would send a communication from Millbank explaining the program and announcing my regular visit as regional IT advisor.

When Gordon sent the communication to the companies, I used it to discuss the issue with my management team at Bilden, this way everyone was informed and knew the challenges and opportunities that this generated.

ADVENTURES OF THE FIRST TRIP TO THE REGION

The first visit to the region took place in July 1987 in a tight two-week program with a tour of Guatemala City, San Pedro Sula, Managua, San Salvador, San José de Costa Rica and Panama City.

It was a very intense trip, two or three days around each city, in a picturesque, hot environment full of unforgettable experiences.

Due to lack of experience, my itinerary on the first trip included a six-hour stopover with a change of plane in Belize, which turned out to be a torment, since at that time the airport to make the connection in addition to the runway and the control tower, only had a wooden house in a practically uninhabited area, which only had a small cafeteria that sold coffee, water and Coca-Cola.

Since my tour ended in Panama, I entertained myself at the airport buying souvenirs for the family while I waited for the plane to depart, but as time passed and I didn't hear the flight announcement, I went to the departure gate to ask, then I discovered that the flight had already left, I had been waiting in an area where the flight announcements could not be heard. This was another important lesson that I would never forget, from then on I would always wait by the exit door.

The people at all the BIT companies I interacted with were super friendly and made me feel welcome, I only had some communication problems due to idiomatic expressions and the use of some words that locally had different meanings than what I was used to.

I remember that in El Salvador one night they invited me to dinner and then I invited them to have some "Palitos" at the hotel and this made them very funny, so I explained to them that in Venezuela having some "Palitos" was to drink something, they clarified to me that "Palitos" in El Salvador has an inappropriate meaning, especially if you are in a hotel. In all the companies my program of activities was almost the same, first a courtesy visit to the general manager, another to the director of finance, a quick visit to the facilities and then work sessions with the IT manager to talk about the systems in operation, the ongoing projects, the development plans, the resources available to it and the most important challenges and problems it faced.

At the end of the visit I would have a summary with the finance director and sometimes also with the general manager. The differences between the companies, the great challenges and the opportunities were appreciated when the company was put in the context of the political, economic and social situation in which they operated. With the exception of Costa Rica and Panama, all other countries were immersed in serious political problems that affected the country's economy, the security of company operations, and the quality of life of the population.

NICARAGUA

Nicaragua was the most extreme case, experiencing hyperinflation, an import blockade by the United States, and serious security problems.

I remember that the car that took me from the airport to the hotel was stopped three times by the army at various checkpoints in a 40-minute journey.

On the way from the hotel to the factory in Managua, I frequently saw cars with the windshield rebuilt with flat glass to replace the original ones that had curved areas and could not be imported. It was also common to see trucks transporting people to work, since there were very few buses available for public transportation.

In Nicaragua, inflation had collapsed the value of the local currency, generating logistical problems that were difficult to imagine. For example, in the finance department, they had to create a special section to count and organize the bank notes from cigarette sales, since the space required for the banknotes was enormous.

In the sales routes, the sellers could not deposit the bank notes because the bank offices could not handle so many bills in a reasonable time, additionally, the bills took up more space than the cigarettes they had sold and the trucks had to go back to the office to unload the money.

The blockade of imports made the repair of machines and vehicles very difficult, forcing to look for alternative solutions that in some cases involved the cannibalization of equipment and in others the local manufacture of something similar that sometimes worked and sometimes not.

Nicaragua has a territory of 130 thousand square kilometers and at the time of my visit, it had just under 4 million inhabitants, the majority of the population was below what was considered the poverty level and the BIT Co. company did wonders to stay in operation. Kiosks that sold cigarettes could sell one or more, since most people did not have the money to buy a pack.

EL SALVADOR

Another interesting and complex case was El Salvador, a country of 21 thousand square kilometers and 5 million inhabitants at that time, the country faced serious political, economic and security problems, not as serious as those of Nicaragua, but at a very delicate level.

I remember being picked up at the airport in a car with armored windows, and upon arriving at the factory building, the guards inspected the underside of the vehicle with mirrors to make sure there were no explosives.

While I was holding work meetings in the offices, on several occasions I heard the sound of explosions, but no one paid attention. Finally, I dared to ask and they told me that the guerrillas exploded bombs every day and they were used to it, generally there were no injured and could happen anywhere in the city.

At the end of the work program, the IT manager offered to show me the city of San Salvador before going to the hotel and so I had the opportunity to visit a supermarket that had several guards armed with machine guns and then I asked why so much military equipment, and The response was interesting, the Salvadorian guerrillas raided supermarkets from time to time to restock groceries.

HONDURAS

Honduras, with an area of 112 thousand square kilometers, was at that time a fairly poor country, with a population of 4 million inhabitants and enormous political, economic and social problems that competed in severity with those of Salvador.

The Honduras's economy was based on the agricultural sector, especially the export of bananas and coffee.

The BIT company was located in San Pedro Sula, a small city of 300 thousand inhabitants at that time, it is located about 250 kilometers from Tegucigalpa, the capital of the country.

I remember that, on my plane trip from Tegucigalpa to San Pedro Sula, I was sitting next to a woman who was carrying a bag with two live chickens as part of her hand luggage.

The company was a model of cleanliness and efficiency, where everything worked like a Swiss watch, old but very precise.

In my interview with the general manager he told me that he was very strict with expenses and that this had allowed him to make the company profitable. In his philosophy, if something was not budgeted, it was not purchased and if it was budgeted, they had to convince him that it was really necessary. Mr. Nicolas had managed the company military style for many years and was close to retirement.

GUATEMALA

Guatemala, with an area of 108 thousand square kilometers, was at that time a country with an agricultural economy, with almost 8.5 million inhabitants, with a high percentage of illiteracy, political and social problems, but not as serious as those of Nicaragua or El Salvador, although it had the infamous death squads.

The BIT factory was in Guatemala City, it was the largest in Central America and due to its level of production, it generated a significant part of the government's tax revenues, which gave it a certain relevance in the country's economy.

PANAMA

Panama was the second smallest country, with an area of 75 thousand square kilometers and 2.3 million inhabitants in 1987, but it had a very important and more diversified economy in the Central American region, among other things due to the canal, tourism and the financial services sector.

The BIT company was in Panama City, the factory was the smallest in the region, it was very well organized, but it lacked economies of scale in a region with potential for integration if relations and political conditions in the countries of the region improved.

COSTA RICA

Costa Rica with 51 thousand square kilometers was the smallest country in the region, its population in 1987 was 2.7 million inhabitants, the economy still depended on the agricultural sector, it had a high percentage of literacy, the highest educational level in the region and a stable socio-political environment that was beginning to attract foreign investment.

The BIT company was in San José, it was small, but it was very well organized and could benefit from a regional integration process.

THE SYSTEMS IN THE REGION

As is easy to imagine, from a systems point of view, I found a wide range of needs to be covered and few resources available both on the user side and in the IT departments.

Additionally, four of the six countries faced difficult economic, political, and social conditions that generated instability and made reengineering processes difficult.

In short, although Gordon was right and there was potential to transfer Bilden systems to these companies, it was not going to be an easy process.

With the exception of Panama and Costa Rica, the other countries had significant problems in their daily lives and enormous limitations of human and economic resources necessary for any reengineering or systems development process.

When analyzing the situation of each country and the organizational culture that I was able to observe in my short visit, I thought about how lucky we were in Venezuela and in Bilden to have so many resources while facing fewer problems than our Central American neighbors, who despite their limitations were, friendly and very professional.

A REGIONAL WORKSHOP IN PANAMA

As a next step to the visit, the organization of a Workshop with the region's IT managers in Panama City in the month of August was planned. The Workshop was an activity organized with the headquarters and Eddie was the general coordinator.

The program was designed to stimulate the exchange of information and resources between companies. The workshop took place in a warm and participatory environment that channeled the enthusiasm and possibilities of regional cooperation. It did not represent the solution to fundamental problems, but it identified some useful initiatives that could be easily implemented.

REFLECTIONS ABOUT CENTRAL AMERICA

From 1987 to 1988, I visited the six companies every six months to support the development of their systems and identify new opportunities for regional cooperation, but very humble progress was achieved.

Some objectives of system reuse and experience sharing were achieved, but the difficulties imposed by political and economic conditions left little room for maneuver.

In all countries in Central America, people ate bananas and beans, spoke the same language and manufactured cigarettes, but each company was a different universe.

In theory one could dream of a single system and even a regional computing center, but in practice we were light years away from this being feasible.

A system that covered the full range of legal and operational situations that had to be handled would be very expensive to develop and difficult to maintain.

The functionality and security expectations of each company were very different, for example, in Nicaragua you could improve many processes with spreadsheets, but in other companies this would be considered an operational risk that would not pass the auditors' review.

Human beings have an enormous capacity to adapt, but we are also very good at setting our preferences and rights to have a different culture.

126

EUROPE AND CENTRAL AMERICA FROM LONDON

TRANSFER TO THE HEADQUARTERS IN LONDON

In September 1988, when I had just turned 32, Gordon proposed to Bilden that I transfer to the headquarters in London from January 1989. The initially agreed period was one year, but it was open to review.

The objective was to familiarize myself with the operation of the headquarters and assist Gordon, serving as a regional IT advisor covering several countries in Europe and Central America.

Additionally, it was expected that I would participate as a representative of Corporate IT in a project sponsored by the parent company that had the objective of identifying strategies to take advantage of the opening of the European market in 1992.

The European Union had been working for several years on the creation of a single internal market comprising 27 member states and certain additions, such as Iceland, Liechtenstein, Norway and Switzerland.

The Europe 1992 project had enormous potential importance since it could substantially modify BIT's business model in that part of the world.

My transfer covered my family group, but as my wife was in the final years of her medical degree, we decided that I would travel to England alone, visit family every two or three months and they would come to the UK in the school holidays.

At Bilden, the O&M manager, Jorge, was appointed manager in charge of the IT Division. Jorge had sufficient management experience and a good relationship with Isaías, Frank and Amira, so the appointment was well received.

A VERY EMOTIONAL FAREWELL

In the last days of December 1988 they gave me a very emotional farewell party, many friends from all functional areas attended, some joked with the idea that I would be back the following month since the English were not going to put up with me.

Others talked about how computing had influenced their area and everyone wished me the best, but I had the feeling that I would not return to work permanently in Venezuela and that made me feel a little sad, Bilden was like an extension of my family I spent more time there than at home.

The transfer had been announced for a period of one year, but in reality it was a door that opened a new path with many probable destinations and few possibilities of return.

The hardest parting was with my mother, since she was used to me visiting her almost every day and now we would only talk on the phone and see each other every two or three months. Fortunately, my sisters and my aunt were very attentive to her and visited her regularly.

For my daughters, my absence would especially affect them on weekends since on a daily basis I always left very early and returned late from the office and they were already asleep. This created certain internal conflicts for me, but I thought that in life you can't have everything at the same time. In my personal experience when I was a child, I learned to value the quality more than the quantity of time I spent with my parents.

My wife also had a quite complicated schedule with the rotating boarding wards at the hospital, so Isabel, the aunts and the grandmothers were very attentive to the girls' daily life and frequently complemented their mother's care.

The day I left for London the whole family went to say goodbye to me at the airport, but the flight was delayed and we ended up spending the night in a hotel and the next day we said goodbye again at the Maiquetía international airport.

I was used to traveling two or three times a year, but this time was different, during the flight I had an attack of nostalgia and I began to doubt whether it was worth staying away from my family for so long and this lowered my spirits for several days.

THE FIRST WEEK IN LONDON

When I arrived at Heathrow Airport, a representative from BIT Co.'s human resources department was waiting, and took me to a small but comfortable apartment they had rented for me in Bessborough Gardens, near Vauxhall Bridget Road in the heart of London.

The apartment of about 50 square meters had a bedroom, living room, kitchen and bathroom and was fully equipped, decorated with very good taste and located at ten-minute walk from the headquarters offices in Millbank. Over time I learned that I had been very lucky since it was not easy to find apartments within the budget I had assigned with these characteristics.

The first day in the Millbank office reminded me of joining Bilden since I spent a good time in the Human Resources Department doing the entry procedures and receiving part of the induction process.

They assigned me a closed office near the Corporate IT area that at first I didn't like very much, but then I found out that they had made an exception for me, borrow it from the Production Department. At the headquarters in Millbank, office space was a very limited resource and having a private office was neither easy nor very common.

The same day I was assigned a vehicle from the company's fleet, but there was a problem, I did not have a parking space and that was more complicated since at Millbank only the directors had an assigned parking position, therefore, I had to decide if I wanted the vehicle to use only on weekends since I lived 10 minutes from the office. I asked if I could think about it and they gave me a week.

When I finished the admission procedures, Gordon's secretary went to pick me up for the welcome meeting and to review the program of activities that had been prepared for me.

The first week was intended to cover an induction program at the headquarters with interviews in the corporate units of Africa, America, Europe, Asia, Agriculture, Production, Marketing, Finance, Public Relations and IT, during the induction process I understood that the matrix structure that I saw from Venezuela actually had three lines of command, functional, territorial and local.

The second week would be an induction at the headquarters of BIT UK, which was the operating company of BIT Co. in the United Kingdom, located in Woking, at 45 minutes by train from London.

A WEEK OF INDUCTION AT BIT UK

I spent the following week in Woking, getting to know the BIT UK team, but the emphasis was on the IT area with Jim.

Jim was a mature guy, very intelligent, with a good sense of humor and a long history at BIT UK. He had recently been appointed head of IT as his predecessor had just retired after a lifetime at BIT.

Jim was super friendly and gave me an excellent introduction to the IT organization at BIT UK, the systems, the projects, the methodology and the challenges they had to solve.

I was struck by the high level of structuring of the organization, the tendency to use software packages and the level of standardization.

When we talk about methodology, my idea of using programmer analysts to do all the development of a system seemed very risky to him, while to me their methodology where someone did the analysis and others did the programming with an intermediate step of written specifications seemed to me, slow, expensive and not risk-free.

Despite conceptual divergences, Jim and I respected each other's points of view, accepting that cultural and economic differences had a major impact on what could be considered viable and acceptable in each country.

BIT UK was much larger and more complex than Bilden in Venezuela, to begin with it had two cigarette factories, one in Liverpool and another in South Hampton, production covered the domestic market and several export markets, they had a research and development center, the Tobacco was imported from several countries, and they had "Just in Time" agreements with some suppliers of tobacco packaging and flavoring materials.

Furthermore, BIT UK had an atypical organizational structure when compared to the other operating companies, possibly due to its geographical proximity to the headquarters in Millbank.

Several times I had the impression that BIT UK executives would have preferred more distance between London and Woking.

During my time in the UK I developed a good relationship with Jim, not only because of his good personality chemistry but also because I frequently met him at meetings in Millbank, in Woking and at the training center in Chelwood. I remember that he always joked about my tendency to say "I have a little question", which generally was neither small nor was it just one.

THE INDUCTION PROCESS FINISHES

Once the induction process was completed, Gordon provided me with material to familiarize myself with the BIT companies in Switzerland, Belgium, Holland and Spain, as a preparatory phase for an IT workshop that was being organized for the first week of February in Amsterdam.

Gordon suggested that I organize a workshop for the Central American countries in February or March, so I could take advantage of the trip to visit family in Venezuela.

Getting familiar with the operating companies in Holland, Belgium, Switzerland, Spain and the United Kingdom was an interesting and very useful activity in my preparation process for the Europe 1992 project, but I was struck by the fact that Germany was not involved yet, I was beginning to have the impression that there were political problems on this issue.

At the end of the week, I decided to accept the car they had assigned me, since I could have it parked in Bessborough Gardens, it was a blue Audi 80 with gray fabric upholstery, it was almost new and had a manual transmission, something I was not used to, but I quickly adapted and started using it on weekends to shop at the supermarket and explore London, which was a lot more complicated.

I remember that the first time I went out in the Audi to look for a supermarket, I drove around for more than an hour until I found a Tesco, I made a small purchase and when I returned to Bessborough Gardens, I discovered that the supermarket was two blocks from my apartment.

London has quite complicated roads, with very few gridded areas and if you have not planned the route well it is very easy to get lost. After my first experience looking for the supermarket, I bought a map of the city and every time I went out I carefully planned where to go, however, more than once I got lost, unfortunately at that time neither Googlemaps nor mobile phones existed.

As my scheduled activities left me a lot of free time, I requested authorization to have access to the IBM AS/400 from the headquarters and thus have the opportunity to experiment with some tools that I did not know and were available in Millbank. Gordon thought it was a good idea and asked the operations manager, to create a user with programming access for me and also to connect my PC to the IBM AS/400 via an emulation card.

ADAPTING TO LIVING AND WORKING IN LONDON

I was used to working late, but the activity at the headquarters practically died at 5:30pm, so I was almost always left alone in the office and could experiment with the IBM AS/400 with complete freedom.

Having a social life in the center of London on weekdays is easy if you enjoy bars or gyms, which was not the case for me, so my nights were a combination of reading, experimenting with the computer, and watching TV.

On weekends it was different since I could meet a friend for lunch, I could visit museums and explore some areas I didn't know with the Audi, however, I could also use the subway which was easier, cheaper and less stressful than driving.

London has a huge and extensive metro system with countless stations that take you almost anywhere, in addition there is the rail system that allows you to travel throughout the country.

Most of the people who worked at the headquarters lived on the outskirts of London or in nearby cities connected by train, so to get home and have dinner with the family they had to leave at the right time to avoid missing the train.

An important activity on the weekends were phone calls to my family in Venezuela, which I had to schedule well due to the time difference, I also had to measure the duration since at that time they were quite expensive, around US$3 per minute, unfortunately it was not like today that we can talk and see other people anywhere on the planet for free through applications like WhatsApp or Facebook.

The days began to pass quickly between familiarization readings, preparation of material for the workshops, tests on the IBM AS/400, meetings and lunches with visitors from the operating companies to the headquarters.

WORKSHOP AND VISITS TO CONTINENTAL EUROPE

The first week of February, just before flying to Amsterdam for the workshop, I received a call from Judith, one of the Bilden analysts who was about to start her vacation touring several European countries and wanted to take advantage of her trip to visit me if we could fit the dates, I thought the idea was great and I told her that I would be between Amsterdam, Brussels and London in the next 10 days, first for the workshop and then visiting BIT companies.

When I explained my itinerary, she told me that Amsterdam suited her very well since she could start her tour in that city.

I told Gordon about Judith's visit, and he suggested that we invite her to the workshop so that she could meet the people and observe the event.

On the second day of the workshop in Amsterdam, Judith arrived and shared with me and all the attendees, who were delighted to meet a young Venezuelan girl from the Bilden team.

Gordon already knew her through his travels to Venezuela and Judith's English was good, so she interacted easily with everyone in attendance.

At the end of the workshop, we said goodbye and she continued her vacation trip to her next stop in Germany where she would see a Venezuelan friend.

Seeing Judith made me feel nostalgic for all my teammates in Venezuela with whom I had shared so many unforgettable moments. The experience I had lived at Bilden was going to be very difficult to repeat; it is not easy to set up a team of people where everyone feels good and enjoys their work at the same time.

The workshop in Amsterdam took place as planned, with presentations from each company, and the search for opportunities to reuse systems that had not materialized.

Each company was a world in different stages of development where company size, market dynamics, culture, language, competition and government policy created challenges, opportunities and priorities that did not match, just compare the list of requests pending development, each company was different.

THE EUROPE PROJECT 1992

The area that aroused the most interest in the workshop was a short introduction to the Europe 1992 project, since it was a topic that made the imagination fly, but we didn't have anything very concrete to talk about, we could only make some speculations.

In Europe 1992, if the entire European space was truly opened as an internal market, available for all member countries without tax or customs barriers, it would be necessary to rethink the need to have so many factories scattered everywhere, since it could be more profitable to produce in one or two places and transport the product to the rest of the markets.

If the objective was to maximize profits by reducing costs and expenses, the closure of factories and operating companies would be on the table, but this would be Pandora's box since the elimination of jobs was a very sensitive issue, not only for BIT workers, also for suppliers, municipalities and governments of each country.

In any scenario there were winners and losers, it was not simply a matter of increasing the profitability of companies or fattening the pockets of shareholders, in theory a single market should benefit consumers and improve the prosperity of member countries, but this is Easier to say than to put into practice.

When I analyzed these scenarios, I thought about what I had read about the development of the Chinese economy after the creation of the special economic zones starting in 1979.

The Chinese special economic zones allowed the creation of millions of jobs with cheap labor in new companies that produced mostly low-cost products to be exported, especially to developed countries.

The new jobs, although very poorly paid in terms of developed world scales, were a bath of prosperity for a Chinese poor class that lived off a subsistence agricultural economy.

Chinese products, upon reaching the developed world, expanded the variety and availability of products available at prices that benefited millions of consumers, this in turn stimulated the local economy and created new sales and distribution companies.

But not everything was good for developed economies, since those local producers who could not compete with the low prices of Chinese products ended up closing their companies and eliminating jobs.

When I understood the similarities between what had happened with the transformation of China into the cheap factory of the west and what could happen with the single market of the Europe 1992 project, I realized that this project would be a more interesting experience than I expected, but with very little chance that I could contribute anything concrete, since the big challenges were not in the information systems, it was a survival problem for many of the parties involved and possibly that is why I did not see at the moment that Germany would form part of the package.

VISITING HENRY WINTERMANS IN NETHERLANDS

At the end of the workshop in Amsterdam, I had organized a visit to the Henry Wintermans cigars factory that BIT had in a small town called Eersel, since it was a very interesting case of systems development and was located at only 150 kilometers from the Dutch capital.

This factory had a very small IT department, managed by Sven, a very dynamic young man who had developed, practically alone, almost all of the company's systems.

Gordon frequently used the case of Henry Wintermans when giving examples of high productivity and internal application development, it was really an embarrassing case especially for companies with many resources and huge systems departments.

The Henry Wintermans factory was relatively small compared to a cigarette factory, the production process was similar, but less automated, since in the world of cigars there is less volume, but quite a variety of size, flavors and packaging.

Touring the factory and offices with Sven, I was impressed by the level of penetration of the computer systems and his level of knowledge of both the processes and the personnel in all departments.

Sven had friends everywhere, he knew all the people he introduced me to closely, he had worked in the company since he was very young and he had an excellent relationship with everyone.

In my opinion, the secret of the productivity of computer development at Henry Wintermans was Sven, since he had been able to accumulate in a single head an excellent knowledge of the IBM AS/400, the processes, and the users to make a job that he greatly enjoyed and represented the center of his life.

The only problem was the risk derived from the high dependence on Sven. But fortunately that was not a problem that I had to solve and the entire management team knew about it.

VISIT TO BIT BENELUX IN BELGIUM

After the visit to Eersel, I continued my trip with about 120 kilometers to the next scheduled stop, this time in Brussels to visit the BIT Benelux factory and its IT Department.

At that time, BIT Benelux was a medium-sized factory, competing in a domestic market of 9 million inhabitants, but it had a high degree of logistical complexity, as it produced a long list of brands of cigarettes and other products for smokers. such as RYO and MYO for their acronym in English.

RYO "Roll Your Own" is a product that includes a bag of tobacco and special paper that the smoker uses to make cigarettes, while MYO "Make Your Own" is typically pipe tobacco that is used to make custom blends of cigarettes.

MYO tobacco is generally considered to be of higher quality than RYO tobacco, and is often used by experienced smokers who prefer the unique flavor and experience of pipe tobacco.

The IT manager of BIT Benelux was a young guy of about thirty, tall with a huge mustache, his name was Lucas, and I had just met him at the workshop in Amsterdam, by the way, he was a MYO consumer.

Lucas's presentation at the workshop had been very comprehensive so I already had a clear and updated idea of the IT environment in the company.

They used an IBM AS/400 with a software package called BPCS for production management and inventory control of a manufacturing process that was quite complicated due to the large number of brands, presentations and diversity of technologies involved in manufacturing.

Most of the production was aimed at the domestic market and the rest at duty free and some for export.

When we sat down to talk about the organizational environment, problems and challenges of BIT Benelux, he told me that a relevant issue was the effect of the high level of taxes that people paid on their attitude towards work.

According to Lucas, many people preferred to have a job with a medium level income than to have a position with greater responsibility and a higher salary, since taxes took up most of the difference and the additional effort did not compensate for the difference in net income.

This point of view surprised me a little, although I understood it, there are people who do things mainly for money and others who do it because they enjoy their work, if the majority is from the second group, paying more taxes is not a big enough force to stop the innovation and creativity that involves facing challenges and solving them.

In Belgium, as in Holland and the United Kingdom, people tended to remain in the same company for long periods of time, upward mobility was neither rapid nor highly desired according to Lucas's explanations.

When comparing this vision with my experience in Latin America, it was clear that they were two very different worlds. The proportion of people on each side of the scale was not the same.

My short visit to BIT Benelux ended, and I returned on a direct flight to Heathrow, during which a confusing panorama of what I had seen in Woking, in Amsterdam, in Eersel and in Brussels ran through my head.

DOUBTS ABOUT SYSTEMS STANDARDIZATION

Each company was a different world where similarities were only seen in high-level diagrams, when you went down to the level of detail things were very different and it was not just a language problem, it was influenced by culture, politics, taxes, characteristics of the market, the level of development and a few other things.

Returning to the office in Millbank I had a short summary session with Gordon about what I had seen and my level of concern about the real possibilities of reusing the systems, Gordon listened carefully and said, let me think a little about what you told me, we will return to the topic later.

My next assignment was the Central American workshop to be held in Panama City at the beginning of March, which I was quite excited about since it was connected to a visit to Venezuela.

As I had my doubts about the effectiveness of the application reuse strategy, I focused on finding the useful side of the workshop from the motivational and learning point of view for the IT managers who would attend, although I would also have to give some weight to the things that were politically correct.

ANOTHER WORKSHOP IN CENTRAL AMERICA

I began to organize the Central American workshop by surveying the interest of the participants and proposing topics for the program. Everyone responded positively to the invitation, but they did not make any special proposal regarding the content, so the program would be in the style of the headquarters.

All the countries in the region accepted the invitation, so we would have delegates from Guatemala, Honduras, EL Salvador, Nicaragua, Costa Rica and Panama, which I was happy since through my visits in previous years I had developed a good relationship with all of them.

Although there were differences in personality, they were all simple, responsible, hard-working people with a desire to do new and useful things for their companies, so this energy had to be harnessed and stimulated.

In mid-March, I traveled from London to Miami and from there to Panama City, it was a long and tiring trip, but without inconveniences.

The BIT people in Panama, as always very friendly, had made reservations at the Sheraton Hotel next to the Atlapa convention center, which by the way comes from Atlántico + Pacific, which is a key geographic element for the Panamanian economy.

The workshop took place in one of the hotel's conference rooms and mainly covered the following topics:

- Presentations of each company summarizing systems in operation, ongoing projects, pending requests, development plans, expense budgets and capital investments in IT.

- Experience of each company in the use of personal computers and their interface with IBM AS/400 systems.

- Presentation from Panama and Guatemala on their experience reusing applications transferred from Bilden.

- Brainstorm opportunities for inter-company cooperation.

- SWOT analysis of the IT area of each company.

- Proposals for topics to cover in the next workshop.

The last day we had a visit to the Miraflores locks in the canal area, then a farewell lunch and finally a "we stay in touch, until the next regional meeting".

This type of workshop did not serve to change the world, but it was an enriching experience for all attendees, including me, since we always learned something new and the spirit of cooperation between companies was cultivated as a value of the organizational culture.

An additional benefit of the workshop was that it forced IT managers to do an objective analysis of what they had done, what they were doing, and what they had planned to address user requests. In my experience, this practice was very useful to maintain perspective of the forest and not get lost in the details of the leaves in which we live every day.

After saying goodbye and thanking the people at BIT Panama for their cooperation, I flew to Caracas to spend a few days with my family who had been waiting with great anxiety.

VISITING THE FAMILY IN VENEZUELA

Two and a half months had passed since I left Venezuela and at the end of February there had been a wave of riots that they called "El Caracazo", an incident that was on the verge of overthrowing the government of President Carlos Andrés Pérez.

The riots were very violent and generated several days of enormous tension with continuous calls from London to Caracas.

Fortunately, everyone in the family was fine, and beyond the scare, "El Caracazo" did not have major consequences for them in the short term, however, it marked the beginning of a chain of events that would sink the peace and economy of the country for several decades.

I spent a little over a week with my family trying to make up for lost time, talking about what each of us had done in the last two months and the scare they had been through.

Time flew by between lunches and dinners at the family's favorite restaurants and some courtesy visits to my old friends and Bilden colleagues.

On the days I went to see my mother, as usual, my daughters Alejandra and Tatiana accompanied me, and their grandmother almost always received them with some miniature tomatoes covered in sugar that she harvested in a small garden on the balcony of her apartment.

During my absence, Isabel had started a new routine of taking my daughters frequently to visit their grandmother while their mother was working at the hospital. This initiative made me very happy as it was a very valuable source of joy for my mother and the girls.

My family had adjusted to going about their routine as normal even though I was 7500 kilometers away, but the country was showing signs of deterioration in the peace and security to which I had been accustomed.

For many people, "El Caracazo" had been an outbreak of protests manipulated by a small group of opposition radicals with the intention of overthrowing the government.

For others it was a symptom of the growing inequality in which the country lived, where a middle class lived "well", the rich lived "super well" and a growing segment of the poor class lived "badly".

When I compared what I had seen up to that moment in Central America, in Brazil, in Colombia, in Peru and in Chile, Venezuela's problems were relatively small, there was certainly corruption, inefficiency and disorder in many things, but in general the country was functional.

There were opportunities, and it was feasible for people who wanted to get ahead both in terms of access to education and economic freedoms to start their own business.

But if I had learned anything in recent years, it is that everything is relative, good and evil are not absolute concepts, each person tends to give more importance to their problems than to those of others.

BACK TO WORK IN THE UK

Upon returning to London, I found the news that, in the first week of April, the Europe 1992 project meetings would begin and that I would also have to prepare a presentation on Corporate IT for the finance managers conference that would be held in May in Chelwood Training Centre.

The Europe 1992 project working group was made up of high-level representatives from BIT companies in the United Kingdom, Belgium, Holland, Switzerland and Spain, and functional representatives from Finance, Production, Marketing, Legal and IT. When the composition of the group was announced, a wave of comments began about the absence of Germany, some said that the Germans had their own project and the results of the analysis would be integrated later, others said that this was a waste of time and that was why the Germans did not want to participate.

Others, like me, wanted to collaborate, but for the moment it was preferable to listen and not give an opinion, there were so many questions that one could easily screw up.

THE EUROPE 1992 PROJECT BEGINS

The general manager of BIT Netherlands was the project coordinator, he called a meeting in a conference room in Millbank, where he presented to the working team a schedule with six branches of activity:

- Familiarization with companies and markets in scope.

- Research and analysis of the expected changes in the regulations of the sectors linked to the tobacco industry due to the single market.

- Identification of opportunities and threats derived from regulatory changes and strategic movements of operators in the markets.

- Identification of strengths and weaknesses of BIT companies to be affected by changes in the regulatory framework.

- Formulation of strategies to protect and improve BIT's competitive position in the single market.

- Preparation of report with conclusions and recommendations.

When the General Manager of BIT Netherlands presented the work scheme, the enormous complexity of what lay ahead became evident to everyone.

In my opinion, the work scheme was very well thought out and made clear the importance and interdependence between the six branches of activity.

The branch of familiarization with companies and markets was relatively easy to cover and that is why it was decided that in the next two months we would concentrate on this branch of work, for which the team would travel to all the companies and receive presentations and material for each company.

For the second branch, the legal department was asked to form a parallel team to approach lobby groups in the European parliament to obtain information on possible changes in the tobacco sector and related industries.

At that time cigarette taxes, income tax and cigarette advertising regulations were different in each EU member country, and the differences were most likely to be reduced along an evolutionary path towards harmonization at some point. in the indeterminate future.

We started visiting BIT companies within the scope of the project, and so I returned to BIT UK, BIT Benelux, BIT Netherlands, BIT Ibérica and BIT Switzerland.

Germany remained out of reach as did territories where there were only marketing units.

In each company we attended a series of presentations, guided tours, lunches with the local management team and I imagine there were some closed-door meetings in which I did not participate.

On my own, I began to build a matrix of indicators with information about each company, where I could see the size of the workforce by functional area, sales volume, production capacity, domestic market share, export markets, product mix, tax levels, the main challenges, threats, strengths and weaknesses, etc.

When analyzing the information matrix, it was clear that each company was a different world and that regardless of the implications of the single market, there was a surplus in installed production capacity without considering Germany.

Beyond that, there was a complex strategic planning problem and many political unknowns that were not going to be resolved in the short term, nor to the level at which I could contribute, so I tried to take advantage of the trips to meet people, learn interesting things from each other. country and expand my information matrix.

I was feeling frustrated and under a lot of stress due to the political difficulties of the project, and to make matters worse, on the second visit to BIT Netherlands, I had a scare when I was returning to London, as the pilot aborted takeoff at the last moment, all passengers hit the front seat due to the sudden deceleration.

It was an Amsterdam London flight that would allow me to get back to the office in Millbank before midday, but instead I was waiting for the flight to be rescheduled from 8am to 5pm. I have never felt so frustrated in an airport before.

After we completed the familiarization phase, team meetings were suspended while possible changes to the legal framework were investigated, but the project was ultimately put on hold indefinitely when the closure of the Liverpool factory was officially announced. in the United Kingdom.

Some thought that this was one of the recommendations of the Europe 1992 project, but as far as I knew, the task force was light years away from making this type of recommendation, however, from my analysis matrix it was easy to see that there was excess installed capacity and the closure of factories was a problem that they had to face sooner or later.

In developed countries, the total cigarette market had been on a downward trend for some time, on the one hand, due to the fall in the incidence of cigarette smoking and, on the other hand, due to the fall in the fertility rate of the population below the replacement level since the 1970s. This meant that, if you were a tobacco company, the long-term future was uncertain at best.

Under this scenario, it is how I imagined that BIT Industries had conceived the group's diversification strategy to turn it into a conglomerate that did not depend on the tobacco industry in the long term and began to focus on the financial sector by acquiring insurance companies such as Eastern Star. in 1984, Dumbar in 1985 and Farmers in 1988.

At that time, high rates of growth and profitability of the financial sector were expected in both the developed world and emerging countries.

In 1996, the insurance companies acquired by BIT were consolidated under an operating entity called British International Financial Se rvices, but the expected synergies, growth and profitability did not materialize, and in 1998, BIT Industries divested British International Financial Services into in a company that was listed separately on the London Stock Exchange.

This implied that BIT's diversification strategy and long-term survival remained an unfinished business.

VACATIONS IN THE OLD CONTINENT

At the beginning of August, my wife and two daughters arrived from Venezuela to spend a month on vacation with me. I had two weeks off and I could leave early and work from home from time to time.

The first week after breakfast, I went to the office for a while and returned as quickly as I could to go out to explore the surroundings of Bessborough Gardens, so we visited the Tate Galery, Big Ben, Parliament, Westminster Abbey, St James Park. Buckingham Palace, Picadilly, Sojo, Trafalgar Square, and many more places.

We left the Natural History Museum and the British Museum for the weekend as each was an experience that easily required more than a day.

The second week we went in the Audi on an adventure to the continent, which began by crossing the English Channel by ferry to Calais, from there I drove to Brussels where a friend had lent me his house for a few days.

The friend was Mark, the finance director of BIT Benelux, who had worked with me at Bilden and when I told him that I was going to Brussels with the family, he kindly offered me his house, since he was spending a few days in Germany.

Mark had a beautiful house rented by the company on the outskirts of Brussels, it had a huge backyard with some fruit trees and all the furniture was new as Mark had just moved in.

The living room had a beautiful sofa with white cushions that played a trick on us, since, on the second day of being in the house, I discovered a chocolate stain on one of the cushions and I thought it had been one of my daughters who had done it. I immediately took the cover off the cushion and tried to clean the stain in the kitchen, which was a terrible idea.

The cushion was made of a special fabric with one side white and the other brown, and when I wet it, the brown side released color and stained the white side, in this way I transformed a small two-centimeter stain into half a stained cushion.

When I asked my daughters how they had stained it, none of them knew anything and although at first I didn't believe them, I finally confirmed that the cushion was already stained and the one who had created the problem was me.

To resolve the problem, I had to speak to Mark's secretary to find out where the furniture had been purchased, go to the factory and purchase a replacement cushion that would be delivered a week later. This whole process cost us two days of holiday and £150.

After Brussels we headed towards Paris, there we spent three days visiting the Louvre museum, the Eiffel tower, the triumphal arch, the Bastille Palace, the Notre-Dame Cathedral and not much else since time flew by, and we had to return to London.

We all wanted to spend more time in Paris, since it is a spectacular city and it takes much more than a week to get to know it.

The return trip was a little longer, but without any setbacks, the Audi behaved very well and we enjoyed several stops to eat and rest in very picturesque towns on the road to Calais through the French countryside.

In Calais we took the ferry back to Dover in England, and a few hours later we were back in Bessborough Gardens. The family's last week in London was dedicated to shopping for gifts for the family and visiting some special places such as Madame Tussauds Wax Museum, London Bridge and the Greenwich Observatory.

THE LAST STAGE BEFORE LEAVING LONDON

At the beginning of September my family returned to Venezuela and I returned to focusing on office activities that were now in a different priority scheme.

The Europe 1992 project had disappeared from the scene, so I focused my attention on my role as regional IT advisor, and began developing instruments to facilitate the evaluation and monitoring of IT in operating companies, and preparing presentations on added value of IT in operating companies.

The presentations were the material I used when I was invited to participate in some of the management development programs at Chelwood while the monitoring and evaluation instruments became surveys that I tried to test in some companies in Central America, as an optional project that did not got a lot of receptivity, people were very busy with their day-to-day problems, so I filed it as an idea to develop in the future.

In the last term, Gordon suggested that I take part full-time in two programs that could be useful to me at the Chelwood training center, one was on marketing and the other on finance. This meant that in addition to the session in which I presented the potential and advances in IT, I would also be another student in the program, attending the master sessions and participating in the teamwork.

Although I already knew a good part of the content, both programs were very useful experiences, you always learn, by doing teamwork with competitive people who come from all over the world and want to leave a good impression of their ability.

Most of the management development programs at Chelwood were attended by key people from BIT, it did not always happen, but sometimes the chairman, or a director, would show up to give a talk and then share with the attendees at dinner or in the Pub at the end of the day.

At the end of November, Gordon proposed that I extend my transfer time at Millbank for another year to continue collaborating as a regional advisor and cover other countries in Asia and Africa, but I was not very enthusiastic about the idea, and I asked him for time to think about it.

The environment at the headquarters had some interesting things, I had learned a lot about how corporate politics works, but it was not what I liked to do, I preferred the challenges and dynamism of operating companies, but I was aware that I have to be flexible and wait for a good opportunity to present itself.

AN OPPORTUNITY IN THE INSURANCE SECTOR

At the end of 1989, Gordon told me about an opportunity that was opening in the Financial Services Division of British International Financial Services in Spain.

They were looking for a CIO for an insurance company they had bought about 5 years ago and needed someone to drive an injection of technological renewal.

The general director of the company was Jeffrey, an expatriate that I had met in 1983 at BIT Co. Venezuela, when he was in accounting management and I was the IT manager.

My relationship with Jeffrey had been good, but I had lost track of him when he was transferred to one of BIT Co.'s companies in Africa.

Although my professional goal at that time was to look for a way out of the IT area and advance to the next level on the path to a CEO position, when reflecting on the possible opportunity, I thought it would be interesting to explore the terrain, also the idea of reconnecting with Jeffrey increased my curiosity.

The following week I traveled from London to Barcelona and spent two days talking with Jeffrey and meeting the management team at the headquarters of "Chasum Seguros".

The company had a 10-story building on Av. Diagonal and was in the middle of a renovation process, you could see everywhere how the old furniture was being replaced by modern desks and modular partitions mounted on a false carpet floor.

At first glance it was evident that the company had been stuck in the past for a long time, at least when it came to office furniture and equipment.

AN INSURANCE COMPANY IN CATALONIA

"Chasum Seguros" was a medium-sized general insurer with about 320 employees, 800 agents, and 15 branches spread throughout the Spanish provinces to manage a portfolio of about 350,000 policies.

Chasum had been a pioneer in the development of multi-risk policies and specialized in the personal insurance market, especially in the automobile, home, accident and illness lines, although it also had a small SME portfolio that included transport insurance, theft, fire and civil liability.

The company had been founded by the Mullet family in the 1940s and became over time a life and general insurer with some brand recognition especially in the Catalan market, however, with the creation of the European Union, it was losing competitiveness and market share due to the strong competition of multinationals and banks in the insurance market.

In the mid-1980s, Chasum was acquired by BIT through the English insurer Eastern Star and shortly afterwards dismembered into two business units, one domiciled in Madrid to manage the life insurance portfolio, called Eastern Star Vida. and the other in Barcelona, to manage the general insurance portfolio that maintained the original name of Chasum Seguros.

In the insurance industry, there are two organizational philosophies regarding life insurance and general insurance. Some believe that it is not a good idea to mix the two types of insurance in a single company since they have important differences in terms of distribution, administration and capital requirements.

On the other hand, there are others who do not see these differences as a problem and view the economies of scale and synergy in some distribution channels as a competitive advantage.

In any case, depending on who's in charge, I've seen this pendulum swing these business units apart and back together during various corporate policy battles.

Returning to Chasum, at the end of 1989, its computer center used an IBM 4381 mainframe with the support of a small army of data transcribers and a set of batch systems to handle the typical transactions of an insurance company, this involved generating hundreds of reports and document which were distributed from the headquarters in Barcelona to the different branches.

There were no screen terminals for querying or recording transactions, processing cycles were measured in days, weeks, and in some cases in more than a month.

MEETING THE CHASUM MANAGEMENT TEAM

At the end of the first day of my visit, Jeffrey organized a dinner with the management team at a restaurant near the main headquarters, where I was able to observe that there was a good interpersonal climate where two generations mixed amicably and used Catalan as their favorite language, all team members had extensive experience in their functional area, all spoke Spanish and Catalan, some also mastered French but all avoided English since this was a pending subject for many Spaniards.

Mateo was the HR director, he was the youngest on the team, but with many years of experience in the company since he had started as an administrative assistant distributing mail when he was a teenager and rose through the ranks to his current position.

The technical director and the finance director, Enrique and Joseph, had two things in common, they were in their early forties and were relatively new to Chasum, one came from the insurance sector and the other from an auditing company.

The other members of the management team were Lucas, Antonio and Joan, responsible for the Commercial, Claims and Marketing areas respectively. They all knew their area in great depth, they had trained at Chasum and together they had almost 100 years of experience.

SPAIN LOOKS VERY RISKY

When I finished the visit I told Jeffrey that the proposal was interesting but that I had to think carefully about it since my interest was more focused on managing a business unit and what lay ahead at Chasum was a huge system replacement effort that would possibly take several years.

Upon returning to London, I discussed the issue with my boss, who happened to be a good friend, and I temporarily closed Chasum's door because, although it was an interesting opportunity, it also had a few risks, since the international development of the division financial services had not been very successful.

Additionally, Gordon thought that, if I was patient, my future could be brighter if I continued at BIT Co.

At the end of the year I traveled to Caracas to spend Christmas with my family and visited the facilities of Bilden, the subsidiary of BIT Co. in Venezuela to which I would return if I did not agree to extend my transfer period at the headquarters.

VENEZUELA HAS CLOUDS ON THE HORIZON

It was nice to reconnect with my old teammates, but things had changed a lot since my departure to London. There were new faces on the Board of Directors, and I felt a little out of place, the good chemistry of my former colleagues on the management team had disappeared along with them. Additionally, the political and economic situation of the country was not going in a good direction.

Changes in the management team are quite frequent in multinationals, and as everything has its advantages and disadvantages, on the one hand, change brings new blood to organizations, allowing executives to acquire more exposure and training by experiencing different political, technical and economic scenarios.

On the other hand, talent transfers between companies mean that the organizational culture and the level of cohesion of management teams is in continuous transformation, sometimes creating good teams and sometimes creating combinations of poorly compatible personalities.

DESTINY OPENS THE DOOR FOR THE SECOND TIME

The idea of continuing as a regional IT advisor at BIT Co. Europe or of returning to Venezuela to do the same in Latin America did not excite me too much, since these were times of great turbulence in corporate politics, so I decided to give a chance to destiny and called Jeffrey to say hello and ask how the search for the CIO in Barcelona was going.

Jeffrey was very friendly and told me that he had recently hired a local for the position, but still didn't know if the new recruit would meet his expectations.

During the conversation, Jeffrey asked me what my plans were. I told him I wasn't clear yet since I had to choose between continuing as a regional advisor based in London or returning to Venezuela in a similar position, but neither option excited me too much.

We said goodbye amicably and for the moment I put the topic aside since I assumed that the door in Spain was closed.

The next day, Jeffrey surprised me with a call from Barcelona and said to me. "Man, I think I have something that might interest you, what do you think about coming to Chasum as deputy general director to be my second in command, we divide the general management half and half, I am in charge of finances, planning, human resources, reinsurance and the interaction with the headquarters and you are in charge of IT, commercial, claims and the technical area".

Jeffrey's proposal seemed like a Christmas gift to me, and something compelled me to immediately say yes, but I managed to control myself and told him "it sounds super interesting, but give me two days to consult with the family and my boss in London".

If I accepted Jeffrey's proposal, I would leave the tobacco division and enter the British International Financial Services division with a promotion. This was very attractive to me intellectually and professionally, but it meant changing an environment that I knew well, where I had stability and a certain prestige for another where I was unknown in a company with profitability problems. I had no idea what could happen if things did not work out in Spain. Additionally, moving the entire family to Barcelona at this time was not convenient since my wife He was finishing her medical studies and my daughters were halfway through the school year.

When discussing the issue with the family, the idea of living in Barcelona was well received and we agreed that I would leave first, in the second week of January to start my new job with Chasum and prepare the ground for the family's arrival at the end the school year, but we would see each other every 3 months just like I had done since London.

On the other hand, my boss in London, as usual, was a good friend and facilitated my departure from BIT Co. to be transferred to Chasum, a subsidiary of Eastern Star belonging to the financial division of BIT.

154

155

RENOVATING AN INSURANCE COMPANY IN SPAIN

156

BACK TO THE OLD CONTINENT

The second week of January 1990, I flew from Caracas to Paris to meet with Pascal, the regional director of Eastern Star Insurance in Continental Europe.

Pascal was Jeffrey's boss and the interview was a formality since my transfer was already approved, but it was useful to learn about the regional structure and the vision of the regional director.

Pascal was a mature man, of thick build with many years of experience in the insurance sector. During the interview he was very friendly and gave me a general introduction to the situation of the company in Spain, which unfortunately was not very simple since it had a serious problem of lack of critical mass and profitability.

At the end of the interview, I took a taxi back to the airport and after checking in for the next flight to Barcelona, I sat down to have a coffee and reflect on the stage that was about to begin.

At 34 years old, I had taken the first step towards a CEO position in a multinational company, accepting an appointment outside my comfort zone in a country I barely knew and in a company with profitability problems. This sounded risky or at least complicated, but I was confident that everything was going to turn out well, I had the conviction that with effort and dedication almost everything can be solved, and in the last case if things didn't work out, my family and I would have had an enriching experience.

THE FIRST DAYS IN BARCELONA

Barcelona is the second most important city in Spain, with a metropolitan population of 3.3 million inhabitants, it was founded just over 2000 years ago in the time of the Roman Empire, it has a very European classical architecture with few tall buildings. The city is marked by the influence of Gaudí's architecture and Cerda's urban planning.

In Barcelona the company accommodated me in the center of the city, at the Ramada Hotel, while I found a permanent residence.

From the Ramblas, I could walk to the office on Av. Diagonal every morning in about 25 minutes, it was a little long for my taste, but it allowed me to familiarize myself with the area.

The second week the walks ended as they assigned me an old manual transmission Renault 25 while an Audi 100 arrived that would be my personal vehicle for the next 4 years.

In the Chasum building they assigned me an office that had just been remodeled on the tenth floor with a beautiful view of Diagonal Avenue. I was very lucky since a good part of the building was still under renovation and many people were exposed to dust and noise.

The headquarters building was divided between the Barcelona branch, the General Management and the central offices, of the Commercial, Claims, Technical, Finance, IT, Reinsurance, Marketing, Human Resources and Legal areas.

Although I had some knowledge of the insurance sector from some work experiences in Venezuela and some subjects at university, I could objectively consider myself a novice compared to any of the members of Chasum's management team, so I should be very careful in my interaction, especially being the second in command, this was a double-edged sword, it gave me authority but at the same time it exposed me to making mistakes and accidentally hurting people's feelings.

In my past experience, entering as second in command in a team that is already formed is quite problematic since some people may feel relegated to a lower level.

DESIGNING THE STRATEGY TO ADD VALUE

On my first day of work, after following Jeffrey around the building to be officially introduced to all the departments, we sat down in his office to design a strategy and an action plan on how to start helping him in the management of the company. We conceive a process in three stages.

The first would be an induction period of several weeks during which I would have interviews with all the managers and section heads in Barcelona to familiarize myself with the people, the organizational structure and the distribution of roles and responsibilities.

The second stage of the plan would be the preparation of a BSP "Business Systems Plan" using a methodology similar to what Jeffrey had experimented with me when we worked together at BIT Co. Venezuela.

The BSP would make it possible to make a quick diagnosis and formulate an IT strategy combined with improvement actions in what was considered high priority.

Carrying out a BSP does not guarantee the solution of all problems or that the IT strategy derived from it is perfect, but it involves the entire company through the management team, giving all areas the opportunity to express their opinion and influence on determining priorities and conceptualizing possible solutions.

Performing a BSP is not a very common practice in most companies and had to be sold to the management team, starting with the CIO.

The third stage of the strategy to support Jeffrey would cover leading the implementation of the BSP results and my progressive participation in the management control of Commercial, Claims, Technical and IT functions.

Jeffrey gave me a vote of confidence by sharing the scheme that we had designed, in the first meeting with the rest of the Executive Committee, we had set in motion a wheel of change that would have enormous repercussions.

The explanation of the plan to the Executive Committee generated expectation, curiosity, confusion and uncertainty, the BSP was something new that they did not know and the incorporation of another foreigner from the tobacco division with no experience in the Spanish insurance sector did not inspire much confidence, but this was predictable and manageable if we produced results quickly and convincingly.

THE PREPARATION OF A BSP IN CHASUM

Jordan, the CIO that Jeffrey had hired, was a mature guy, with management experience and a friendly personality, who quickly supported the idea of doing a BSP, but since he was just starting out in the company, he opened the door to involve the middle management of IT, so I was introduced to Jerónimo, Jesús, and José so that they would participate and cooperate in the preparation and development of the BSP.

Jerónimo was the head of Systems Department, a mature, tall guy, very serious and very competent in his work, he knew in detail the processes of all areas of the company since he had gone through various positions in claims, accounting and production before doing computer programming courses that put him on the path to reaching his current position.

Jesús was the head of Computer Operations, just as Jerónimo was a mature man with excellent knowledge of the company and the operation of all systems including the details of data entry forms, printed reports and production processes. Additionally, he was a super positive person, optimistic, responsible and very reliable.

José, was in charge of Organization and Methods Department, he was Jesús's brother, and also had excellent knowledge of the company in terms of the functions, responsibilities and administrative circuits.

With the help of Jordán, Jerónimo, Jesús and José we prepared the macro process diagrams of all the functions and identify the people who should participate in the BSP and who I should meet in my induction process.

FAST INDUCTION IN CHASUM

The induction at Chasum lasted two weeks and was an interesting and highly productive process. It gave me the opportunity to get to know all the middle managers and the management level of all the functions of the central office and the Barcelona branch up close.

Every day I had two, three and even four interviews that took place in the office of the person with whom I was meeting or if this was not possible in a meeting room.

Through the interviews I built a small paper database with comments, volumes of transactions, problems and unsatisfied desires in each area.

Most people I met were very kind and friendly, although some seemed surprised that my induction was so long and that I was so interested in the details of what they did. I explained to them that in my experience a good induction process was an excellent way to get to know the organization.

Analyzing the information collected, it was evident that the levels of service we provided to the client and the agents had a lot of room for improvement. In those days, it was not unusual for an automobile or home policy to be delivered to the client a month after receiving the application.

If an error or omission occurred in the application or in the transcription of data, it was necessary to go through the administrative circuit between Barcelona and the branch more than once.

As I progressed in my induction process, I exchanged information almost every day with Jerónimo, Jesús or Jose to make sure that I had correctly interpreted what I had learned.

I tried to keep Jordán involved in my induction process so that he could also benefit from this experience, but it didn't work, he had his own program of activities and I don't think he was very interested in the topic.

As the days went by, I became more and more familiar with the people, processes, and products. I remember reading the general conditions booklets and putting together a folder with copies of the insurance applications for all the personal insurance products since these represented close to 80% of the transaction volume.

I knew the importance of having a good understanding of the products and services we were selling.

BREAKING THE ICE WITH THE IT TEAM

At first Jerónimo was a little skeptical that the BSP would have any practical use, and it seemed strange to him that I was so interested in the details, but he gave me the benefit of the doubt and collaborated 100%.

Jesús and José always demonstrated a supportive attitude and showed no doubts, I don't know if it was out of conviction or because of the positive nature of their character, greatly influenced by their Andalusian origin. Jordán did his best to collaborate and make things easier, but I had some concern because little by little he was losing ground in the control of the IT area.

Things were moving faster than Jordán could digest and my interest in details and volumes of transactions made him somewhat nervous since this was not his management style, he always liked to see the forest and left the branches and leaves to his team.

BSP DEVELOPMENT IN CHASUM

When everything was ready Jeffrey announced the BSP as a special Friday and Saturday activity at a hotel near Barcelona. All those responsible for key processes and some branch managers attended.

The BSP went as planned, Jeffrey explained the objective and then I presented the sequence of activities to be carried out and the different forms that people would have to fill out.

The attendees were divided into work groups by functional area and Jordán, Jerónimo, Jesús and José assisted them to describe the deficiencies and expectations for improvement of all the company's business systems and processes.

Finally, each group made a short presentation summarizing their diagnosis and proposing possible solutions and priorities.

THE CHASUM BSP CONCLUSIONS

The BSP confirmed what we imagined, people were very dissatisfied with the level of delay in the systems, the slowness of the administrative circuits, the lack of dynamism in the launch of new products, the scarcity of advertising material, the inflexibility of the Technical Department and the few statistics available to facilitate decision making.

In 1990 there were already companies in the Spanish insurance market that had online systems that allowed data to be entered directly by users, online queries of databases and remote printing of policies.

A complete renovation of the company's computerized systems was needed, and there was no software package available with sufficient credibility, flexibility and functionality to adequately assimilate Chasum's multi-risk policies.

The company had a lot of historical information but it was not available in a database, it was a disjointed set of master, transaction and history files designed to facilitate batch processing.

Jerónimo knew that saving historical information at some point could be useful and fortunately there were millions of inactive records on magnetic tapes waiting for the day to come when they could be useful.

Having an online system connecting all branches to the mainframe was everyone's dream, but the cost of telecommunications in 1990 was still prohibitive if there was not enough volume, and many of Chasum's branches were just small commercial representative offices. with a low volume of transactions.

To further complicate matters, the IBM 4381 platform was expensive in hardware, and tough to crack in terms of productivity of software tools for developing applications.

With this scenario in mind we had a huge problem to solve, the company could not afford a very expensive or time-consuming solution and the BSP had created a high level of expectations, which would become a negative blow to the credibility of the management team, especially that of a recently arrived foreigner.

AN UNORTHODOX IT STRATEGY FOR CHASUM

I spent the weekend thinking about how to approach the solution to the problems reviewing transaction volumes by branch and type of product, and finally after giving things a thousand thoughts I came up with a strategy that had a good chance of success, although it was unorthodox.

The idea was to take advantage of the development speed and low cost of the PC (Personal Computer) platform + an IBM AS/400.

It would be an unorthodox strategy, based on a progressive process that would launch new high-impact applications in the company's daily life in the short term, keeping the old system files updated on the IBM 4381 but progressively replacing it until it was eliminated.

This approach implied a greater degree of operational complexity for the IT operation, but in exchange, it would produce concrete benefits of efficiency, productivity, and competitiveness in all functional areas progressively while the plan was developed.

The next step was to evaluate the feasibility of the strategy I had in mind, so I began to put it in black and white with enough detail so that it could be explained and approved by different audiences that included the IT team, Jeffrey, the Executive Committee and those who participated in the BSP.

I started at the end, drafting a small presentation that in theory would be for middle managers and users who participated in the BSP.

The presentation summarized the new IT strategy and the time scale in which it would be developed, thus pushing the members of the IT Department team to imagine the problems and obstacles they would have to solve.

CHASUM'S NEW COMPUTER STRATEGY

Replace the obsolete Chasum secure computer systems that operated on the mainframe, with a new generation of systems developed on PCs and an IBM AS/400 computer according to the following schedule and scope:

Phase 1 June 1990: Implementation in all branches of a decentralized system for issuing policies on PCs with laser printing for automobile, home, community and personal accident insurance.

The new system will cover about 80% of the volume of production transactions and will improve the quality and competitiveness of service in the issuance of policies.

Information on issued policies will be transmitted once a day to the central office in Barcelona using modems over telephone lines.

Phase 2 September 1990: Implementation of a database consultation system for policies, claims and collection receipts through screen terminals in Barcelona. This consultation system would streamline the management of a good number of processes in the technical office and in the production and claims departments.

Phase 3 November 1990: Progressive extension of the system for consulting policies, claims and receipts in the branches, by time slots according to the volume of business, using remote connection from the PC to the AS/400.

Phase 4 January 1991 to December 1993: Progressive implementation of new online systems for issuance, renewal, collection, claims, reinsurance, coinsurance, commissions, accounting and the rest of active applications on the IBM 4381. The new systems will be developed on an integrated database using the IBM AS/400 platform. Details of this phase will be announced later.

SELLING THE STRATEGY TO THE IT TEAM

On Monday morning I met with Jordán and asked his opinion on the experience we had had with the BSP at the hotel, his response was. "positive and interesting, now we have to take advantage of it".

I explained to him what I had in mind, showed him the draft strategy, and asked him to arrange a meeting with Jerónimo, Jesús, and José to discuss the results of the BSP and use the draft I had prepared as a starting point to develop the IT strategy.

Jordán asked me some questions about the IBM AS/400 and he reacted positively, but it was clear that he was feeling under pressure. Chasum's IT area was about to enter a period of a lot of work, technology changes, and high pressure to repower the company.

Jeffrey showed up at my office at lunchtime and we went out together to eat at a small restaurant on Aribao Street five minutes from Chasum. There was a tasty executive menu and a quiet atmosphere to chat.

Jeffrey was encouraged by the participation and analysis that the attendees did at the BSP as it was what we expected, but he was curious about the next phase, I told him that I already had a draft IT strategy, but I had to evaluate it first with the team of work to be able to show you something with sufficient solidity.

This weekend marked my first month in Barcelona and for the moment everything was going more or less as I had imagined, I had rented a house on the outskirts of the city, I spoke on the phone with my family on the weekends, my relationship with Jeffrey was excellent, he had good chemistry with everyone he interacted with and he was in the process of becoming familiar and learning.

The next day at 10 am the IT management team appeared in my office, but this time expanded with María José and Félix, two systems analysts, who according to Jerónimo would play a very important role in what was to come.

As the meeting began, we exchanged views on what had happened in the BSP and it was clear to everyone that people wanted an online system with a decent database available in all branches.

The idea of using a software package to replace the IBM 4381 batch systems was quickly discarded, the known references were not good and everyone agreed that internal development was needed, but this required acquiring new development tools, increasing the workforce of analyst-programmers and expand the capacity of the IBM 4381.

This implied a significant increase in the annual budget of IT and everyone knew that the company's finances were not going very well since the claims ratio left very small margins and the size of the business portfolio was not large enough.

When we got to this point I thought it was time to let the cat out of the bag and showed them the draft 4-phase strategy I had prepared for us to use as a starting point identifying potential benefits, risks and feasibility elements.

The idea of issuing policies on a PC seemed crazy to them at first, but as we delved deeper into how it could be done and the benefit it implied, everyone changed their minds.

We already had a quotation system available that worked on a PC and allowed us to print automobile and home insurance proposals.

Expanding this system to issue the policy, the receipt and save the data was quite simple, the problem was seen in the printing since it used continuous forms pre-printed on the central computer.

To solve this problem, I told them about a laser printing system that I had seen in a travel agency in "El Corte Ingles" where they had an application on a PC that printed the image of a high-resolution form combined with characters generated by a program in Basic language.

If we did something similar we would not need to use pre-printed forms since the laser printer would use a single standard type of paper, this would simplify things substantially.

Another aspect that worried them was the reliability of data transmission via telephone. At this point, I shared with them my experience at BIT Co., where at that time this transmission mechanism was used to receive the financial summary of all the companies in London from all over the world via international phone calls and there was no problem.

If you can talk on the phone you can transmit data, things only get complicated when there is a lot of data and the call is interrupted.

In the case of Chasum, when considering the number of new policies issued by 15 branches each day, the volume of data was perfectly manageable, what had to be careful was in the administrative control to ensure that all the policies that were issued were transmitted.

The idea of using an IBM AS/400 computer to replace the IBM 4381 required more effort and concrete examples since they had no personal experience with this technology.

Fortunately, I knew the IBM AS/400 technology well and had several interesting stories to share with them.

Once I explained to them the case of BIT Co. Venezuela where all the systems were developed from scratch with a team of 10 analysts who had no experience in the IBM AS/400, I think they were convinced at a first level, additionally, I committed to bringing to Chasum from Venezuela several IBM AS/400 applications that we could use as a reference, starting point and training material.

Accepting the idea of using the IBM AS/400 due to its low cost, the power of its relational database manager, and application development tools, it was easy to convince the team about the convenience and benefits of generating a database that would replicate information from the old systems on the IBM 4381 on a daily basis.

VERIFYING THE VIABILITY OF THE IT PLAN

At the end of the meeting, unanimous support had been achieved for the draft strategy and we had identified concrete actions to verify some key points by researching and requesting information.

Jordán and Jesús were in charge of speaking with IBM to obtain a quote and estimated delivery times for an IBM AS/400 with sufficient capacity to begin the development of the plan. They should also do a comparative cost analysis to demonstrate the economic benefits of moving systems from the IBM 4381 platform to the IBM AS/400.

José was in charge of preparing a dossier with all the pre-printed forms and conditions used in the issuance of automobile, home, accident and community policies. Additionally, statistics for several months should be prepared to evaluate what percentage of policy production could be covered.

Jerónimo, María José and Felix would study the feasibility of expanding the PC quoting system to issue policies and would investigate the cost and feasibility of using desktop laser printers.

For my part, I was in charge of informing Jeffrey about the strategy and obtaining approval from BIT Co. in London to obtain a copy of the systems developed in Venezuela.

We finished the meeting around six in the afternoon, it had been very long but apparently very productive, I had the feeling that the team was enthusiastic and convinced that the strategy could be viable, now we had to make sure that this was true and then convince the rest of the company that this was a good path.

SELLING THE PLAN TO MY BOSS

The next day I invited Jeffrey to lunch at the Corte Ingles on Av. Diagonal, he was surprised that I suggested that place since we would have to drive about 10 minutes, but I told him that there was something important to see there before eating.

After parking, we went straight to the travel agency where I had seen the laser printing system and I asked them when they had implemented it. The manager was very friendly and explained to us that he had installed it about six months ago and it was developed by a computer services shop of the Corte Ingles that was on the same floor.

After browsing for a while and imagining the impact that issuing policies on PC using desktop laser printers could have, we went to eat in one of the restaurants on the top floor.

During lunch I shared with Jeffrey the strategy I had discussed with the IT team and he reacted very positively to the plan, wanting to know all the details.

Upon returning to the office I gave him a copy of the presentation I had used with the IT people and the research points that Jordán, Jesús, Jose and Jerónimo were following.

We agreed that when I had confirmation from the team that the plan was viable and the time scales were achievable it would be time to share the strategy with the Executive Committee.

To save time on my part, I called my old boss at BIT Co in London to tell him how things were going and ask for his support in obtaining a copy of the systems developed in Venezuela.

Gordon, as always, was very kind and thought it was a good idea. He had always promoted the reuse of software within the corporation and this could be another opportunity to take advantage of what had been done in Venezuela on the IBM AS/400.

THE CHASUM IT STRATEGY LOOKS VIABLE

On Friday afternoon, we had a follow-up meeting with Jordán and the IT team, things were going smoothly, Jerónimo had visited the systems development company in El Corte Ingles and they could give us the service of creating high definition formats that would be superimposed on the information of the policies and receipts when printed and they could advise us on printer models and software tools to use, this would allow us to reduce learning risks and save time.

On the other hand, the analysis and programming group had already evaluated the effort necessary to expand the PC quoting system to issue, store, and transmit policies. In principle, this project was feasible for June as long as the scope did not change substantially.

Something that was still not clear was the cost and number of pages to print per policy since the pre-printed forms used carbon paper copies and would have to be printed several times on the laser printer.

Jordán and Jesús had already met with the IBM salesperson to obtain quotes for an IBM AS/400 system and an upgrade to the IBM 4381 so they could evaluate the cost difference. The following week we would have the numbers and delivery times available.

I told them that I had already made contacts to obtain a copy of the Venezuelan systems and that in principle there would be no problem.

José had the information on the production statistics and these confirmed that the sum of automobile, accidents, home and community ranged between 77% and 83% in the 6-month period that he analyzed.

José also suggested that if the project went ahead, two important aspects that we had not analyzed would have to be considered.

The first was to use the new policy issuance system to launch new products or at least tweak them to amplify the commercial effect.

The second point was to verify with the Technical Office as soon as possible restrictions that should be considered in the subscription policy, especially in automobiles and communities where accident rates were not going very well.

José's comments were very accurate and we all appreciated its convenience, even Jerónimo commented that if new products were not made, at least we should use different codes.

Excitement was growing in the team as was the stress level for everything that was coming up. I commented that I would keep Jeffrey informed of the progress and we agreed to meet again on Tuesday of the following week since we would have quotes and delivery times available from IBM.

That day, as usual, I was leaving the office late and I ran into Jeffrey in the parking lot, so I took the opportunity to update him and he told me, "That's great because next Wednesday Pascal is coming to see how the remodeling is going and the issuance of policies on PC".

Then I realized that Jeffrey had already talked about the project to the regional director, this worried me a little since I was still not totally sure that everything was feasible, but Jeffrey had a very good relationship with his boss and I understood that the he did the same as me.

Pascal was a Canadian with extensive experience in the insurance sector and as regional director he was responsible for Eastern Star's insurance operations in continental Europe which at that time included Belgium, France, Greece, Italy, Portugal and Spain.

That weekend I was eager to finish analyzing the costs of the project, but I didn't have all the data so I dedicated myself to buying furniture for the house I had rented, since it was still almost empty, I had only had time to buy a bed and two sofas.

While I was shopping, I suddenly realized that it was not right for Pascal to find out the details of the project before the members of the Chasum Executive Committee in case there was any problem that I had not anticipated.

CHASUM EXECUTIVE COMMITTEE & IT STRATEGY

On Monday morning I suggested to Jeffrey that we hold a special meeting of the Executive Committee, to canvass opinions on the IT strategy we were evaluating, since if they had objections it would be best to handle them before Pascal came.

Jeffrey agreed and we arranged the meeting for late afternoon as everyone was available at 6 pm. In the meeting, I explained to them that the IT team was working on the new systems strategy based on what was presented in the BSP and we had a draft that we wanted to evaluate with them before moving forward.

Then I gave them a copy of the summary of the strategy with the four phases, explained the details of each one, and suggested that we begin a round of clarifying doubts and identifying the problems, risks, and benefits posed by the strategy.

Lucas asked why there were only four types of policies to issue in the branches and I explained to him that the four products covered about 80% of the transactions and since we already had the quote system on PC this could be easily extended.

Antonio was very thoughtful and suddenly said "This idea of issuing policies in the branches, I think it will be very well received by the staff and the agents as long as it is not a tall tale that is breaking all the time".

We all laughed at the colorful comment and then Lucas commented, "If they can implement this system in all offices in June we can make a lot of noise in the market, especially in the province, accelerating the issuance of policies in this way is very innovative and can also help improve the speed of collection of premium receipts".

Antonio intervened again and commented "If this can be done with a PC and a laser printer, why don't we also give the system to the most important agents", in this way, we save a good part of the administrative cost and the flow of papers between the agent's office and branches.

At this point, Enrique commented: "Giving the system to the agents could create problems with the underwriting policy, how are we going to ensure that they do not issue policies outside the policy".

Jeffrey intervened and said, "we can put controls in place that prevent the issuance of risks that are outside policy, but we must first see how it works in the branches before giving it to the agents".

Lucas spoke again and commented. "In addition to the controls that can be put in place, remember that an exclusive agent has insurance proposals that when delivered to the client already imply coverage".

Enrique intervened again and said, "if this can be implemented between now and June, why we do not take advantage and launch new products in home, automobile, and accidents by making some changes in makeup and rates, we can select the risk that interests us and control better the subscription policy".

Lucas intervened again and said, "I think it's a great idea, there are some rate and coverage details in all of these products that are worth updating to be in line with the market".

Joan intervened at this moment and said "If the products are defined quickly we can make new brochures and promotional material, at this moment we do not have brochures in stock".

I had been silent taking note of the interventions, and it seemed prudent to intervene at this point.

"I also think that launching new products with promotional material is an excellent idea, we just have to move quickly and avoid very radical changes if we want policies to be issued in June".

Jeffrey chimed in again and said, "I think we all like the idea of issuing policies at branches as soon as possible, but I would like to know if you see any major problems with it and if you think it really benefits us".

Enrique intervened again and commented. "If the subscription policy is controlled and no policy is lost, I see it as positive. They have not said how much it costs, but I imagine they have already studied this aspect".

I intervened and commented.

"We have not finished the cost analysis because some supplier data is missing, although in principle we believe that the cost is acceptable, with respect to hardware, we already have the PCs for the quoting system that currently works, the new thing would be the laser printers and the modems to transmit the data to Barcelona. A pending issue is the cost of toner and stationery since A4 paper would be used to print the policy several times since there would be no carbon copies as is used in the continuous forms today. Another economic element to consider is that this is the first step towards eliminating the entire data transcription department here in Barcelona in the future, but that will be later".

Mateo, who had remained silent, intervened at this moment and commented "Assuming we can afford it, printing the policies in the branches would be a positive step for the morale of the staff and the image of the company. It has been a long time without important improvements in the company's systems".

With Mateo's opinion, the circle of support for the issuance of policies in the branches in the Executive Committee was completed, the rest of the phases depended on the IBM AS/400 whose cost-benefit analysis was not yet available, therefore I intervened again and, I told them.

"It seems that we have unanimous support for the first phase of the IT strategy conceived from the BSP, we can evaluate the rest later when we have all the information. If you like, I propose that we approve the following points:

- Launch of new automobile, accident, home, and community products with the issuance of policies on PCs with laser printers in the branches.

- The Technical Directorate will prepare the specifications of the new products and organize a work team to launch the products at the end of June 1990.

- Report weekly to the Executive Committee on the progress of the project".

Everyone agreed and then Jeffrey said.

"The project to launch new products and issue policies in the branches has officially been born, thank you all for your participation, and for everything you will have to do in the coming months, I think we have done enough for today, let's stop the meeting here".

Things had turned out better than expected, the Executive Committee knew about the project, and supported it, and, incidentally, the idea of launching new products had come spontaneously from the Technical Directorate, and that increased the user ownership of the project.

The next day I informed Jordán, Jerónimo, Jesús, and José of what had happened in the Executive Committee and they all reacted positively, the energy of the project continued to grow.

At mid-morning I received a copy of an email from Enrique inviting Sales, Claims, Marketing, and IT to form a working team to start the development of the new products.

GOOD AND BAD NEWS WITH AN IBM AS/400

On Tuesday afternoon Jordán and Jesús came to me with cost information and quotes from IBM.

They had prepared a spreadsheet comparing the acquisition and maintenance costs of the two platforms IBM 4381 and IBM AS/400. The analysis indicated that the IBM AS/400 was clearly more economical, but Jordán and Jesús had doubts about the capacity for growth.

On the other hand, Jordán had bad news, the IBM representative told him that the delivery time for an AS/400 like the one they had quoted was around 12 months and this had a very negative effect on the project.

My reaction was surprise and concern, I had no idea what things were like in Spain for the acquisition of an IBM AS/400, in my experience at BIT Co. In England and America, I had never seen such bad delivery times.

I spent a few minutes thinking about the problem and I came up with a possible solution. I told Jordán and Jesús, "Tell the IBM representative to make us a counteroffer to improve times by considering other options, for example:

- They lend or rent us a smaller AS/400 to start development as soon as possible.

- They sell us another smaller machine that is available and then buy it back when we receive the one we are going to order from them.

- They evaluate the purchase within the global purchase agreement that is made each year at the corporate level.

At the end of the meeting, I told them, "I'm going to talk to the Corporate IT manager at BIT Co. to see if they can give us a hand with IBM through the corporate account manager".

THE REGIONAL DIRECTOR COMES TO BARCELONA

On Wednesday Pascal came to the offices as planned and spent the morning with Jeffrey. Around noon they invited me to meet them and we discussed the BSP, the IT strategy in development, especially the policy issuing at branches.

Pascal showed interest in the project and asked about the estimated costs and the level of reliability of the dates, at that point I told them about the problem with the AS/400 dates and the pressure I was trying through BIT Co. to obtain a quote with better delivery dates.

I asked Pascal what the procedure was for approving the purchase of the AS/400 at Eastern Star and he commented that if we kept it under one hundred thousand dollars he could approve it and we would consider it as another element in the remodeling of the building.

Later he added. "We have already spent a lot in office renovation, I don't think the head office is going to give me problems for investing in improving the capacity, efficiency, and competitiveness of the company".

When he made that comment I realized that I had no idea about the cost of the remodeling that was underway and I thought I'd better stay out of this topic.

We ended the meeting and Jeffrey suggested we go to lunch at a French restaurant on Paris Street near Chasum where they made very good turbot.

We left the building and a five-minute walk away was a small restaurant that I didn't know. We all ordered the turbot and enjoyed it in a pleasant conversation in which Pascal shared with Jeffrey and me some interesting anecdotes about the ups and downs and problems of the other companies in continental Europe.

In Greece there was a Joint Venture with a medium-sized local company, which, like Chasum, was not doing very well in profitability, in Portugal, Italy, Belgium, and France there were branches dedicated to the commercial segment through Brokers and each one was a world different according to Pascal.

At the end of lunch, I said goodbye and did not see Pascal again on this visit to Chasum.

AN IBM AS/400 ON THE WAY

At the end of the day, Jeffrey came to my office to tell me that Pascal had already left to return to Paris, that he had made very good comments about the IT strategy, and that we could move forward, so he gave the green light to place the purchase order for the IBM AS/400, provided it didn't go over a hundred thousand dollars, I immediately called my former boss in London and asked if I could help with the corporate account manager to improve the delivery date. As expected, he was very receptive and promised to do whatever he could.

On Monday of the following week, the IBM account representative came and brought a new quote with a slightly smaller machine than the one we had originally ordered, but it would be available for delivery at the end of April since it was from a canceled order from another client in Spain.

We reviewed the configuration with Jordán, Jesús, and Jerónimo, at first it seemed sufficient to develop the next stages of the plan, so I took it to Jeffrey, I explained what it was about and he was delighted to sign it.

Things were going even better than I expected, I had never been approved for an AS/400 so quickly before.

It was evident that the relationship with Jeffrey, and the support of Pascal made a difference, although I shouldn't complain because in the past at BIT Co. things always went well, it was just that there were more meetings and presentations involved.

Pascal and Jeffrey were very practical, they always got to the point and long presentations were not their thing, if they understood the logic of what you proposed, and were convinced by your answers, they would support you.

PROGRESS AND PROBLEMS WITH NEW PRODUCTS

The development of the new products was advancing in the working group led by the Technical Directorate, but the typical problems began between the Commercial area and the Technical area. Some wanted more flexibility, alignment with the market average, and competitive advantages and others wanted more controls and restrictions on what could be dangerous risks.

Each wanted to do their job and although in theory, both sides wanted a profitable and growing company, each had a different and not always compatible vision of how to do it.

I knew what was happening from Jerónimo and José's comments, and I stayed out of it, giving them time to find a point of agreement without compromising the project dates.

THE IT DIRECTOR RESIGNS

The tension continued to increase and the following week Jordán presented his resignation as IT director.

I asked him what motivated his decision and he told me.

 "Orlando, I know that he has the best intentions, but the situation in the IT area is very stressful, we have very tight dates, and now the hard work begins, I feel that my health is going to suffer and they have offered me a position at the same level in another company where the situation is calmer, since the previous director is retiring, there the work is more maintenance than development".

I understood his point of view, wished him well, and accepted his resignation. Jordán was right, his position was high stress and the challenges were just beginning to rear their heads.

At the moment I had no intention of hiring a new IT director, since Jerónimo, Jesús and José were doing a good job and I wanted to give the opportunity for an internal promotion.

I asked Jordán to make a transfer plan for the matters he handled personally, indicating which ones could be delegated. Jerónimo, Jesús, and José. They knew the company in depth and could add a lot of value both at a technical and managerial level.

When I informed Jeffrey of the resignation, he said, "To be honest, I expected it, you don't take prisoners".

So I asked him what it meant that I take no prisoners, and he explained to me, "Man, you very diplomatically generate enormous pressure and people can't always take the train".

I thought about his comment and then I told him "You may be right, there are many ways to cook chicken, and possibly my recipe is not the most popular".

The next day I officially announced Jordán's resignation, indicating that I would temporarily assume the IT Directorate.

I established a weekly meeting with Jerónimo, Jesús, and José to discuss issues of IT, which in practice was mixed with the coordination meetings of the different phases of the project.

VISIT TO THE FAMILY IN VENEZUELA

In mid-May, I went to Venezuela for a week to visit my family since I hadn't seen them since January. During the visit, my daughter Alejandra's first communion was celebrated and I had the opportunity to see the whole family at a meeting on the terrace of a hotel since it was a fairly large group.

During the celebration, I was able to share very special moments, which were recorded in videos and photos for the family album, but with my parents, the reunion was deeply emotional since I felt that the weight of the years was affecting them in an accelerated way, which made me feel deeply sad.

My father had already had two heart attacks and although he was much younger than my mother, he looked quite aged.

My mother suffered from arthritis and kidney problems that caused problems with blood pressure and electrolyte balance.

The rest of the family was fine and preparations for the move to Barcelona were already beginning, which also generated a certain level of stress in me since, although I was doing well at work, the long-term situation was uncertain due to profitability problems of the company and sometimes my optimistic side faded a little.

The week passed in the blink of an eye and I returned to Barcelona to continue with my job responsibilities.

ANOTHER EMERGENCY FLIGHT TO VENEZUELA

I had just been back in Barcelona for a week when I received a call from my sister to tell me that my father had died, he had suffered a third heart attack and this one had been massive.

I immediately took an unplanned flight to Venezuela to attend the funeral. It was a very sad and painful experience that, although I knew that one day it would arrive, there was no way to cushion the blow felt in the heart.

1990 was a year of great changes in my life and that of my entire family. My father and mother were taken to the spiritual world and it would be the last year of residence in Venezuela for my family.

Venezuela would continue to have a very important place in my memory, since I lived my childhood and adolescence there, created my family, completed part of my academic training, and had my first work experiences, but the death of my mother and father in 1990 It would break an anchor of great emotional value.

PROBLEMS WITH NEW PRODUCTS

Upon returning to Barcelona, in the next follow-up meeting, Jerónimo expressed his concern about the difficulties between the Technical and Commercial areas to agree on the issue of the subscription policy, indicating that, if it was not resolved quickly, we could not maintain the date of the end of June, so I asked him to give me examples of what was so difficult for them to remember.

Jerónimo said. "There are many details and specific cases for each product, for example, in a car when it is not the age limit of the driver, it is the circulation area, or the use of the vehicle, or the engine power, or the percentage of no claim bonus, or the amount of the deductible. For home, it is the theme of jewelry, or the years of construction, or alarms, etc.

Given the situation, I asked Jerónimo if it was possible to make a table for each product where a record could be placed for each combination of subscription parameters that was considered unacceptable and based on that, put a control to not issue the policy if it was not authorized by the Technical Office in Barcelona.

Jerónimo thought for a while and then drew on a sheet of paper an imaginary table with different variables to consider, then said. "I think it could be done, but the issue remains of how to approve the transaction from Barcelona without further complicating the system"

Then I remembered a movie I had seen a few years ago where they used approval codes saved in the computer and whoever knew them could use the codes to approve transactions.

I explained the mechanism and Jerónimo said.

"If we generate a file with enough alphanumeric codes and give them to the Technical Office, also we put them on all the PCs that issue policies, in we can create a mechanism to approve by telephone each case that was outside the underwriting policy".

Jerónimo agreed to study the matter in more depth and take it as a proposal to the working team.

The proposal led by Jerónimo helped solve the problems of how to control the limits of the subscription policy and the approval of each case that was outside the standard, using special codes that they called "Random Code Approval System (RCAS)".

The working team finally agreed to have a new policy for private automobiles, two new types of home policies, one flexible and one standard, one for personal accidents and one for community.

In total, they agreed on the details of 5 new products to be issued on PCs with laser printers and controlled by a restricted subscription policy according to tables that specified the areas outside the subscription policy that should be approved from Barcelona by a telephone call to the Technical Office which would give a SACA code to enter into the branch computer.

CHASUM BEGIN TO ISSUE POLICIES ON PCs

At the end of May, the laser printing policy issuance system was ready. In just four months, the combined efforts of IT, Sales, Technical Office, and Marketing had managed to resolve all the challenges that arose.

The work team prepared a demonstration of the system in the conference room and it was shown in several sessions to a good part of the Barcelona staff and to the branch managers who attended a special meeting with Lucas.

Since the second week of June, the system began to be installed in all commercial offices and fortunately, everything worked as planned, the delivery time of the policy to the client was dramatically improved, and a lot of noise was made in the provincial market, and the staff He felt an air of renewal that was added to the substantial improvement of the offices in Barcelona.

The approval of cases outside the subscription policy by random codes also worked well, but to the relief and surprise of almost everyone, it only represented less than 2% of the transactions.

As the days passed, the issuance of policies in the branches became routine and attention changed direction in each functional area.

EYES FIX ON THE IBM AS/400

Starting in June, Jerónimo and his team began to familiarize themselves with the IBM AS/400 that had been installed in early May.

When Jerónimo began to pay attention to the IBM AS/400, Jesús had already installed the application libraries that we had received on magnetic tape from BIT Co. Venezuela.

At that time, I still had a good level of technical knowledge of the IBM AS/400 and the content of the libraries that we had received and I was able to help Jesús create a development environment and a production environment where the following applications were installed:

- User access control.

- Automatic documentation.

- Accounting

- Expense budget.

- Control of fixed assets.

- Management information.

We could use some of these applications with few changes if we followed the conceptual principles with which they were designed in Venezuela, others would serve as examples of database and programming in RPG400 so that Jerónimo and his team of analysts and programmers could experiment and become familiar. with the IBM AS/400. I knew that if I taught Jerónimo and his team the basics they would master the IBM AS/400 very quickly.

THE IBM AS/400 BEGINS TO BE USED

At the beginning of July 1990, the IBM AS/400 was operational with an environment for production and another for development with the systems from BIT Venezuela. At that point, I organized a seminar for the IT staff where I gave them a demonstration of the systems and also explained how they could look at the programs and the database.

The objective of the seminar was to whet their appetite and stimulate their curiosity by giving them the basic knowledge to begin interacting with the machine and the applications that served as an example.

During the seminar, I could see from the interest and participation that the objective had been achieved. Jerónimo, Jesús, and the rest of the analysis and programming team were impressed with the IBM AS/400 and eager to get their hands on it.

In the next weekly meeting with the IT team, I asked them to prepare a plan of action with the goals that we should achieve in the remainder of the year to continue developing the IT strategy that emerged from the BSP.

Jerome, Jesús, and Jose responded to my request with a very practical and comprehensive plan.

Jerónimo and his team took the IBM AS/400 as a kind of personal challenge and dedicated extraordinary time to the design and development of database migration processes for products, policies, claims, collections, reinsurance, coinsurance, accounting, etc.

I had access to the IBM AS/400 from a screen in my office and could see how the number and size of the database files were growing.

Jerónimo and his team were doing an excellent job with the database migration process. In addition to the master and transactions files, they also included historical files that would be very useful for statistical analysis.

CHASUM'S PROBLEMS AND ITS BUSINESS PLAN

As I was beginning to feel comfortable with the organization and progressing with the IT strategy at the beginning of the summer, Jeffrey took his family on vacation to Australia, leaving me in charge of preparing the annual business plan that would be sent to the headquarters in September. I was familiar with the Business Plan format at BIT Co. but I didn't handle the details of how it was done at Eastern Star, additionally, except for the CFO, the other directors had not been involved the previous year, so I had a little problem.

I tried to contact Jeffrey for clarification, but I was on a sailboat in the coral reefs, and at the time I didn't have any contacts at Eastern Star headquarters who could guide me, so I had to improvise with what was available.

The "Business plan" is basically a five-year projection of business operations with monthly figures in the current year and the next and then quarterly figures until the end of the period.

For the exercise I had to do, the year 90 was the "Current", the year 91 was the "Budget" and from 92 to 94 the "Forecast".

To make a projection of the company's operations, I would have to prepare with the other directors a set of assumptions of what we planned to do and what we assumed would happen over the planning period.

All these assumptions should be translated into estimates of fixed and semi-variable expenses, premium volume, claims levels, and investment portfolio performance.

With all these numbers, the CFO should prepare a profit and loss statement and balance sheet covering the time periods for the actual, budget, and forecast.

As you can imagine, the "Business Plan" is a very theoretical exercise that, depending on how it is carried out, it can be very useful or a waste of time. Additionally, for the headquarters in some cases, it is simply a reporting requirement, and in others, it can be the difference between maintaining the company or closing it. It all depends on the conditions of the strategic moment that the company is experiencing.

Although I did not know it, Chasum was in the crosshairs to be removed from the group, since some members of the Eastern Star Executive Committee in the UK, did not see enough strategic value in the Spanish general insurance market.

DIRECTORS HELP IN THE BUSINESS PLAN

I organized a meeting with the area directors to discuss the issue that we had to prepare the "Business Plan" and everyone was willing and interested in collaborating.

But they didn't have much idea of how to contribute with concrete figures, they barely had an idea for the next few months, but beyond that, it was pure imagination.

In Chasum's management style that came from the time of the Mullet family, everything was decided from the top with little or no participation from middle management.

Making a business plan once a year like the one I was proposing was a totally new experience and for some of them possibly a way to waste time.

Joseph, the finance director, commented that the previous year he had collaborated with Jeffrey on some specific aspects. Still, he did not know how the figures had been generated for all the years that had to be covered. Given the situation, I proposed the following work scheme:

1. Joseph would talk to the finance people at headquarters to confirm the formats that should be used to send the figures and would verify the delivery dates, additionally, he would prepare a month-by-month expense estimate for the remainder of the year based on current expense levels and the impact of new items such as IBM AS/400 maintenance.

2. Enrique, as technical director, would prepare an estimate of technical results by business line that would follow the trend that we had until the end of the year. Additionally, he would try to prepare an estimate of the growth of the Spanish market by business line for 1991 using the figures from the statistical yearbook of the General Directorate of Insurance (GDI).

3. Antonio, as claims director, would review the accumulated accidents frequencies so far this year and the reserves established for peak claims,

if there were any important changes he would discuss them with Enrique.

4. Lucas, the commercial director, would prepare an estimate of the volume of business that each branch could achieve until the end of the year and would prepare an estimate of growth per branch for each month of 1991.

5. Joan, the marketing director, would prepare a promotional activities plan with quarterly expense estimates for the remainder of 1990.

6. Mateo would prepare a projection of the number of workers by branch and central functions for each remaining month of 1990.

We all agreed and agreed that we would have a follow-up meeting next week, to discuss what they had prepared and that in the meantime if there were any problems or unforeseen events they would let me know.

If everyone did their part for the next meeting, we would have a good idea of how the year could end and a first vision for 1991 in terms of sales volume and market growth, from there we could start the imagination with goals. and strategies for 1991.

THE IMPLICATIONS OF SUMMER IN BARCELONA

At the end of the meeting, Mateo walked with me to my office and told me that since we were entering summer, many people would go on vacation and this could affect the preparation of the plan. He told me that in the summer we had special hours and that in previous years they had even closed for a week in Barcelona since not a fly was moving.

This information surprised me quite a bit, I had no idea that summer would affect operations so much, and at first, I thought that Mateo was exaggerating, but as the days went by I realized that he was right, most of the directors and their subordinates had already prepared their summer vacations so I had to incorporate this new limitation in the preparation of the plan.

At the next meeting, each director presented their part or what they had been able to achieve up to that point and they discussed the topic of summer vacations. I took a very flexible position and told them to do what they could in the time without canceling their vacation, I assumed that if in previous years Jeffrey had survived I would have to do the same.

The summer atmosphere was felt everywhere and I was impressed to see how the city almost stopped, weekdays seemed like Sundays with many establishments closed.

TAKING ADVANTAGE OF THE IBM AS/400 DATABASE

Given the circumstances and with so few people in the office, it occurred to me that I could take advantage of my time browsing the database that Jerónimo and his team had generated on the IBM AS/400.

At this time, there was already up-to-date and historical information on policies, claims, and collections, so it occurred to me that I could build some working files to analyze the issuance of policies by branch by month and by year, this would be useful to take the pulse on business volume figures.

Possibly, I could also calculate and analyze the technical result of each branch and its evolution over time.

When Jerónimo found out what I was doing, he was curious of why I dedicate myself to this, so I explained to him the problems I had with the "Business Plan". He guided me to use the database correctly and clarified that the figures in claims were before applying the reinsurance contracts, so I should be careful when interpreting them.

In a few days, I set up a small query module that allowed me to analyze the total business volume, policy issuance, and renewal, by branch, agent, type of product, month, and year.

For claims, I did something similar, but obviously, the claims rate fluctuated drastically due to the effect of the lack of critical mass when analyzing small groups of data.

LEARNING FROM THE COMMERCIAL DIRECTOR

Having the ability to analyze the issuance of policies by branch for any period of time that existed in the database, it occurred to me that this tool could be useful to Lucas in making a sales budget by branch and that the sum of all the branches could be the total budget, so I decided to discuss the idea with Lucas and I got a very interesting surprise.

Lucas explained to me that he had a sales budget per branch that he used to evaluate the business performance of office managers, but that the sum of all branches was never Chasum's total budget.

I asked him what the reason was and he explained that at the branch level each year he set a growth objective based on the previous year's volume, fluctuating between 10% and 100% depending on the starting point.

If you were a new, small office just starting out, you could be asked to double volume or 100%, but if you were a large office, growing 10% could be a difficult goal to achieve.

On the other hand, the mix of products played an important role in growth; if we wanted to fill ourselves with bad risks, we could grow very quickly, ensuring what no one wanted in the market, and we would pay dearly for the consequences with a bad technical result.

Finally, there was the issue of the stability of the portfolio of clients and the agents themselves. Chasum's business is the sum of the business that all the agents in all the branches give us. This implies that, if an agent loses a client, or we lose an agent, Chasum's business volume decreases instead of growing in that office.

Under normal conditions, no office manager in their right mind would make a sales budget to lose business from one year to the next, however, in the real world the agents lose clients and the office loses agents from one year to the next, this is very difficult to predict at the branch or office level, therefore, the sum of the sales budgets of all the branches would never be realistic as a total budget unless a drop correction factor was included. The correction factor was estimated by Lucas every year.

The preparation of the sales budget was influenced by the law of large numbers, Lucas knew that in some branch he was going to lose agents and that some agent was going to lose clients, but he could not predict exactly in which branch this would happen.

To further clarify the issue of growth, Lucas explained to me that, beyond the stability of the client and agent portfolio, the growth of business volume also depends on three possible sources:

- Products whose insured sum grows each year due to the effects of inflation, which implies an increase in the premium to be paid.
- Each agent is interested in finding new clients and selling more policies to those they already have.
- Each branch manager must achieve a goal of recruiting new agents.

For Lucas, the most important part of growth was the recruitment of new agents, for this reason, it became an annual objective that he set for each branch manager.

Lucas monitored this objective keeping a record of new agents by branch and year which included the volume of sales they had generated.

Lucas told me. "new agents are like your children, you have to pamper them, guide them, and make sure they grow up healthy, if we don't recruit new agents, there is simply no growth"

That morning I spent with Lucas listening to his explanations about the growth in premium volume and the budget transformed my vision of the commercial area and helped me understand some of the challenges and complexities of his work that I had not considered until that moment.

The model that I had developed on the IBM AS/400 to analyze business volume by branch could be useful to Lucas as a reference, but it was a light year away from covering everything he needed.

On the other hand, having seen records of years in a notebook to keep track of new agents by branch was an enriching experience that demonstrated how ingenuity, experience, and deep knowledge of the commercial process had worked despite not having access to sophisticated technological tools.

After understanding the importance of agents from a more realistic perspective due to my conversation with Lucas, I decided to modify the model that I had prepared and attend to an invitation from Lucas to visit agents and all the branches. This was going to take time, but it was going to be an unforgettable and very useful experience.

REVIEW OF THE BUSINESS PLAN WITH DIRECTORS

In the second meeting to prepare the "Business Plan" Lucas presented his estimate of how we could close the year, and an initial business volume figure for 1991 that would make us grow with the market index, but that in his opinion was not easy to achieve. Competition was very strong, especially in large cities where banks continued to penetrate the insurance distribution.

He also commented that, if we managed to grow in line with the market in 1991, this would be a positive change in trend since in previous years' growth had been lower than the market average and therefore we had gone backward.

The other directors listened to Lucas carefully and then Antonio asked.

"Lucas, what can we do to grow above the market average".

Lucas answered.

"Well, many things, for example, we can have a more aggressive underwriting policy, we can open more branches, we can put the issuance of policies in the most important agents, we can hire more commercial inspectors, we can launch new products, we can do a marketing campaign on TV, etc., etc. The problem is that we are in a very competitive market and all this requires additional expenses and investment, and some strategies may not improve the technical result. In short, it all depends on how much meat we put on the grill and how much Eastern Star has an appetite".

At this point, I commented.

"Clearly growth is a complex issue, and I agree with what Lucas says, I suggest for the moment that we adopt the scenario of growing in line with the market in 1991 and when Jeffrey comes, we review it with him".

Everyone agreed and we moved on to the next point, the claims reserves, here Antonio had bad news, we had had two car accidents with personal injuries and one of them looked like it would become a peak accident, it involved the death of a senior executive of a banking entity run over by a private car insured by Chasum.

At that time, compensation for death and personal injury in the automobile insurance industry could have a catastrophic effect on the technical result since judges frequently awarded compensation that exceeded the limits of reinsurance contracts.

Chasum had a relatively healthy Automobile portfolio with around fifty thousand policies in force, but in recent years it had had a negative result mainly derived from peak personal injury claims.

Then it was Enrique's turn in the Technical Directorate, and he commented that the growth for 1991 that Lucas used, was expected at the market level and that this was derived from a small increase in insurance penetration, increases in the insured sum, and some adjustments to the automobile rate, which at the moment was in deficit for many companies in the sector.

The Spanish insurance market was in the midst of a consolidation process at the beginning of the 90s. There were more than 400 insurance companies and many of them were not large enough to have a critical mass that would give them stability in technical results and savings in economy of scale in their expense structure. Additionally, multinational insurers and banks aligned with insurance companies substantially increased the level of competitiveness.

In short, Chasum did not have an easy time growing or surviving in a market full of sharks.

Joan and Mateo were on vacation and there was nothing special to report about their areas, so we went to the financial area.

Joseph commented that he already had a projection of expenses and that he had reviewed with Lucas, Enrique, and Antonio the projections of business volume, accident rate, and expenses for the rest of the year, so he had a first scenario that showed losses. Nevertheless, we still had to refine some numbers, for example, if we were going to hire more staff, open an office, or modify the level of IBNR.

The IBNR stands for "Incurred but Not Reported" is a loss reserve that refers to accidents that are statistically expected to have occurred until the accounting close but have not yet been officially reported to the company.

In summary, claims reserves give some room to influence the outcome of the year by injecting a certain level of optimism or pessimism into the reading of statistical trends.

This means that the annual result declared by an insurance company is subject to a certain level of financial engineering, in other words, you do not always win everything you say or lose everything you declare.

Chasum had several exercises declaring losses and as far as I could tell they were not exaggerations, in the claims reserves. The profitability of the company was a quite complex issue, difficult to solve and I was just beginning to understand it.

JEFFREY IS SURPRISED WITH THE BUSINESS PLAN

When Jeffrey returned from vacation, he found a business plan developed for "Current" and "Budget" with a list of the assumptions that had been used in each area.

Jeffrey was impressed with the work that had been done and the involvement of the area directors.

When I showed him the query module on the IBM AS/400 screen with the statistics of production, business volume, claims, and claims reserves, he was even more impressed and told me.

"I knew the IBM AS/400 was going to be a useful tool but I didn't expect it to be so fast".

Then I told him.

"I didn't think it would happen so quickly either, but working on the "Business Plan" pushed me to use the database that Jerónimo was generating and I think fate extended a hand to us.

THE FAMILY ARRIVES FROM VENEZUELA

In mid-September at the end of summer, my family arrived from Venezuela, my two daughters, my wife, my cousin, and my nephew landed on a Saturday at noon at the Prat airport, after a long and tiring trip from Caracas with a stopover in Madrid.

For them, it was their first visit to Barcelona and it marked the beginning of a new life in a country they did not know, and with many cultural differences that among other factors included new idiomatic expressions, vocabulary, food, way of greeting, television programs, way of dressing, four seasons, a new school, a rented house and the absence of aunts and grandparents who frequently visited them in their old city.

My wife had just graduated as a doctor after finishing her rotating internship, and my cousin had lived with my family for 10 years and had been key in raising my daughters since they were born, thanks to her my wife was able to continue her studies in medicine, my 14-year-old nephew was like my third child and the older brother of my two daughters, ages 8 and 10.

Everyone quickly adapted to the house we had on the outskirts of Barcelona since it was much more spacious than the apartment we had in Caracas, which, although comfortable and cozy, could not compete with a 3-level house where there was plenty of space and everyone had his own room.

The original plan was for the children to study at the American school that was 5 minutes from the house, but when we went to register them, registration was already closed. The school year in Spain starts earlier than in Venezuela, and I didn't know it.

But we were lucky and through some of Jeffrey's friends, we got places for the three kids at a Jesuit institute in a central area of Barcelona. It wasn't the ideal solution, but it worked for the first school year.

Since there was no school transportation for the area where we lived, I took the children in the morning and picked them up in the afternoon. During the trip I gave them English classes, preparing them for American school the following year.

Taking the kids to and from school was something I enjoyed, but it made my life at the office difficult since I usually had meetings that ended late, so Jeffrey gave me a hand and assigned his driver to pick up the kids in the afternoons and take them home.

My wife was also very lucky professionally and another friend of Jeffrey's introduced her to the head of the gynecology and obstetrics service at the San Juan de Dios hospital and he offered her an internship to learn obstetric ultrasound. The internship worked very well and after a few months, it became a position in the regular cycle of the specialty of gynecology and obstetrics, since San Juan de Dios was a university hospital. After 4 years my wife completed her specialty at the San Juan de Dios in Barcelona.

WORK PERMIT AND FAMILY ENTERTAINMENT

The processing of my employment contract in Spain and thpermits of the entire family took more than a year, this meant that I would have to maintain an unofficial status in Chasum and I would have to leave and return to the Spanish territory with the entire family every three months until the procedures were completed.

This was an inconvenience, but it also had its positive side, since it involved a trip for the whole family to a nearby destination every three months, this opened our eyes to all the facilities that were within our reach to get to know many other cities.

When my employment contract was approved, the family trips continued two or three times a year, one paid for by the company in my benefits package and the others covered by the family budget.

VISITING OVER 20 CITIES IN 5 YEARS

Barcelona has a privileged location to travel at a very reasonable cost. Between 1990 and 1995 we had the opportunity to take advantage of school holidays and some multi-day holidays to visit a long list of cities including, Madrid, Figures, Paris, Canes, Brussels, Bruges, Amsterdam, Andorra, Rome, Florence, Pizza, Venice, Prague, Zurich, Geneva, Basel, Bonn, Frankfurt, Cologne, Mainz, Vienna, Salzburg, London, New York, Houston, and Miami. In all the cities we visited museums, parks, monuments, a few restaurants and of course many souvenir shops. Most of the trips were by plane, but some in Spain and neighboring countries were done by road.

Visiting all these cities was a very enriching and unforgettable experience for the whole family, it allowed us to experience first-hand the great linguistic, culinary, architectural, and historical variety of the world in which we lived.

I remember that the first time we went to Andorra, we were all very excited about the idea of skiing on the snow slopes, but it turned out that this was much more complicated than we imagined, especially for me, as when I got off the transport chair I fell rolling, and I twisted my ankle.

On another occasion, on a car trip through the south of France, strangers opened the trunk of our car during the night and took all the coats and snow equipment we had.

On a trips to Paris, organized by a travel agency, the day we returned to Barcelona, the bus driver got lost on the highway for more than two hours and we almost missed the return flight. When we realized that the driver was lost on the highway we laughed for a while since it was better to take it as an adventure and no one knew how to help him, finally, we arrived at the airport and we did not miss the flight because God gave us a hand and delayed the departure of the plane.

On a trip to Vienna, my eldest daughter, who was studying piano at the time, couldn't stop talking about Mozart and convinced us to drive 300 kilometers to visit her musical idol's birthplace in Salzburg. The journey was long, but impressively beautiful, as we were able to see a parade of hot air balloons and spectacular landscapes. Mozart's house had been converted into a small museum and my daughter fulfilled her dream, in addition to purchasing several scores and souvenirs from the visit.

On another occasion, we visited some friends in Germany near Frankfurt and we went to dinner in a town called Mainz, which at first had nothing special, but suddenly we passed by a small museum that said. "Here was Johan Gutenberg's workshop". And then we realized that the first printing press had been invented in that place, which began the process of massification of written knowledge.

WEEKENDS IN BARCELONA

During the time I worked in Barcelona, almost every Saturday I had to go to the office since there was always some important project that couldn't wait, however, Saturday afternoons and Sundays were for family activities.

Sometimes we would watch movies, go out to eat, or invite a group of friends to a barbecue and play a game of tennis or racquetball.

Sharing with friends was pleasant, entertaining, and revealing since it helped us become familiar with the cultural differences between Latinos and the groups of Europeans with whom we lived.

I remember that the first time we organized a meeting at home, we had bought beer, wine, whiskey, rum, gin, and soft drinks, but when we asked people what they wanted to drink, most of them ordered a glass of cava and I had to run to the supermarket to buy some bottles. In Catalonia, cava is the favorite drink at many social gatherings, and we had no idea about that custom, over time we learned about the subject well and discovered that cava and champagne are the same, the difference is the area where it is produced.

SCREENS OF THE IBM AS/400 IN BARCELONA

At Barcelona, in September 1990, when everyone was returning from their vacation, they found several IBM AS/400 screen terminals that allowed consultation access to the policy and claims database.

Jerónimo and his team had developed the query modules and the database was updated daily by extracting changes from the IBM 4381.

Additionally, the management information module that I had developed during the preparation of the "Business Plan" had been improved and it was connected to the policy and claims consultations that Jerónimo and his team had developed.

This allowed the user to make a helicopter flight from the general to the particular. For example, if the user enters the system in a statistical query by product, branch, or agent, then could go down to the next level breaking down the information to the details of the policy, the accident claim, or the receipt.

If you have worked only with printed listings and suddenly you have access to a screen that gives you all this information updated daily, you feel like you are part of a revolution, and that was the feeling among the staff at the Chasum building in Barcelona in September 1990.

THE SYSTEM PLAN MEETS WHAT IT PROMISED

As planned in the BSP, the goal of providing consultation access to the company's database was achieved and this added to the issuance of policies on PC in the branches, giving an injection of enthusiasm to the staff and credibility. to Eastern Star.

At the beginning of October Pascal came to visit us again and Jeffrey asked me to give him a demonstration of the management information module, we had a new toy that was on the one hand instrumental in daily life, but was also a political tool to obtain support at headquarters.

THE AUDITORS FROM THE HEADQUARTERS COME

Pascal was very impressed with the demonstration and commented that we would soon receive a visit from the head office's systems auditors since issuing policies on PCs had set off alarms in London.

Jeffrey was a little worried when Pascal left and at first, I thought it was because of the auditors' visit, but later I understood that his long face had other reasons.

In the last week of September, Francis, Eastern Star's systems auditor, showed up in Barcelona and since he didn't speak Spanish I had to take care of him most of the time, although I tried to pass him on to Jerónimo, Jesús, José, and even to Jeffrey.

Francis was an experienced and quite reasonable man unlike many auditors who focus excessively on standards and procedures, this allowed him to accept the usefulness, efficiency, and low cost of the PC policy issuance system.

All the problem or risk arguments that I raised were adequately covered and the number of policies issued, the cost analyses, and the opinions of users were very valuable support.

The database queries on the AS/400 also left a good impression and he had to admit that Eastern Star didn't have anything like that despite having had online systems for a long time.

Francis wrote a report where he described his observations and conclusions in an objective manner that obviously did not create problems for us.

BAD NEWS AND A COLD WATER BATH

After the auditor left, Jeffrey called me into his office and explained the reason for his long face these past few days.

Pascal had informed him that Eastern Star had decided in a strategic planning exercise that the Spanish general insurance market was not attractive or profitable enough to justify the injection of capital or the risks that had to be assumed to achieve enough market share and critical mass.

In other words, it was more profitable and less risky to invest in other markets than to try to grow a company that was losing money, had a very small market share, had no critical mass and incidentally did not have the Eastern Star brand.

Under this scenario, Jeffrey received instructions to start a sales process for Chasum Seguros. This involved, on the one hand, hiring an investment bank to prepare the sales documentation and make contacts with potential buyers, and on the other hand, maintaining this process in total confidentiality.

From a personal point of view, this news was like a bucket of cold water, which broke the stability of my family that had just settled in Barcelona and the project to renew all of Chasum's systems.

Obviously, neither Jeffrey nor I could do anything to change Eastern Star's decision, there were only two options, we collaborated with the sales process by keeping it secret and continuing all the projects as if nothing was happening or we quit and looked for a job elsewhere.

Jeffrey decided to collaborate and asked me to do the same, resigning at that moment would be a family chaos for both of us, and in Chasum it would complicate things significantly, generating stress and instability for hundreds of people who, beyond being co-workers, many of them were good friends.

Jeffrey followed the guidelines of the parent company and hired an investment bank to prepare the sales documentation.

In my case, I should be focused on maintaining the day-to-day operations, and promoting all the systems projects as if nothing was happening, the only thing I could not do was incur new investments or extraordinary expenses.

Jerónimo and his team were advancing rapidly in the development of the new systems on the IBM AS/400 and managed to adapt accounting, expense budgeting, and fixed asset control to Chasum's needs with very few modifications.

On December 1, 1990, when I turned on my IBM AS/400 screen and entered the system to see the production statistics, I was pleasantly surprised.

The image of a Christmas tree decorated with gifts and imitations of flashing light bulbs appeared on a message that said.

"MERRY CHRISTMAS 1990, AND THE BEST WISHES FOR PEACE, JOY AND PROSPERITY FOR 1991.

THERE ARE 30 DAYS UNTIL THE NEW YEAR"

The message had been programmed by Judith, one of the analysts who worked with me at BIT Co. Venezuela so that it would be activated on December 1st and appear until the last day of the year.

The first time I saw it in Venezuela, it seemed like an excellent idea, capable of injecting a few drops of optimism and cordiality to more than one user at the beginning of their day.

The phenomenon was repeated thousands of kilometers away, five years after being programmed, the message surprised me again and gave me a new lesson about how small things can have great value and a very important effect on the unpredictable development of life.

That day I thought, I don't know how long or under what circumstances my family and I will be in Spain, but I will do my best to make every day a positive and enriching experience.

A SAD DECEMBER IN VENEZUELA

In mid-December, I traveled with the whole family to Venezuela to spend Christmas and see my mother who was in poor health, but when I arrived I found that she was hospitalized and the prognoses were not good.

On December 30, my dear old lady passed into the spiritual world and I felt the strongest pain imaginable. I don't know the physiological mechanisms of what happens, but I literally felt like my heart hurt.

It was the saddest December of my entire life, but thank God the emotional pain I initially felt transformed over time into a feeling of resignation and inner peace as I imagined my mother in a spiritual world without pain and surrounded by a beautiful and peaceful environment.

CHASUM FOR SALE THE SPANISH MARKET

The first week of January 1991, after my mother's funeral, we returned to Barcelona, where probing contacts were progressing to find a buyer for Chasum Seguros.

Some multinational insurance groups showed interest and signed the confidentiality agreement. From here, a process of additional questions and answers began regarding the content of the memorandum that described the company and the conditions of the sale.

In mid-March, Jeffrey told me that there was still no concrete offer, but in order not to be left in the air, it would be prudent in his case and mine, to make some contacts at BIT Co. to explore possibilities of returning to the division of tobacco as the opportunities to transfer within Eastern Star or to continue with the new buyer were very few.

Jeffrey's comment did not take me by surprise since neither he nor I were very well regarded by Eastern Star's old guard, and if an insurance group decided to buy the company, the most logical thing would be for it to focus on absorbing the policy portfolio and the distribution network, while eliminating anything it considered redundant.

Despite the environment of instability, I decided to give it time and keep my attention on promoting IT projects and continue to become thoroughly familiar with the commercial, technical, and claims areas.

I thought it didn't make much sense to run to another position that also had no guarantees of stability. In my experience of working with multinationals, most of the movements are opportunistic and in the direction that the company needs, if you do a good job and have good relationships that helps a lot but nothing is 100% sure, when you accept a transfer, you know when you arrive, but you are never sure when you are leaving, for the family it is a little different if you have school-age children, measures are normally taken for them to finish the year, although it is not always possible.

THE HEADQUARTERS CHANGES THE STRATEGY

In May something unexpected happened, as none of the potential buyers made an offer, the Board of Directors of Eastern Star decided to suspend the sale and try to repower the company.

They could not keep Chasum Seguros for sale for a very long period since, if the information was leaked, it would damage the value of the portfolio and the commercial network. No one is interested in buying insurance from a company that is in danger of going bankrupt or disappearing.

On the other hand, maintaining the company will require a long-term vision, investing to grow on a profitable scale, and changing the name of Chasum Seguros to Eastern Star Seguros Generales.

When Jeffrey told me about it, I thought it was excellent news and I was very glad that I hadn't rushed to cancel a project or run away looking for a return to BIT Co.

UNEXPECTED PROMOTION TO MANAGING DIRECTOR

On the other hand, I wasn't very impressed with Eastern Star's strategic planning skills and I told Jeffrey, after what we've been through, I think you deserve to be named president of the company, and I managing director

I imagine Jeffrey discussed this with Pascal and to my surprise, the following month Jeffrey was named president, and I was named managing director.

In practice, we continued doing the same thing with the exception of having powers of attorney to sign certain documents or approve certain levels of spending or investment.

The supposed change in strategy didn't really make much difference, since the concept of profitable growth was not a blank check, it only implied that growth objectives and projects capable of passing the scrutiny of justification would be well received.

On the personal side, the promotion was something valuable for the ego and the resume, but economically it was something almost symbolic since the company's finances did not allow for much more. Jeffrey and I assumed that if we did a good job and took the company forward, the reward would come later.

THE NEW STRATEGY FOR CHASUM

To give shape to the new strategy that we could only partially explain since the entire workforce didn't know what was going on, we agreed to define four new projects.
1. Name change from Chasum to Eastern Star
2. Expansion of the commercial network
3. Portfolio profitability
4. Efficiency and economies of scale

NAME CHANGE TO EASTERN STAR

We assigned the name change project to the marketing director as it was a complex, expensive, and gradual process that would have to be carefully planned and executed. This project included the media argument, the official announcement, the identification, redesign, and replacement of all the elements that would be affected, from the signs in the offices, the stationery, forms, computerized reports, policy conditions, business cards, letters issued by the system, promotional items, etc.

The cost and impact of the name change were enormous and involved hundreds of people in the company, all the agents, customers, suppliers, and even government offices that would need to be notified.

The name change project was organized and executed following a work schedule that spanned more than a year.

EXPANSION OF THE COMMERCIAL NETWORK

The expansion of the commercial network was assigned to Lucas, the commercial director, and consisted of the design and development of strategies to expand the company's distribution network, this meant in a few words recruiting more new agents and creating the mechanisms to make this happen more quickly than had been done in the past, but there was a small problem, the results in this area depend on the law of large numbers which implies that having a budget and making the best efforts is not enough to guarantee the result.

Lucas could plan how many new offices he could open, how many new commercial inspectors he was going to hire, how many visits from new agents he was going to make, and even how much business he wanted to obtain from all these actions, but he couldn't guarantee the final result, he simply wasn't in it. his hand.

If you were focused on recruiting rookie agents, they are small, unstable, and unreliable. If you focus on professional agents, the most serious ones do not easily switch to work with another company. This is what I began to call in my professional life, probabilistic outcome projects, since no matter how much effort you put in, there is no way to guarantee the result.

In other words, the business growth strategy of recruiting agents, even with the best effort and with a good budget, would have an uncertain result.

The only way to guarantee a high volume of growth was to buy other companies and this option was not contemplated at the moment.

Lucas did his best to develop an expansion plan for the commercial network, based on his experience and that of his team of branch managers. The plan deserved all my respect since it was ambitious, realistic, and reasonable.

Lucas saw the company as if it were his own business and under this principle, he only proposed things that he would do if it were his money that was at stake. Under this principle, the plan was implemented progressively and generated modest growth somewhat above the market average.

During the development of the plan, I had the opportunity to visit with Lucas all the branches and a few agent offices in large and small towns in the Spanish province.

PROFITABILITY OF INSURANCE POLICIES PORTFOLIO

The portfolio profitability project was assigned to Enrique as technical director and was divided into two projects, one focused on developing new products to induce improvements in contribution and competitiveness, and another focused on loss control of the insurance policies in force.

The profitability of an insurance product cannot be guaranteed exactly, but it can be predicted within certain limits and depends on factors such as the frequency of claims, the average cost of compensation, the amount of the risk premium, the agent's commission, deductibles per claim, the characteristics of the insurable risk, bonuses for non-claims, etc.

From this perspective, the product development team has an almost infinite range of possibilities to design technically profitable and more or less attractive products depending on the needs of the client, the commercial attractiveness of the agent, and the size of the insurable market.

If a product is easy to sell, has an attractive commission for the agent, and has a reasonable profitability, we are in the presence of a win, win, win.

This is ideal, the problem is how to find the balance point in a very competitive market where there are some who do not always respect the rules.

The product development plan worked with relative success, as it was able to correct deficiencies in old products, improve risk selection, and fuel an image of dynamism with the frequent launch of new products.

This experience helped me understand that new products have enormous replacement power over existing ones and are always excellent excuses to talk to the customer again and raise the morale of the sales force.

However, despite all the efforts made, it was not possible to create a new trend or market niche that would differentiate us indisputably from the competition. We went up one or two steps in product quality, but we were not the masters of the valley.

The accident control project was based on using the IBM AS/400 to optimize the analysis of the cost and frequency of accidents in the database of policies inforce, in this way, we could identify situations in which we should take measures either by canceling the policy or modifying the renewal conditions, but this is not so simple since very often there were commercial considerations involved.

For the insurance business to function within the socio-economic machinery of a country, there must be claims and these must be adequately compensated with the premiums that have been collected to cover the risk.

This implies that having claims is something desirable since without them insurance makes no sense as a protection instrument. The problem arises when a risk is too bad and there is no reasonable risk premium to cover the claims.

If it is a bad risk, such as a driver who continually has accidents, the easiest thing is to cancel the policy, but what happens if this driver is the owner of a company that has many policies that are profitable and is a client of a very important agent.

In this case, a solution would have to be found, such as setting a higher deductible per claim, increasing the risk premium, or eliminating some coverage from the policy.

The loss control system worked quite well and allowed the portfolio to be cleaned of some bad risks in some branches, and improved the underwriting conditions of many others, however, it did not improve profitability dramatically, which indicated that the control that was practiced before the system was not as deficient as was thought.

EFFICIENCY AND ECONOMIES OF SCALE

This project was subdivided into three work areas assigned to Jerónimo, Jesús, and José.

Jerónimo was in charge of evaluating the impact of the new systems developed in AS/400 regarding reducing work hours in administrative processes.

Jesús was in charge of implementing the reduction of the data transcription workforce and computer center operators as the new systems were implemented and the printing of lists was reduced thanks to the use of screen terminals and the installation of departmental printers.

José was in charge of studying and documenting the process times and costs in the new administrative circuits that progressively eliminated the flow of documents and printed lists between the branches to the central office.

The progressive implementation of the new systems in the IBM AS/400 made it possible to substantially improve the speed and quality of service in all functional areas, from the issuance of policies to the processing of claims.

In three years it was possible to replace all the systems that operated on the IBM 4381 with new versions that operated on a database integrated and updated by users through screen terminals, data transcription, and the flow of hundreds of lists and forms between the branches and the head office in Barcelona.

OPTIMISM AND SENSE OF STABILITY

In mid-1992, all the projects we had started at Chasum were progressing satisfactorily and I had the impression that we were close to solving the profitability problems, which gave me a feeling of optimism and stability in Spain.

Under this scenario, it made sense to have another car at home, and I decided to buy a Mercedes E220 for myself and leave the Audi 100 to my wife since she was used to having her car from a very young age. Besides, I loved the idea of having a brand-new Mercedes.

Under the same principle, the family grew with two pets, first came "Cugui", a little Pekingese dog that we adopted on a walk to San Cugat. A while later "Tito" arrived, a white Persian kitten that stole the family's heart at the Corte Ingles.

In those days, sometimes the girls accompanied me to the office on Saturday mornings so that I didn't stay too long. On one occasion when I was reviewing some prototypes of a plastic almanac to promote the name of the company, my daughter Tatiana had the idea that we should put a catchy phrase under the name of the company. It occurred to her that this could be "An Intelligent Decision", the following Monday I mentioned it to the marketing director and the idea prospered, so from that year on, the company's plastic almanacs would carry that slogan.

During this period of optimism, on one occasion I went with Manyi to an aero modeling club on the outskirts of Barcelona and fell in love with remote control helicopters, so I ended up buying one and discovered that things were much more complicated than I thought. For every minute of flight, I had to spend hours repairing the helicopter, taking off was easy, but landing without breaking it was quite a challenge.

THE RESULTS ARE NOT ENOUGH

At the end of 1992, the old Chasum of the 70s had been converted into a modern, more competitive Eastern Star Seguros Generales, with business systems that surpassed most of the competing companies in functionality. However, improvements in Growth and profitability were still not enough to solve the financial problems.

Some important challenges remained to be resolved, mainly in the average cost and productivity of the human resources structure.

The productivity increases that had been achieved with technological renewal, although they freed many people from long work hours and completely eliminated certain tasks such as transcribing data or resending documents due to errors, had not translated into a substantial reduction. of the number of people on staff.

A high percentage of workers had a permanent contract and many years of accumulated seniority, in an organizational culture where the normal thing was to grow old in the company and receive salary increases by CPI plus adjustments from the insurance sector employers, this generated internal inflation. over the years in the operating cost of those positions in which their added value did not increase.

Furthermore, compensation in the event of unjustified dismissal was expensive, a sufficiently large reserve had not been established for this item, and the voluntary turnover rate was very low.

In short, we had the capacity to absorb a greater volume of business that would not arrive quickly, we did not plan a costly and painful restructuring process based on unjustified dismissals, but we could not continue scratching the financial breakeven point for long.

BARCELONA 1992 OLYMPIC GAMES

The 1992 Olympic Games arrived in Barcelona and I enjoyed relative tranquility, due to the good progress of the projects, which made me forget from time to time the sword of Damocles of the financial result.

I hadn't realized how quickly time had passed and how special the city I was living in at the time was.

Barcelona had made impeccable preparations for the Olympic Games including major infrastructure works such as the new airport, the Ronda de Dalt, and the Olympic Village.

The games went perfectly and I had the opportunity to attend with my family the opening, closing, and some competitions thanks to special tickets I received as a courtesy of IBM, which was one of the Olympic sponsors.

The Olympic games of 1992 was an unforgettable experience that put Barcelona on the map of international attention and catapulted its image and tourist attraction.

EXPLORING OTHER SOURCES OF PROFITABILITY

After the games, everything returned to normal, including the pending issue of critical mass and profitability, so we began to study other avenues of solution and we only had two left: to propose, the purchase of another insurer or a merger of Eastern Star Vida with Eastern Star General Insurance.

Buying another insurer did not have much chance of passing scrutiny at the parent company, since the Spanish market was still seen as unattractive to risk a significant amount of capital and at that time a high level of attention was being raised about the potential of the Chinese market.

The merger scenario of the life and general insurance companies in Spain, was cheaper, with fewer risks, and more viable now that the two companies had the Eastern Star brand. Also, it would be easier to convince the head office that this was a good idea to realize economies of scale in office space, operational structure, and synergy in distribution channels.

The merger would involve a cost of reorganization to eliminate redundancies in marketing, IT, accounting, finance, and legal, but would result in a profitable company with a channel of general insurance agents who were also Eastern Star Vida's most important channel.

Internal politics did not allow us to involve Eastern Star Vida's management team in preparing a bulletproof proposal, so we only presented the idea of the merger to Pascal in conceptual terms with very superficial calculations of the benefits it could generate.

Pascal listened carefully, he gave us to understand that it made a lot of sense, but he did not want to go into details about the possibilities of carrying it out.

The name change project had been successfully completed in 1992 and Chasum became a name that was fading into the past, although many of us remembered it fondly for all the experiences and effort made.

For me Chasum Seguros, at that time it was a period of 3 years of a lot of work, and some professional achievements that I felt very satisfied with, for other people it had been their entire working life since it was the only company they had worked for.

Jeffrey and I continued to promote the four retraining strategies, now including some cases of workforce reduction using early retirement when possible.

These situations were neither easy nor pleasant to handle, but there was no other option, to keep the ship afloat the weight had to be reduced and some very senior people occupied high-cost positions with little added value. On the other hand, there were younger people who could take on other functions and grow in the organization.

CHANGE OF REGIONAL DIRECTOR

The year 1993 came and with it a change in the Eastern Star organization, with implications for Jeffrey and me. Pascal had been appointed director of Eastern Star Asia and was no longer our boss.

He moved to Hong Kong to direct Eastern Star's expansion strategy in the Asian market, especially China with its 1.2 billion inhabitants at that time.

For Jeffrey and me, things could get complicated, since we had an excellent relationship with Pascal that would not be easy to replace, he had continually supported us, trusted us, and communicated well, and there was very good chemistry.

When you have a new boss, it's almost like changing jobs especially if you don't know them.

Carter was the new regional director with responsibility for the territory that Pascal managed, but he was a new face coming from the headquarters.

Carter was a mature Englishman, tall, corpulent, with a kind and calm personality. His strong area was finance, and he had no operational experience since he had spent his career at the headquarters and this was his first position at the regional level.

On his first visit to Barcelona, he met with Jeffrey and me to become familiar with the company and all the recent history of what had happened, what we were doing, and how we were moving in the search for growth and profitability.

During the presentation we prepared for him, Carter focused on listening carefully while taking long notes and asking questions to clarify any points that stood out to him.

When it was time to eat, he suggested that we order sandwiches and fruit juice to save time since there were a lot of topics to cover.

At the end of the presentations he asked for a space to review his notes and we offered him the reinsurance manager's office, which was next to Jeffrey's and was available.

At the end of the visit, Carter kindly said goodbye, and said that we would be in touch.

NEW BOSS NEW RULES OF THE GAME

The next day Jeffrey appeared early in my office with his face a little long, his private meeting with Carter had not gone very well.

Carter, unlike Pascal, wanted to put his hand into the operations and not limit himself to managing large objectives and strategies.

His first point was that he didn't like the structure of a president and a Managing Director, so he had in mind that both Jeffrey and I would report directly to him and have a clearer distribution of roles and responsibilities.

In practice, Jeffrey and I were a team that worked well, I respected him as my boss and he trusted me, he handled the financial, legal, reinsurance, and institutional relations part and I handled the operational part but always in accordance with him.

Now Carter came to break up the team based on theoretical principles of organization that, although apparently valid and logical, were not going to help us.

Carter began having frequent one-on-one calls with Jeffrey and me and became interested in levels of detail that Pascal was never interested in. Things were definitely changing for both Jeffrey and me.

DIRECT SALES INSURANCE COMPANY PROJECT

As the automobile industry was very important in the portfolio and I had spent a lot of time studying the market and the competition's strategy, Carter became interested in this topic and asked me to prepare a preliminary study to evaluate the feasibility of creating a direct sales automobile insurance company, that is, without intermediaries.

When I brought it up to Jeffrey, he thought it would be a waste of time and he was probably right, but the cat was already in the water and it had to swim to the other side.

From this point, I began to travel frequently to London to have meetings with Carter about the direct sales project for automobile insurance and to report to him on activities and projects in the areas of my competence at Eastern Star General Insurance.

My visits to Eastern Star UK also served to find out how Eastern Star Direct had been developed, which was the equivalent of what I was studying for Spain, but which was already working in England, however, things were not as simple as copy and paste, each market was different in composition, competition, potential profitability and barriers to entry.

LIFE AND GENERAL INSURANCE INTEGRATION

After the summer of 1993, all the projects that Jeffrey and I had planned had been implemented or were underway, but growth and profitability were not reaching the necessary levels, so we put back on the table the idea of a merger with Eastern Star Vida.

On this occasion, the idea was evaluated at the headquarters and they decided to put it into practice to be implemented in 1994.

When I found out about the decision, I was initially very happy since this would solve the problem of the expense structure of Eastern Star Seguros Generales and would also benefit Eastern Star Vida.

However, the joy did not last long because when I returned with my family after the Christmas holidays in Venezuela, Jeffrey informed me that in London they had decided to appoint the President of Eastern Star Vida as responsible for merging and directing the two companies.

Furthermore, Jeffrey had been appointed CFO of Eastern Star Asia and would be transferred to Hong Kong to assist Pascal in developing the Asian market.

In my case, I would continue as Managing Director of Eastern Star Seguros Generales and would have to report to Juan, who would soon be named President and CEO of Eastern Star Seguros Generales.

Carter had disappeared from the map in a transfer to a corporate role and the direct sales project for motor insurance for Spain had been cancelled.

BREAKING THE WORKING TEAM

Jeffrey's departure meant breaking up our work team and placed a strong halo of uncertainty on my role since the new President and CEO was a person I barely knew, and based on the references I had, he was not someone easy to deal with.

Juan had considerable experience in the life industry and had been hired locally to be the head of Eastern Star Vida since it began operations about six years ago, managing the life insurance portfolio that Chasum Seguros had accumulated through several decades.

When Juan assumed the position of President and CEO of Eastern Star Vida, in the late eighties, he moved the company's headquarters to Madrid, and from there he directed operations using the same agent network of the former Chasum Seguros.

Jeffrey ended his stay in Barcelona in mid-1994 and moved to Hong Kong.

We said goodbye to him with a small but emotional toast that marked the end of a period of great changes that allowed the former Chasum Seguros to be transformed into a renewed and more competitive Eastern Star General Insurance.

ANOTHER UNEXPECTED COLD WATER BATH

When Jeffrey left, Juan began visiting the offices in Barcelona, and at the first opportunity, he came to my office to talk privately and said to me.

"Orlando, I have been very attentive to talking to you, but as you can imagine I have a very complicated agenda, today when we can finally talk, I am going to be very clear with you, do not take this the wrong way, I know that you have done a good job in the company in recent years especially in the systems area, but in the merger stage that we are going to start I have to reduce expenses and make the most of my local team, so I have spoken with HR in London to coordinate your return to BIT Co In the coming months".

I knew that my relationship with Juan was not going to be easy, but I did not imagine that he would be capable of having such an inconsiderate attitude; I had been key in the reengineering of the company and in proposing the merger of life and general insurance. His words surprised me and I felt very disappointed with the corporation, his attitude of contempt towards everything that had been done to make the company profitable, improve results, and sell the idea of the merger seemed inconceivable to me, but something inside me kept me afloat and I told him.

"No problem Juan, I would have done it differently, but you have the responsibility and authority to organize your team as you see fit. Tomorrow I will talk to the human resources people at BIT Co. I am sure they will know how to handle the situation within the conditions of my contract. By the way, while I'm here, I'm at your disposal to help with whatever you need".

Juan got up from his chair and said to me, "Well, Orlando, good luck, remember it's nothing personal".

Mentally I thought, not even in my worst nightmares had I imagined that my transfer to Spain would end this way, at the same time, an inner voice told me, see what you get for working 12 hours a day every day of the week. Another voice told me what an injustice, you don't deserve this treatment, resign and send everything to hell.

Fortunately, I calmed down and told myself, something good has to come out of all this, I have had an incredible experience in these years, my family is well, they have seen a lot of the world, they have learned other languages and even my wife has completed a specialization in gynecology.

I have a clear conscience that everything I have done has been honest and professional, I have helped many people and saved a few people's jobs, so I should not be discouraged.

Nobody forced me to work hard, I did it because I felt good doing it, I enjoyed it a lot and at the same time, they paid me well.

That day I left the office unusually early, and went home and only the dog was there to keep me company, so I sat in the garden to imagine what I could do, what path to take, what options I could explore.

That day I didn't say anything to my family, it wasn't worth worrying them about what was coming on a path that I had no idea where or how it was going to continue.

I only knew that the immediate future of my work was not in Spain, but I knew that that school year would end in Barcelona.

The next day I started making contacts at BIT Co. which were now a little more difficult since my old boss had retired, but the contacts at HR worked and in the following weeks three possibilities appeared.

THE DOORS ARE OPENED TO RETURN TO BIT CO.

In Central America, there were two CFO positions waiting for replacement, one in Nicaragua and the other in El Salvador.

In Venezuela, they also opened the door for me to return to the position of Regional IT Manager that I had held a few years ago and the General Manager on duty also knew me.

When I discussed the options with the family and explained to them what was happening, of course, there were long faces, Nicaragua and El Salvador had important political and security problems that, among other things, posed the risk of kidnapping and the use of armored cars. Venezuela had serious economic problems, and the political situation was not going very well.

A DOOR TO THE OTHER SIDE OF THE PLANET

Before making a decision it occurred to me to call Jeffrey in Hong Kong, and fate opened a new door, when I told him what was happening and the options I had, he told me.

"If you are willing to accept a position other than CEO, I think Pascal can offer you something interesting here.

Asia has great projects ahead and many opportunities, but Pascal is convinced that CEOs must be local and not expatriates, if you want I will sound him out and call you tomorrow".

The next day Jeffrey called me and told me that Pascal saw opportunities for me, but to explore them I would have to go to Hong Kong to talk in person and learn about the terrain he was going to tread if this path prospered.

I told Jeffrey to get me the ticket and the next day he sent me an email with the details of a three-day trip the following week.

I sent Juan an email to notify him that I would be going to Hong Kong the following week and he replied saying.

"There is no problem, as long as they pay the ticket, there is no budget here for that type of expense"

I put his email in the imaginary folder of unpleasant situations that I should use to train my self-control and I thought everything happens for a reason, surely I must learn something from this experience.

I embarked on a 20-hour trip with a stopover in London to fly to Hong Kong, a British colony in the southeast of China that I had visited 18 years earlier on a brief get away from my student life in Tokyo.

In 1977, when I was finishing my specialization in system engineering in Tokyo with a scholarship from the Japanese government, I took a short trip to see Hong Kong since I was very curious about what was said about the colony and I thought that due to the cost and the distance, it would be very difficult to ever return to Asia from Venezuela.

But fate, as usual, surprised me and here I was flying to a place I thought I would never return to.

The British Airways flight landed on a Sunday afternoon at the old Kai Tak airport, reliving a very special experience since in the last phase of the landing the planes flew over at a very low altitude over a densely populated area called Kowloon in a turn of 90 degrees.

Hong Kong Airport had a high level of security and an approach accident had never occurred, but landing at Kai Tak was quite an experience.

I went through immigration with a small briefcase and went out to the waiting room where it was nice to see a sign with my name held up by Andy, Pascal's driver who very kindly went to pick me up.

On the way from the airport to the hotel we went from Kowloon to Hong Kong Island through one of the underwater tunnels that cross the bay and in a few minutes we arrived at the Shangrila Hotel in Pacific Place where I had a room reserved.

Andy gave me some directions on how to get from the hotel to the office the next day, which was in a tower right next to the hotel.

What I had seen so far bore little resemblance to the Hong Kong I had known 17 years ago, there were many new buildings and a high level of development and prosperity could be seen everywhere.

The next morning, I got up early, went out to explore the shopping center, and checked my way to the office tower where I would meet Jeffrey and Pascal.

FIRST VISIT TO EASTERN STAR ASIA

I arrived at the office punctually at 10.30 am as indicated in the program and I got the first surprise, the Eastern Star Asia regional team was in an open space with five desks, for Pascal, Jeffrey, Julia, Vicky, and Andy.

Jeffrey introduced me to Julia, the human resources director, to Vicky, Pascal's personal assistant, and I already knew Andy from the day before.

Pascal was not there at the time and would arrive around noon as he had some business to settle outside the office.

We sat at a small conference table and Jeffrey told me the part of the story that he knew. When Pascal was transferred to Hong Kong in early '94 to create Eastern Star Asia, he was given the mission of reorganizing and enhancing the development of the insurance market penetration strategy in Southeast Asia.

The territory under his responsibility included mainland China, Hong Kong, and countries such as Taiwan, Korea, Singapore, the Philippines, Malaysia, Indonesia, and Vietnam.

In this territory, there was already a certain presence of Eastern Star through small subsidiary companies and branches of the parent company that had distribution agreements with some international brokers, but there was no regional strategy. There were different lines of reporting to the UK and coordination between units was practically non-existent.

On the other hand, the Chinese government was expected to allow access to its domestic market to international insurance groups that demonstrated their efficiency, professionalism, and long-term commitment to obtaining the necessary licenses.

At that time there was a perception that the opening of the Chinese domestic market was the opportunity of the century for the western insurance industry.

With all this potential market to be explored and developed efficiently, Pascal had an enormous challenge ahead of him and needed a good budget, a multi-disciplinary team that covered a wide range of areas of competence, and clear lines of command over all the operational units that he They already existed in their territory.

The budget was being approved directly by the chairman, the regional team was being recruited, and the line of command over the operational units would be officially announced the following week as it would have to overcome several political barriers in the Eastern Star organization in the United Kingdom.

To close the explanation, Jeffrey mentioned to me that both Pascal and he thought that I had a lot to contribute to the design and development of the projects they had in mind, but that those responsible for the operational units should be personnel of local origin, among others. reasons due to the language and knowledge of the practices and customs of each territory.

When Jeffrey finished the explanation I thought it would be very interesting to participate in the development of many of the projects that lay ahead.

The future of the world economy was germinating in Asia, and my experience in statistics, computer science, project management, and process reengineering could be very useful to them.

Pascal arrived just at lunchtime, greeted us very kindly and we immediately left accompanied by Jeffrey to a restaurant in the Conrad Hotel, located in another tower on Pacific Place.

Upon arriving at the restaurant, Pascal commented that, due to an unforeseen event, he had to travel that afternoon for a meeting in Beijing, so we would only see each other during lunch.

AN INTERESTING BUT NEBULOUS FUTURE

During lunch, he explained to me that they were working under a lot of pressure since the following week the organization of Eastern Star in Asia would be officially announced and as usual, there was no shortage of political problems due to people who would be affected by changing reporting lines.

We ate very quickly since he had to leave for the airport, but before leaving he said to me.

"Next week we will send you a proposal with the job description and economic conditions, I think you might be interested.

Tomorrow Julia will accompany you on a tour of Hong Kong so that you can see the areas where the international schools are and the residential areas frequented by expatriates.

If you have any questions before flying back to Barcelona, Jeffrey or Julia can help you".

Pascal left as quickly as he arrived and I was left in limbo. I was waiting for a longer conversation, but that was his style, always get to the point and bluntly.

Jeffrey and I returned to the office and sat down to talk again, but this time it was Jeffrey who asked me about the situation in Barcelona.

Neither he nor I had had a good relationship with Juan and the last stage in Spain had not been very pleasant for either him or me.

The next day Julia and Andy took me on a tour of Mid-Levels, Aberdeen, Showson Hill, Repulse Bay, and Tai Tam where the Hong Kong International School was.

Julia was a super friendly person, with a lot of experience in human resources and she went out of her way to show me all the relevant aspects of what the social life of an expat and his family in Hong Kong was like.

At the end of the tour, we returned to the office, I said goodbye to Jeffrey, Julia, and Vicky and thanked them deeply for the effort they had made, as they had all personally contributed to making my visit pleasant and productive. Andy took me to the airport and I began my journey back to Barcelona.

REFLECTIONS ON THE PATH TOWARDS THE FUTURE

During the flight back to Barcelona, I gave free rein to my imagination about what I could do in Hong Kong, and imagined that with my experience I could contribute to a wide range of projects that could be a very enriching and interesting experience.

Asia was the growth engine of the world economy and had enormous potential, but I needed to be patient and flexible to see a bright future again instead of the hazy present that was beginning to clear.

Upon arriving in Barcelona, the family waited anxiously to find out the results of the trip, but were left in the air since I still did not have a concrete proposal, the trip had only shown good possibilities.

At the end of the week, I received a fax from Eastern Star Asia, offering me a general manager planning position to start in Hong Kong on November 1, 1994. The benefits package was similar to the one I had in Barcelona, but, Although I didn't realize it at first, the amount represented a 100% increase when considering taxes and benefit details.

After discussing with the family the implications of living in Hong Kong, I accepted the offer, and two weeks later I said goodbye to Eastern Star Seguros Generales in a small and emotional toast with my co-workers at the reception of the building in Barcelona.

This stage in the old continent had a happy, although unexpected, ending; Barcelona had been a very valuable experience for the whole family.

My wife had completed her postgraduate degree in gynecology and obstetrics, my daughters had learned Catalan, developed an excellent level of English, and Manyi was beginning her computer studies.

For my part, I had the opportunity to work with a management team super-identified with the organization that collaborated to the limit of its possibilities to protect the future of the company.

I learned the complexities of a work environment that, in an attempt to protect the worker, significantly hinders the survival and competitiveness of companies.

I saw firsthand that effort, dedication, and professionalism are not always rewarded; there are situations where senior management decisions respond more to personal interests than to the needs of the organization.

I became in-depth familiar with the operational and strategic mechanisms of insurance activity in a complex and competitive market.

I had the opportunity to successfully conduct a reengineering process once again thanks to the support of a tireless, responsible, and dedicated human team that closely identified with the company.

Now destiny was putting us on a path, even more enriching, with many more adventures and opportunities, although we didn't know it yet.

ADVENTURES IN THE SOUTH OF CHINA

222

STARTING A NEW STAGE IN HONG KONG

I had just turned 38 when landed in Hong Kong, in October 1994 as a result of a storm of reorganization in the multinational in which I worked, since the two companies of the group in Spain had just merged and there was an extra managing director. "I".

Hong Kong was at that time a British colony in the south of China with a population of about 6 million inhabitants and a territory of about a thousand square kilometers. Its economy represented about 20% of China's GDP and it had a very low level of taxes, it was considered one of the safest and most dynamic economies on the planet, so choosing Hong Kong was easy.

This was the first time in my career that a change wasn't a promotion or even a lateral move, it was a demotion, and I felt a little hurt and betrayed by corporate politics.

Fortunately, my practical sense prevailed over my heart and I accepted the position they offered me, since the financial package was good, my family would have the opportunity to get to know another culture and the key people were people I knew and trusted.

My arrival in Hong Kong as general manager of planning also coincided with a reorganization of the group's companies in Asia, but in this case, I was part of the winning team in the last battle, although at the moment I was not very aware of it.

At that time, Eastern Star Asia consisted of three companies in Hong Kong, one in Singapore, and two development projects, one in China and one in Taiwan.

Asia had been identified as the first priority to boost the group's growth worldwide, due to the gigantic potential of the area's markets and the accelerated economic growth experienced by the countries in the area.

Asia was seen as an opportunity that could not be missed.

The regional director of Asia was a Canadian of French origin, hardened in a thousand business policy battles. I met him when he interviewed me in Paris in the early 90s to authorize my transfer from the tobacco division to the financial services division.

Pascal was an imposing man of few words with an impressive bearing that left no doubt that he was the boss.

This curious attribute almost always worked in his favor, although from time to time it put him in delicate situations since on more than one occasion journalists confused him with the chairman during press conferences.

There was an excellent relationship between Pascal and the chairman based on a high degree of trust and loyalty, which fueled the jealousy and envy of other members of the Board of Directors in London.

Pascal was a visionary who had distanced himself from details many years ago. His strength was neither numbers nor computers, but he knew how to see through the tunnel and ask the right questions at the right time.

His management style was based on assuming that the people in his charge should know what to do, he would indicate the major objectives and strategic lines. In other words, if you were an insecure and questioning person you couldn't easily work with him.

FIRST DAYS AT THE PACIFIC PLACE OFFICE

My first day of work at the group's head office in Hong Kong coincided with a black day, I had arrived in the middle of an organizational storm.

That morning one of the CEOs was notified that he would have to accept early retirement and other members of the management team were given the opportunity to resign or be fired.

I was used to having very busy days and I was dying to do something, but without having been officially presented and having more or less clear what I could stick my nose into, common sense advised me to dedicate myself to reading all the promotional brochures of insurance policies that I could find at the reception.

A little before noon, Vicky, Pascal's secretary, approached the office that had been assigned to me and in English with a strong Chinese accent told me.

"Mr. Orlando, Pascal asks you to forgive him because his agenda is very complicated today and he can only meet you tomorrow at lunchtime.

Today we have arranged for you to have lunch with Mr. Jeffrey the Regional Director of Finance.

Shortly before one in the afternoon, I met Jeffrey in the 18th floor reception and we went down to the Pacific Place shopping center where we would have lunch at an Italian restaurant.

Jeffrey had been my boss in Spain, he was an old friend of English origin who had arrived three months before me in Hong Kong also as a result of the reorganization in Continental Europe.

I had known Jeffrey for many years and we had been through quite a few battles and adventures in the corporate world together.

It was during that lunch with Jeffrey that I found out that they were beheading a few people that day, among other things in an attempt to transfer the sales force to a competing company.

Upon returning from lunch, Jeffrey gave me a tour of the offices and introduced me to some of the department heads.

As the afternoon fell, the employees disappeared from their work tables while the city lit up in an impressive swarm of skyscrapers that I could see from the window of my office.

I was temporarily staying in a suite on the 32nd floor of the Island Shangrila Hotel, a building adjacent to Tower II of Pacific Place where we had part of the group's offices in Hong Kong.

Pacific Place is a shopping center with dozens of high-end stores, two office towers, and three luxury hotels, a truly spectacular site that symbolizes the success and economic power of Hong Kong.

As a newcomer, I still didn't know many things, such as that I was living in one of the most exclusive hotels in the territory and that Pacific Place was one of the most expensive places to have offices in one of the most expensive cities in the world.

However, I appreciated the comfort in which I lived, which partly compensated for being away from my family while my daughters finished the school year in Spain.

The next day I went to the office very early, so early that I had to wait half an hour for the receptionist to arrive since I still didn't have my access card.

Since I had already been introduced to some members of the staff, I felt a little more comfortable and wandered around the offices again trying to familiarize myself with that maze of cubicles and offices full of people with slanted eyes and the occasional Western face.

By mid-morning, thanks to Jeffrey, I received a copy of the latest monthly management reports and an old organizational chart which I reviewed several times trying to locate names that looked familiar to me with little success.

Although it may seem curious, until this moment the only thing I knew about my job in Hong Kong was the title of the position and the economic benefits package, which was not entirely strange in international personnel transfers, but in my case there were some special nuances.

Firstly, planning positions are usually like a mixed bag and their content varies significantly depending on the taste and color of the organization. Secondly, although I knew and trusted Pascal, it was the first time that we would have the same base of operations.

When I was in Spain, Jeffrey was my boss for a long period and Pascal was the director of Continental Europe based in Paris.

AN IMPORTANT AND VERY NEBULOUS POSITION

Around noon I decided to make a list of questions and discussion topics for my lunch with Pascal, I knew I had to be prepared, otherwise, he could spend the lunch talking and I would run the risk of losing my chance to get relevant guidance for my job.

Finally, it was time to see him, I had not finished entering his office when we almost ran out, followed by Jeffrey in the direction of one of the restaurants at the Conrad Hotel in Pacific Place.

During lunch, I tried to raise the topic of how I fit into the organization and what was the mission behind my position as general manager of planning, but just as I had imagined, Pascal took over the use of the word and he gave me his version of the disaster we were facing in Hong Kong, the difficulties he had with the interference of the other directors in London and how important the China project and the joint venture in Taiwan were.

Finally, almost as we were leaving, he said to me.

"By the way, welcome to the team, in Asia, we need people with your experience in systems and reengineering. You need to get familiar with the business, think about how to improve things, and take advantage of integrating the operations in Hong Kong, this afternoon I'm leaving for Shanghai. We will talk next week".

"For the moment, don't mess with China, Taiwan, or Singapore, I'll explain why later".

When I returned to my office I felt lost, here I was 10,000 kilometers from my family, surrounded by a lot of people I didn't know and with objectives more general than the Ten Commandments.

That night I suffered an attack of melancholy and my self-esteem plummeted. I spent some time regretting my situation, at times considering the idea of giving up.

But as usually happened to me, in the end, my sensible side prevailed, reminding me that I couldn't afford that luxury and that despite everything, Pascal and Jeffrey trusted me. I was costing the organization a fortune and they were giving me an opportunity that if I took advantage of it could be useful and interesting, I just had to put my vanity aside and believe in what I told people.

"There are no small positions, the position is the size of the person who occupies it".

"Power is only useful when you know what to do with it".

 "People are really important when they are useful".

At the moment it was clear that the only thing I could do was become thoroughly familiar with Hong Kong operations and find a way to make myself useful as quickly as possible, it was obvious that my job title was just a cover to give me some status. and that Pascal saw me as a consultant and not the general director of the company in Spain.

I had already done what Pascal asked me on other occasions and I knew that the key was to have access to the people, the management reports and the computer systems, which I should do diplomatically since, although I had a high-level position, I did not He had no line of command over any department, I was a one-man team.

KNOWING AN ORGANIZATION IN TRANSITION

After the black day, the three companies operating in Hong Kong officially reported to Pascal, but in a temporary organizational structure while we found a way to integrate them efficiently.

During the transition period, Pascal took over as CEO of Eastern Star Life Hong Kong and appointed Jeffrey to manage the operations, IT, finance, marketing, and actuarial services departments.

This meant that those responsible for the distribution channels also reported to Pascal temporarily.

Eastern Star Life Hong Kong at that time had a staff of about 110 employees, an exclusive agent channel of about 600 people, a channel of about 30 brokers, and distribution agreements with three financial institutions.

Each distribution channel was a different world, managed by people with considerable experience, who operated under general objectives and guidelines.

The Channel's exclusive agents represented more than 70% of the premium production capacity, through a network of producers, supervisors, and district managers who had been recruited and trained by the company. This channel could sell complex products, generally long-lasting and with a good profit margin.

Brokers represented about 20% of the production capacity, through independent professional firms that could distribute complex long-term products from various insurance companies.

The financial institutions channel represented close to 10% of the production capacity and was materialized through agreements with banks and credit cards that allowed us to contact specially selected segments of their clients to offer them via mail and telemarketing products that were generally perceived as attractive low-cost offers that combined some element of savings and protection framed in a life policy.

The network of exclusive agents and brokers was under the responsibility of a New Zealander called Glen, and the Financial Institutions channel was directed by Belinda of Chinese origin.

The other company in the life area was Eastern Star Life International, run by British named Mike, it had a sales and administration team of about 20 people to service a network of international brokers specializing in offshore products in Hong Kong, the Philippines. and other Asian countries.

Most of Eastern Star International's insurance policies were complex savings, protection, and investment products aimed at the expatriate segment and at medium-high level people who wanted to maintain policies expressed in easily convertible currencies such as the US dollar or the British pound.

The third company was Eastern Star Hong Kong General Insurance which sold motor, theft, fire, home, accident, hospitalization, liability, travel, and transportation policies.

This company had a staff of approximately 100 employees and also had multichannel distribution. The offices were located in the Hopewell Center, a cylindrical tower about five blocks from Pacific Place.

The general director of Eastern Star General Insurance was a very experienced Englishman named Peter who had been in the territory for about seven years and had been under Pascal for only six months.

Another key person at Eastern Star Asia was Julia, director of the organization and human resources. Julia was a mature, bright, and highly experienced woman who perfectly knew both the multinational environment and the local modus vivendi.

Julia was of Chinese origin and was married to an American who had run Bank of America's operations in Asia, but when they tried to return him to the United States he decided to resign and make his own way in Hong Kong advising a local group on financial issues.

The youngest of the regional team was a thirty-something English actuary named Nigel who was currently based in Taipei helping to launch a new life insurance company but came to Hong Kong quite frequently as he had responsibility for the actuarial issues of the life insurance company in Hong Kong.

Nigel was a brilliant guy with an enormous capacity for work, however, his excessively technical and sometimes inflexible vision was going to give us some headaches.

LOOKING FOR A WAY TO ADD VALUE

My days began to pass between interviews with the company's staff at Pacific Place, and long hours of analysis of the information collected, this would allow me to put together the organizational puzzle for the life companies, but on the general insurance side, Peter was not very open to exploring the topic of integration.

At the moment I didn't give much importance to this attitude since I had enough to keep me busy in Pacific Place and of course, I didn't want to create an incident while I could avoid it.

One of the first things I discovered was the exaggerated staff turnover, it was not unusual in Hong Kong to find annual rates of over 30%.

At that time, the territory of Hong Kong had an unemployment rate of around 2% and people had no major problems changing jobs, moving from one company to another almost as easily as changing suits. This situation made maintaining well-trained work teams identified with the company a real challenge, which differed substantially from what I was used to seeing in Europe.

Another interesting aspect was the communication problems between locals and foreigners. As expected, the natives of Hong Kong preferred to use Cantonese, which is their mother tongue, and although English was the official language, only 20% spoke it well, the remaining 80% were in a range that ranged from speaking what was necessary to communicate until almost total ignorance of the language.

Although it may seem curious, most of my Western colleagues had not given much importance to this aspect and remained in their English-speaking circles without realizing the mistake we were making by maintaining our communication strategy based on English.

In my case, in addition to the limitations imposed on me by not speaking Cantonese, my English had a marked Hispanic accent that forced me to make an even greater effort to make myself understood.

A FIRST DIAGNOSIS OF THE ORGANIZATION

By mid-December 1994 I already had a pretty good idea of what was happening in life companies, which, by the way, in my opinion, was not as bad as was thought.

There were some problems with efficiency, quality of service, management control, and high operating costs, but the vast majority of the staff were capable people who knew how to do their jobs.

The origin of the problems had a lot to do with communication failures between locals and Westerners, which when combined with the delusions of grandeur of the old management team had created a structure that was too expensive for the size of the operations.

For example, the rent we paid at Pacific Place was a suffocating burden on the bottom line, as was the duplication of support departments between the three companies.

The ideas he had in mind to improve management required some surgery and more changes in the organization, but it was premature to call the shots on the part of a newcomer, apart from the fact that politically Pascal would not be willing to make many changes in that situation. moment.

I should be patient and focus my energy on something useful that I could do and implement in the short term. I was thinking about the topic and it occurred to me that I could do a survey in the exclusive agent channel to identify needs, problems, and opportunities.

With Glen's help, I designed and distributed a survey that more than half of the exclusive agents completed, and I conducted the tabulation myself over the weekend.

The survey collected information on the usefulness of advertising material, management control information, quality of service, and some aspects of the agent's profile such as monthly productivity, customer base, hierarchical level, length of service, age, and sex.

When analyzing the information collected, I found several areas susceptible to improvement, especially in relation to management control due to the absence of a good management information system to monitor the sales force in terms of production levels, persistence, composition of the portfolio, and size of the customer base.

On the other hand, I observed a great dispersion in the productivity levels and the size of the client base reported by the agents, this aroused my curiosity and increased my motivation to generate real statistics by extracting information from the IBM AS/400.

IN BARCELONA WITH THE FAMILY AT CHRISTMAS

In mid-December, I took a 10-day trip to Barcelona to see family, celebrate the end-of-year holidays, and make progress on preparations for moving to Hong Kong.

Everyone was in good health, although a little nervous because, although Hong Kong had many advantages, it also generated inconveniences.

Isabel and Manyi had visa and language problems, which made it necessary for them to stay in Barcelona. My wife would have a difficult time practicing medicine since there was no way for her medical and gynecologist degrees to be homologated at a reasonable time lapse, my daughters Alejandra and Tatiana already had a few friends in Barcelona and the idea of leaving them caused them a certain nostalgia.

One day I visited my old Eastern Star colleagues in Barcelona and it was nice to see them again, but the organizational environment had transformed, there was no longer the sense of team that existed before.

I didn't want to ask what was happening, but I imagined there would be a lot of changes, and not everyone was happy.

MANAGERIAL INFORMATION OF THE SALES FORCE

Upon returning from Barcelona, I continued with the development of a small management information system for the sales force, extracting information from the IBM AS/400 and using some of the programs that had been developed in Spain.

At the end of January 1995, the system was already in operation and had a spectacular impact, much better than I had imagined.

The secret of the unexpected success was that in just six weeks all sales district managers had access to a system that they had been asking for years, and for one reason or another had never been developed.

Since the straw poll I had used was related to the development of the system, this opened the door for further studies.

I knew that there was nothing spectacular about this, but for the locals, it was the first time that a GUAILO (foreigner of Western origin) offered them something in computing and it was fulfilled in record time.

Although Pascal was not a man of details and did not show much interest in computers, such was the fuss over the system that he asked me to show it to him, and he was impressed.

THE REGIONAL TEAM BECOMES COMPLICATED

In February 1995, a new individual from the headquarters landed in Hong Kong to advise Pascal in the area of life insurance sales, and as in my case, it was not very clear how he fit into the organization.

Richard was a Scotsman in his forties, almost two meters tall, with a very jovial character. Apparently, he was very well connected with the chairman, which gave rise to a wide wave of rumors and speculation about what his role was going to be in Asia.

Although I think we were all full of good intentions, the lack of clarity in the organization that was being formed was beginning to create confusion and the beginning of a power struggle was in sight.

Jeffrey controlled part of the functions of Eastern Star Vida Hong Kong while Peter remained distant from the rest of the team and avoided broaching the topic of integration.

Nigel had completed his part of the project in Taiwan and shared control of the actuarial and investment area with Jeffrey, Richard had been appointed Glen's direct boss, but he felt limited by not having a line of command over the support units and was resistant to see Jeffrey as number 2.

I kept a low profile, deepening my knowledge of companies and the market while extending the functionality of the management information system, but without career expectations, since Pascal had made it very clear to me from the beginning. "The CEO of Hong Kong will be a local".

IDEAS TO INTEGRATE COMPANIES IN HONG KONG

When I had enough information on the structure, cost, and distribution of functions of the three companies, I prepared an integrated organizational chart showing a model of what the organization could look like and some numbers on opportunities for cost reduction and increased productivity.

My intention was to prepare the scene for when the time came to officially talk about how the three organizations could be integrated and what benefits we could obtain.

The opportunities translated, into the reduction of duplication in areas such as IT, finance, marketing, legal, office services, and personnel administration.

Additionally, there were potential benefits in the development of synergies and economies of scale in some distribution channels.

One Friday afternoon while I was updating one of the diagrams showing the integration process, Jeffrey happened to pass by my office and was interested in what I was doing.

When I explained the diagram to him, he grabbed the paper and said. "Let me show this to Pascal" and left my office.

Later, Jeffrey returned the diagram to me he said "This is interesting, but be careful because there is very sensitive information in this document".

Jeffrey was right, and that's why I hadn't shown these analyses to anyone in the office, not even to Pascal.

THE CHAIRMAN COMES TO HONG KONG

At the beginning of March, something happened out of the blue, the chairman had announced a visit to Asia and was going to be in Hong Kong for three days, which usually meant presentations and discussions about the current situation, the business plan for the region, and of each company in particular.

As soon as I found out about the visit, I volunteered to help Pascal prepare the presentation, but to my surprise, Pascal disarmed me by telling me that this time it was not necessary, the chairman wanted only informal meetings.

This surprised me since, in my experience, presentations were always made for important visits and if they were well prepared, misunderstandings were avoided and a good image was projected.

Despite the instructions, at my own risk and expense, I decided to prepare a presentation on the situation in Hong Kong, and in case Pascal changed his mind I prepared some slides.

As the day of the chairman's arrival approached, I received a copy of the program in which several group meetings and individual interviews with regional team members were planned.

I had been included in the meeting about Eastern Star Life Hong Kong and had a 30-minute one-on-one interview with the chairman as did Jeffrey, Richard, and Peter.

On the day of the meeting to discuss the life insurance business, I gave a copy of the presentation to Pascal, telling him that it contained key figures and aspects of the business in case he needed them.

Pascal answered me with an expressionless look and didn't say a word, so I thought I had made a mistake.

The meeting began with the typical informal ice-breakers making jokes about how impressive it was to land at Kay Tak Airport but quickly pivoted to get down to business.

Pascal began to talk about the market situation and generalize about the functioning of the company. After a few minutes, the chairman interrupted him saying, "That is all very good Pascal, but I imagine that you have prepared a structured presentation. Let's begin".

At that moment, a feeling of cold ran through my entire body as I shrank in my chair, then, Pascal looked up and calmly looked at me while saying:

"Of course George, Orlando has it prepared".

I whipped out the overhead projector and began to recite the presentation saying: "This is a team effort and I'm sure my colleagues will help me with their comments".

During the presentation, Pascal, Jeffrey, and Richard chimed in with comments that gave the impression that we had carefully prepared everything including a demonstration of the management information system which was thankfully available from a terminal in the conference room.

INFORMAL CONVERSATION WITH THE CHAIRMAN

The next day I had my private interview with the chairman which turned into a fairly informal conversation in which he let me know that I was doing a good job and that it was better for me to be in Asia than to have stayed in Spain, suggesting that things were not going very well on that part of the world.

This conversation gave me a certain stimulus since I realized that I could have a future in the corporation, and they counted on me.

At the end of the chairman's visit, Jeffrey and Julia told me that Pascal had asked the chairman to intervene to arrange the termination of my contract with BIT Co. Venezuela so that Eastern Star UK could assume the settlement amount of my old contract, and prepare a new one.

This was excellent news since I did not have a pension in the English system and this payment of benefits in Venezuela would be part of my retirement fund, which until then had been a pending issue.

THE INTEGRATION OF HONG KONG IS ACTIVATED

The following week Pascal called a meeting and told us that the chairman had been very pleased with the visit and that he would return again in June since he was very interested in following our progress in Asia.

During the meeting, Pascal also mentioned the need to accelerate the integration of operations in Hong Kong and suggested that we meet without him to propose a work plan and a new structure.

Peter immediately indicated that the integration was not going to be easy but that he was nevertheless willing to cooperate in whatever was necessary.

Richard spoke up and suggested that someone should be put in charge of coordinating the work, to which Pascal replied.

You're right, and then he looked around the table until he made eye contact with me as he said: "Orlando, you've been working on this for a long time, get together with the others, and prepare a proposal that we can discuss with the whole team in around fifteen days".

At the end of the meeting, Jeffrey approached me and said in a funny tone, "Well boss, let's see how you get out of this".

I responded by telling him:

"Come on man, this is a team effort and we all have to contribute, by the way, it's your fault for having shown him the draft of the organization chart".

Jeffrey smiled and with his usual walk disappeared towards his office.

Peter also approached me trying to hide his discomfort and told me: "Call me so we can schedule a meeting".

With that said, he took his briefcase and left with a hurried step.

Julia waited until we were alone in the conference room and said to me:

"I can help you with everything related to human resources, I don't know if you know that before working with Pascal I was the human resources manager at the life insurance company, and as far as I know, the salary scales between life and general insurance are very different, I also know some people at the Hopewell Center and that can help".

Until now my relationship with Julia had been infrequent, although I felt good chemistry with her, which would be very useful since she had a lot to contribute to the project.

When I returned to my office I found a note from Richard suggesting that we meet that afternoon to talk about the matter.

When speaking to Richard, he told me that he thought the integration of life and general insurance was a good idea and that we should move quickly, appoint a single person responsible, and let him work without interference from the regional office.

Now that everyone was open to the topic of integration, it was time to put my analysis on the table, but first I should explore the vision of my colleagues at the regional office and based on that evaluate the viability of what could be done.

The Integration would affect the interests and stability of many people and possibly each would have a different view on what was convenient and what was not.

JULIA HELPS WITH THE HONG KONG INTEGRATION

After speaking with Richard, I met with Julia and she had very clear ideas, she practically had a similar analysis to mine, but in her head.

She suggested that we go together to visit Peter at the Hopewell Center to get his opinion and then take the opportunity to test the waters with some people she knew from the general insurance company.

The interview with Peter was relatively short, he had a general idea but did not want to go into details, he preferred to wait for a specific proposal, he commented that there were very easy areas such as office services and other more complex ones such as IT since the systems were different.

In Peter's case, one of the added complexities was that integrating the three companies would possibly reduce his level of autonomy if he was not named CEO of Hong Kong.

After speaking with Peter, Julia, and I had interviews with some of the middle management at the Hopewell Center, we obtained updated copies of the payroll and organizational charts for each area, and with this information, we could evaluate the potential impact of the integration on the different areas due to possible problems arising from differences in salary scales and other compensation mechanisms.

INTEGRATION AND OFFICE RELOCATION

The next meeting was with Jeffrey, and he also had quite clear ideas about what could be done. Additionally, he had been working for months on a project to move the offices that would allow the staff of the three companies and the regional management to be located in a single building, this would have a significant effect on the ease of sharing resources and reducing rental expenditure.

The next step was to meet with Mike to get his point of view on Eastern Star Vida International, and this was also quite easy, as the company had a very small structure, Mike was a very reasonable person and his area already had a certain level of integration with the other life company, since several departments provided services, such as risk underwriting, computer support, office services, reception, and personnel administration. Once I had gathered the opinion of all the parties involved, I made a summary and introduced it into the integration model that I had already prepared.

The expected benefits were summarized in increases in productivity, reduction in expenses, and increases in competitiveness through improvements in the quality of service and the range of products available for each channel.

The integration could be announced and presented with an organizational chart, but in reality, it was a process of organizational transformation that would take time and involve various levels of difficulty and resistance depending on the area.

In cases where there were surplus personnel, the feasibility of transferring them to the regional office or temporarily maintaining the excess resources could be considered since natural rotation would relieve the structure without causing organizational stress.

As I progressed in the design of a new organization and its implications, I discussed it with Julia, which was very useful, since she knew the people and knew how they could react.

However, there were factors that forced us to review the time scale, for example, we should link the organizational integration with the move to Cityplaza III, also we needed to identify all the people for the senior management positions in the new structure before the announcement.

RESISTANCE TO THE OFFICE MOVE

Talking to Jeffrey I learned that there was strong resistance from the general insurance company's commercial team to moving from the Hopewell Center to Cityplaza III in Taikoo Shing.

Cityplaza III was an office complex located about 20 minutes by subway from Pacific Place, when I went to visit it seemed perfect, it was a modern shopping center, with access to the subway, with a good view, near a tunnel to Kowloon, it had a wide variety of restaurants at various price levels, and the cost per square foot was half of what we paid at Pacific Place.

I really did not understand the argument of the commercial team of Eastern Star General Insurance, they indicated that several of their main agents had their offices near Pacific Place and for them, it was a major inconvenience to have to take the subway.

If the problem had been posed to me, I would have offered them a screen and a printer to print their policies since they could handle everything else over the phone.

Finally, Pascal forced the situation, the three companies and the regional office moved to Cityplaza III in June 1995. At that time, I lived in an apartment that the company had rented in an area to the south of the Hong Kong island called Repulse Bay, my daily commute to the office became a little longer, but it was nothing out of this world, except for the first day when, due to lack of experience on the road, I entered the tunnel from central to Kowloon and I was lost for an hour.

In the Cityplaza III building, we had three complete floors for the three operating companies and the regional office, everything was new, and modern with a professional and very functional design. Jeffrey had done a good job with the relocation project as rental expenses were reduced and office functionality was improved without losing corporate image.

Besides, there were other insurance companies of international caliber in the same building and the fears of the general insurance commercial team quickly disappeared.

TRIP TO BARCELONA TO TRANSFER THE FAMILY

At the end of June 1995, I traveled to Barcelona to move my family to Hong Kong since my daughters had finished the school year, and I had to end my employment relationship with Eastern Star Spain.

It was also an emotional moment since Isabel, Manyi and a little Pekingese dog named Cugui would be staying in Spain. Manyi was about to turn 18 and was studying computer science in Barcelona, Isabel had found her way to work and had a rented apartment in Esplugas, Cugui, who had joined the family in a park in San Cugat, had become the spoiled pet dog of Isabel and stayed in Barcelona. Destiny pushed us down different paths after 14 years of coexistence full of memories and family experiences.

On the transfer trip with my wife and daughters to Hong Kong, all the luggage arrived without problems except for the family cat named "Tito" who was detained at the airport and sent to a shelter to spend two weeks in quarantine before being accepted in Hong Kong.

When I arrived with my family at the Repulse Bay apartment, they had a positive and negative reaction, the apartment was comfortable, spacious, and had a beautiful view of the beach, but the family was used to living with Isabel, Manyi, Cugui, and Tito in an unforgettable house in Mallola on the outskirts of Barcelona.

To make things more complicated with the family's arrival, a hurricane was near Hong Kong and we were locked up for three days, it was not a catastrophe, but emotionally it did not help as a welcome in the middle of a transfer to another continent.

FAMILY ADAPTATION TO HONG KONG

When the hurricane passed, my family began its process of adapting to a culture and environment substantially different from the one we had experienced in Barcelona.

My daughters began the new school year at the primarily English-speaking Hong Kong International School, and my wife quickly made friends with a list of Latino contacts in the expat community and diplomatic corps.

To help the family adapt to Hong Kong, I bought my wife a second-hand Jaguar, but she had to get used to driving with the steering wheel on the right side.

Unfortunately, the Jaguar thing didn't work out, since the first time she went for a ride around the area, she got too close to the sidewalk and damaged the front axle.

Driving in Hong Kong is not easy, in some areas the streets are very narrow and if you don't know the roads it is very easy to get lost.

The Jaguar was repaired, but a few months later we decided to sell it since the company assigned me a driver and he dedicated most of his time to the family, so there was no need to have two cars.

My benefits package included a share at the Aberdeen Marina Club, so my wife and daughters went frequently there as it was a meeting point for expat families and students from the International School.

To help with the housework, we hired a girl of Filipino origin who made life easier for everyone at home, since cooking was not the strong point of any of the family members.

HONG KONG HAS INTERNATIONAL CUISINE

In Hong Kong, there is a wide variety of restaurants and supermarkets abound with imported products from all over the world.

My family preferred to eat at home in the Western style, but everyone liked the Hong Kong food that was common in many social activities.

Over time, we discovered that Chinese food is very varied, depending on the area of the country and in general it does not look much like what we are used to seeing as Chinese food in Western countries, which is generally associated with fried rice, pork sweet and sour and spring rolls.

Typical Hong Kong food is Cantonese-style, among which Dim-Sum stands out, represented by a set of small portions prepared steamed or fried.

Fried rice is a filling dish and has a low ranking in local preference. In Chinese culture, an important aspect is to order enough variety of dishes and share them with the other people at the table. Dim-Sum is mainly eaten for breakfast and lunch.

Those who enjoy eating in a variety of ways will have no problems in Hong Kong as they can choose from a long list of Indian, Vietnamese, Japanese, Korean, Spanish, Italian, Portuguese, French, Lebanese, American and even a Venezuelan restaurant.

A SYSTEMS PROBLEM IN TAIWAN

On the first day back at the office, after my family arrival, I found a somewhat tense atmosphere and when I asked Jeffrey what was happening, he told me that there was a serious problem with the Eastern Star Life Taiwan Jointventure, apparently, the local partners were very upset because the insurance software installed by Eastern Star did not meet the requirements of the local market and without that, they could not obtain permission to start operations.

I had not participated in that project, but if they asked for my collaboration I would gladly try to help find a solution.

Before noon, Pascal called me into his office and told me what was happening in Taiwan to see if I could give him some ideas for a solution.

From what I understood, Eastern Star UK had a team of systems experts who had installed a software package at Eastern Star Life Taiwan, but when the CEO came on board to run the company, he evaluated the system and concluded that it did not adapt to local requirements and therefore could not obtain approval to begin operations.

When Pascal asked my opinion, I told him.

"Every system can be modified, the problem is the time and cost involved in the changes. If it were my decision, I would evaluate the cost and time and compare it with other possible solutions".

"If you want, I can go to Taiwan to learn more about what is happening and help find a solution".

Pascal thought for a few seconds and told me:

"Let's do that, but go with Julia so she can help you understand the situation, in Taiwan, there are many people who do not communicate well in English".

Going with Julia was a good idea, she had lived in Taiwan, knew people in the company, and was surely going to help me understand what was happening.

In my heart, I thought that the system they had installed couldn't be that bad and that there was probably a serious communication problem.

The travel preparations were made, and I flew with Julia to Taipei, the capital of Taiwan, the trip was just under two hours, but half a useful day was lost due to waiting and transfers from the airport to the city.

TAIWAN AN ATYPICAL COUNTRY IN SOUTH OF CHINA

Taiwan is practically an island located about 150 kilometers south of China, it has an area of almost 36 thousand square kilometers and in 1995 a population of 21 million inhabitants.

Taiwan's political origin dates back to the end of the Chinese Civil War in 1949 when leaders of the losing side and some two million people moved to the island and established an independent government that attempted to gain international recognition in a diplomatic battle that They had been progressively losing.

Taiwan had developed a wide range of trade relations with China in a win-win strategy. In other words, if politics weren't discussed, Taiwanese businessmen and Chinese businessmen got along very well.

POLITICAL PROBLEMS IN A JOINT VENTURE

The Joint Venture between Eastern Star and a group of Taiwanese investors to create Eastern Star Life Taiwan was a 50/50 project with an investment of close to 100 million dollars, which explained the importance that Pascal assigned to the problem we had to solve.

When Julia and I arrived at the company's offices in Taipei, we were very kindly greeted by Mr. Yu Shi, an American of Chinese origin who had recently been recruited by Pascal to fill the position of CEO of the new company.

Yu Shi explained to us the same thing that Pascal had said, the system did not adapt to the requirements of the market in Taiwan, and he found it difficult to modify it since the differences were substantial.

Then I asked him how he thought the problem could be solved and Yu Shi answered that in his opinion the most practical thing was to use a local insurance package that many companies used and had certification from the insurance superintendence.

Considering Yu Shi's opinion, I asked him if they had evaluated the difference in cost and time between modifying the installed system with respect to what he proposed and the answer was negative.

At this point in the conversation, it was clear a certain predisposition against the system provided by Eastern Star, the problem went beyond functionality.

Considering the situation, we asked Yu Shi to assign someone to show us some examples of the functionality problems and to provide us with information about the cost and installed base of the software package he proposed, since with this information it was easier to help Pascal make a decision.

Yu Shi made the necessary arrangements, and in the afternoon we began to see cases of functionality problems in front of a computer screen.

On the other hand, I had asked to have a meeting with the person responsible for the installation of the system on the Eastern Star UK side.

Max, was a mature person, with a lot of experience in IT and insurance systems, but without experience in the Asian market. In fact, this was the first project he developed in Taiwan and he did not speak or write Mandarin, which is the official language.

When I asked Max for his opinion on what was happening, he told me that the users were very difficult and that some people responsible for providing the specifications joined the project late. The system could be modified, but in his opinion, they wanted to make too many changes that were not really necessary.

On the other hand, to make the modifications he would have to bring back part of his team of systems analysts and programmers who had already returned to Europe.

The system they had installed was very powerful and worked perfectly in several European countries, but there was no known version operating in Taiwan.

At the end of the day, Julia and I went to dinner and took the opportunity to exchange impressions about what we had seen.

AN EXPENSIVE PROBLEM & EVERYONE IS INNOCENT

There was a serious communication problem that had transformed into an environment of lack of trust and a certain level of hostility between the local team and Eastern Star UK's imported consultants.

At that time, it was not easy to find people in Taipei with a good level of English and the computer systems that were used had almost everything in Chinese characters.

It was not easy for a Taiwanese to adapt to a system full of titles and fields in English, especially if the system was more complex than usual.

Taiwanese culture and idiosyncrasy also generated differences that affected the design of systems and business practices, for example, at that time issuing post-dated checks was common and the systems were prepared to handle that situation.

Regarding the networks of life insurance agents, the level of professional training was very basic and almost anyone could register as an insurance agent for a company and have a small portfolio of clients.

This meant that the best-selling insurance products in Taiwan were simple policies that anyone could explain without much difficulty.

On the other hand, Eastern Star had a high level of technology and a lot of experience in product development, covering everything from simple policies to the most sophisticated ones, but this involved more complex computer systems with a long learning curve.

For Yu Shi, Eastern Star Life Taiwan should start with a traditional approach that everyone knows and progressively evolve into a sophisticated product portfolio, and this was not an easy path using the Eastern Star's system.

If Pascal forced Yu Shi to accept the Eastern Star system, Max, and his team could modify it, but the time scale, cost, and fights that would be required to agree was a very difficult scenario to anticipate and would significantly delay the start of the company's operations.

If Pascal supported Yu Shi and allowed him to replace Eastern Star's system with a local package, Yu Shi would be obligated to get things up and running as soon as possible, but Pascal would have to bear Eastern Star's system development cost to save the viability of the joint venture.

In short, the system could be modified, but considering the communication difficulties and the business model that Yu Shi had in mind, it was possibly faster, safer, and cheaper to start with the local system that many companies used in Taiwan and keep the system provided by Easter Star in reserve for the medium term.

When we returned to Hong Kong both Julia and I gave the summary of our impressions to Pascal, and the ball was in his court.

The decision was not easy since it had important implications in the short, medium, and long term.

I am not sure how Pascal handled the different sides of the problem, but the crisis was overcome and Eastern Star Life Taiwan began operations with some delay, in a market full of challenges, opportunities, and new difficulties on the horizon.

AN UNEXPECTED PROPOSAL IN HONG KONG

Two weeks after the trip to Taiwan, Julia came to my office to talk to me about the integration project in Hong Kong.

She told me that Pascal had analyzed the organizational charts that we had prepared, and he was happy with the possible managers for each functional area, and the candidates to be absorbed by the regional office.

All the proposed people have enough experience, a good track record, and good potential, the only thing missing was someone to lead the team while Kenny or Ricky accumulate experience and one of them shows the necessary ability to take charge of Eastern Star Hong Kong.

I told Julia that was very good news, they just needed to find the right person for the transition period.

Then Julia told me something totally unexpected.

"Pascal wants to know if you are willing to do that job".

The offer took me by surprise, and for a few moments, I felt confused since Pascal had told me several times that this position was for a local, not an expatriate.

But I landed quickly, they only asked me to do transition work, it was not a definitive appointment, Pascal was consistent with his localization policy, in addition to the fact that the integration of life and general insurance required certain experiences that I had, and additionally I was not very easy to recruit someone of sufficient caliber for a position with an expiration date.

After reflecting for a few moments, I told Julia that the idea excited me since it could complete the integration process of Hong Kong. Julia responded with a positive gesture and told me, the next step is a meeting with Pascal to refine the details of the announcement.

APPOINTMENT AS MANAGING DIRECTOR & COO

The next day Pascal called me to a meeting in his office where he reflected on the objectives he was pursuing with my appointment as director & COO of Hong Kong and gave me several guidelines on the business strategy and some advice on how to handle the political reactions of the reorganization.

- Prepare Kenny and Ricky
- Focus on profitable growth
- Efficiency and economies of scale
- Protect corporate image

After the meeting with Pascal, Julia prepared a draft announcement of the integration of Eastern Star Hong Kong into a single structure, highlighting the objectives being pursued, and the appointments of key people.

CONTROVERSIAL AND UNEXPECTED APPOINTMENT

Information about the restructuring quickly leaked and Pascal brought forward the Eastern Star Asia Executive Committee meeting to communicate the changes and clear up any doubts the committee members had.

During the meeting, Pascal explained the objectives of the organizational restructuring and asked the committee members to support the change process and to focus more of their energy on the development of Eastern Star Asia in other territories, indicating that although Hong Kong was important, it is just a grain of sand in a sea of opportunities that we should take advantage of.

MANY EMOTIONS IN A SINGLE DAY

After the reorganization announcement, the meeting continued with the usual agenda items, but I received an emergency call and had to leave immediately, there had been an accident in my apartment and my wife had called to ask me to come as soon as possible.

Fortunately, there was not much traffic and in less than 20 minutes I made the trip from Taikoo Shing to Repulse Bay while a thousand catastrophic ideas ran through my head about what could have happened.

When I arrived at the apartment everything was wet, a high-pressure water pipe that ran through the inside of a closet had broken and in a few minutes, the entire apartment flooded.

When my wife managed to ask for help at the building management office, they sent a group of maintenance and cleaning employees to plug the leak and help collect the water, but in the midst of the commotion, the cat was scared by seeing so many unknown people and jumped out of the window from the 11th floor and unfortunately didn't survive.

I had experienced three very stressful events in a single day, the flat flooding, the death of the family's cat, and the announcement of the new organization.

After helping resolve the emergency in my apartment, I returned to the office and explained the incident to my colleagues. They all reacted with a supportive attitude, although there were some distasteful comments.

The next day, the reorganization announcement was posted on the billboard and emailed to all staff, generating the expected wave of comments and a few phone calls.

ORGANIZATIONAL INTEGRATION BEGINS

Over the next week, I began meeting individually with my direct reports to talk to them about the integration process, give them the opportunity to ask questions privately, and make some adjustments to short-term goals.

The interaction with the Eastern Star Hong Kong management team began easily, as I knew everyone, the new organization gave them stability, and in some cases, it was a promotion.

To facilitate coordination and begin to cultivate team spirit, I established the Eastern Star Hong Kong Executive Committee "ESHK-EC", which met for just over an hour every Monday morning.

The members of the ESHK-EC were the following.

- 1. Orlando   Managing Director & COO
- 2. Kenny   Business Dev. Agency Division
- 3. Ricky   Business Dev. General Business
- 4. Bill   Technical Services G.I.
- 5. Kevin   Marketing Projects
- 6. Susana   Information Technology
- 7. Benny   Actuarial Services Life Insurance
- 8. Kennedy   Life Business Services
- 9. Vitus   Finance & Administration

Kenny was the main candidate to become the CEO of Hong Kong in the medium term, he was an intelligent, well-prepared, and very entrepreneurial young guy who had created, from nothing, one of the best sales districts in the exclusive agent's division.

Julia and Pascal had convinced him to leave his career as a district manager to become the director of the Exclusive Agents Division, this meant changing an activity where he was almost an independent businessman to become a high-level employee.

The change had risks, advantages, and disadvantages. If all went well, in a few years Kenny would become CEO of Eastern Star Hong Kong and this would open the way for other positions in Asia, but if things did not work out he would have lost his sales team and would be exposed to the political forces of a multinational.

Ricky was also a young, dynamic, very creative guy who had made a career at Eastern Star General Insurance and also had high potential to become the CEO of Hong Kong, he was the second candidate, but I imagine he did not have a positive view of the handover of Hong Kong to China scheduled for 1997. He resigned a few months after the reorganization and emigrated to Canada. This created the opportunity to promote Jimmy, one of his team members with more experience.

CHRISTMAS IS COMING WE'RE FLYING TO BARCELONA

On the family side, things were going well, my daughters had adapted to the Hong Kong International School, and my wife was entertained with her friends in the Latin community since it was not possible for her to practice medicine in the territory.

When December approached we invited Isabel and Manyi to spend Christmas in Hong Kong, but this was not possible since Manyi had lost his passport and there was no time to get a new one, so we decided that since they could not come, we would go to spend Christmas with them in Barcelona.

We spent two weeks in an apartment hotel near Av. Diagonal and we had a great time sharing with Isabel, Manyi, and many of the friends we had met in the previous stage.

During this period, I realized that Barcelona was the ideal place for my daughters to go to university since there were good universities, we had many friends and the cost of education was within my reach.

Upon returning to Hong Kong, everyone returned to their usual activities and I focused on accelerating the integration process and consolidating the management team.

THE LIFE MANAGEMENT TEAM IS STRENGTHENED

Kenny had already established himself as leader of the Exclusive Agent Division and had the brokerage channel under control, but he needed someone to offload some of his activities, so Julia recommended Bobby, a former Eastern Star employee who dominated the world of the sale of life insurance both on the side of the company and the commercial network.

Kenny liked the idea and we hired Bobby as his second in command, also assuming responsibility for all processes related to the organization of promotional events, contests, compensation, recruiting, training, and licensing registration.

THE FACES OF MANAGEMENT TEAM IN ADVERTISING

The synergy and cooperation between life and general insurance was beginning to accelerate and we decided to use an advertising campaign to project the image of Kenny and the other members of the management team as the visible face of the company.

For a few months, all local members of the Eastern Star Hong Kong Executive Committee appeared on a poster in Hong Kong subway stations and public buses.

We were the first multinational company to use this strategy and we took advantage of it to facilitate the recruitment of new agents, especially in the life insurance area, since Kenny occupied a prominent position in the posters.

I decided not to appear in that campaign, since it was assumed that sooner or later I was going to disappear from the scene and thus give prominence to the local team.

PROCESSES INTEGRATED & SYSTEMS ARE IMPROVED

The management information system was expanded with functionality that allowed monitoring the pipeline of policies to be issued and the first steps were taken to view customer information in an integrated manner.

The computing center, local area network, and communications infrastructure were integrated as planned and some operational savings were achieved.

The financial institution's channel was integrated at the management level and the telemarketing system could handle campaigns from the two companies, but market competitiveness continued to increase and banks continued to penetrate the insurance sector, which made growth increasingly difficult. on this channel.

The sale of general insurance was facilitated in the network of exclusive agents and a cycle of promotional activities was developed in shopping centers to promote the sale of life insurance and train new agents.

OTHER CORPORATE POLITICAL BATTLE IS COMING

By mid-1996, Eastern Star Hong Kong had completed the integration process and had experienced a small increase in business volume over the previous year, while reducing operating costs, through the move to Cityplaza III and the elimination of some duplications in the organizational structure.

In the United Kingdom, important changes had occurred; a new chairman had been appointed who had a different vision of the group's business strategy, which was generating a tsunami that would soon reach Hong Kong.

TRIP TO AUSTRALIA WITH THE SALES TEAM

The annual sales force convention was organized with a trip to Australia that involved the mobilization of almost 300 people on an itinerary that included Sydney, Brisbane, and the Gold Coast.

The organization of the event was impeccable, Kenny and Bobby did an excellent job in conveying an image of professionalism and efficiency to the entire sales team, which on this occasion also included some agents from the general insurance company.

I remember that during the trip across Australia, Bobby organized several informal meetings for me with small groups of agents from the different sales districts, which gave me the opportunity to get to know them more closely and explore their perception of what we were doing and what we could improve.

URGENT STAFF REDUCTION

When we returned from the sales convention, Nigel presented a report to the Eastern Star Asia executive committee, according to which the profitability of the Hong Kong life insurance portfolio was significantly lower than previously reported and recommended an urgent reduction in management expenses to preserve the viability of the business.

This information took us by surprise, and Pascal asked me to take action as soon as possible, which required me to identify a group of 10 positions to be eliminated or frozen in the coming months.

Hong Kong has very flexible labor legislation and the level of unemployment is very low, however, downsizing is not a pleasant process or easy to explain, especially after doing a sales convention with 300 people.

I tried to do everything possible to make it easier for the selected people to leave by allowing them to resign and giving them a paid period, but a negative scar was created in the organizational environment.

MY SISTER BÁRBARA VISITS US IN HONG KONG

At that time, my sister Bárbara was touring several countries to attend some conferences in Europe and since we hadn't seen each other for a while, I invited her to visit us in Hong Kong before returning to Venezuela. She was enthusiastic about the idea and using the miles accumulated in the frequent flyer program the ticket was free.

Bárbara spent two weeks with the family in Hong Kong and we had the opportunity to share many unforgettable moments that helped me digest the stress I had been accumulating due to what was looming on the horizon.

A LESSON OF CREDIBILITY

After carrying out the downsizing, I reported the results to the Executive Committee of Eastern Star Asia, and then something unexpected happened, Nigel commented in the same meeting, that he had reviewed the assumptions of the calculations of the intrinsic value of the portfolio and the situation It was not as negative as it had been reported a few months ago, this implied that the reduction we had made was not really necessary.

This change baffled all of us on the committee and I believe it was the incident that triggered his return to the UK.

UNEXPECTED CHANGES IN THE ORGANIZATION

In the fourth quarter of '96, it became evident that relations between Eastern Star Asia and the parent company were not on the right track, apparently the new chairman and Pascal had not been able to develop a good relationship and this resulted in a new restructuring that was announced in the first week of November.

In the new structure, Pascal maintained his position but would team up with Tom, a senior executive based in London who was in charge of international development, Richard was appointed director of Eastern Star Hong Kong, Peter was appointed CEO of Eastern Star General Insurance Taiwan, and I was appointed Director & COO Asia, with emphasis on the life and general insurance business in Taiwan.

I have no idea what logic was used to design this organization, but in analyzing it, I could read between the lines that it was in the middle of a new political battle that probably wasn't going to end well.

Richard's appointment to head Hong Kong did not interfere with the integration that had just been carried out, but it broke the localization policy that Pascal had established and put Kenny in a complex position regarding the development of his career at Eastern Star.

Richard seamlessly assumed leadership of the Hong Kong operations, maintaining the integrated structure and developing business strategies to increase market share in both life and general insurance.

TRYING TO ADD VALUE IN TAIWAN

In my case, the appointment sounded like a promotion since I would now be director & COO of Asia, which is a larger space, but in practice, this title was like general manager of planning, I had a lot of status, but I had no line of command over any unit.

I began to make a weekly trip to Taipei to attend the companies' Executive Committee meetings, but they did not make it easy for me, in one case they were not held periodically and in the other case, there was still no properly structured Executive Committee.

As the months went by, it became more difficult for me to add value to the Taiwan operations, as even one-on-one meetings with the CEOs and other members of the management team were difficult to arrange.

Unlike what I had experienced in Hong Kong as a planning general manager, in Taiwan I did not have access to computer systems or many reports unless they were translated from Chinese and approved by the CEO.

Members of the management team wanted to have good relations with both sides of the joint venture, but Eastern Star was not the dominant side despite having 50% of the business.

The lack of organizational stability and ability to understand the local market was creating credibility problems.

Every time I went to Taipei I returned to Hong Kong eager to quit, but this time it was more complicated since the company had given me a loan on preferential conditions to buy a house in Spain and I was still paying it. If I quit in a hurry my retirement fund would lose a few zeros.

GUEST TO THE ANNUAL CONVENTION IN GREECE

The 1997 Eastern Star Hong Kong sales convention was held in Greece, with an itinerary that included Athens, and Mykonos.

The group of attendees was close to 300 people including exclusive agents, brokers, and several members of the Eastern Star Asia Executive Committee who were invited to the event.

On the last day of the convention, there was a gala dinner at the hotel and as was usual on these occasions, all attendees dressed in their best clothes, which included tuxedo suits for men and long dresses for women.

DIFFICULTIES PAYING THE BILL

After dinner, the night was young and the regional director invited all members of the Executive Committee with their respective partners to visit a bouzouki venue where popular Greek music is played.

The place was packed with people, the music was beautiful and we all had a great time breaking plates.

As they explained to me that night, in Greece, breaking plates at a celebration is a sign of affection, goodwill, friendship, and good wishes for the owner of the house.

When it was time to leave, we asked for the bill and when trying to pay with the credit card we got a surprise. They didn't accept cards or dollars in cash, so for a few moments we imagined cleaning the dishes, even though we had already broken them.

Fortunately, my boss had some good friends who lived in Athens and they quickly came to the rescue to pay the bill, and we all ended up happy with a new story to remember.

These mini vacations helped me to recharge my emotional batteries somewhat, since the difficulties of my work in Taiwan made my professional life very complicated.

THE END OF THE TUNNEL IN THE SOUTH OF CHINA

If I controlled my emotions and found a way to use my time for something useful, the situation could be ideal, since I had total freedom in the use of my time, the highest salary in my entire professional career, a package of expatriate benefits that covered vacations, housing, a driver and accommodation in a luxury apartment in one of the most expensive and sophisticated cities in the world.

 What more could you ask for?

However, I couldn't endure the frustration and discomfort caused by not being able to be useful for long, and in July 1997, I decided to invoke a clause in my contract that allowed me to collect compensation and leave the organization.

I was tired of the corporate political battles and thought it was the right time to retire with the family to Barcelona, where my daughters could pursue their university studies, my wife could return to practicing medicine and we could share a new life with Isabel and Manyi. in the house he had recently bought.

When it was officially announced that I was leaving Eastern Star and returning to Spain, they organized several farewell lunches and dinners for me in Hong Kong and Taipei.

I also received some farewell souvenirs and letters of gratitude from some of my colleagues, and I felt that despite the communication difficulties had managed to connect deeply with many people.

THE FAREWELL OF HONG KONG

On Saturday, August 30, 1997, we left the Repulse Bay apartment and headed to the airport to board a plane that would take us to the old continent, after spending the last three years of our lives in the ex-British colony.

Upon arriving at the terminal, Peter Chu, our driver, was quick to say that he wanted to be with us until the last moment, which was nice of him.

As we approached the KLM counter, Christopher, a faithful and selfless friend who had gone out of his way to offer us his warm hospitality since our arrival in Hong Kong, suddenly appeared among the crowd.

At 9:15 am after obtaining the boarding passes, Christopher took out his inseparable camera, while we promised to write to each other and look for the opportunity to see each other again.

Finally, it was time to clear immigration and with some tears of emotion, we said goodbye and left behind Peter Chu and Christopher who were trying to touch us with their gaze from the door of the immigration corridor.

Hong Kong had permanently marked our lives, it had been a fascinating experience full of many satisfactions and some difficult moments that we could never forget.

After a 13-hour flight, we arrived in Amsterdam and there we connected with another flight to Barcelona, which at the moment was the place chosen as a permanent residence to start a new life.

I was about to turn 41 and I thought I had accumulated enough money to live on income after ending my career as an executive of a multinational company with which I had traveled 3 continents in the last 15 years. My wife was making plans to return to practicing her profession as a doctor and my teenage daughters were torn between the excitement of seeing Isabel, Manyi, and Cugui again and the nostalgia of leaving their friends in Hong Kong behind.

REFLECTIONS OF THE STAGE AT HONG KONG

The three years that my family spent in Hong Kong left us with many unforgettable experiences of high personal, cultural, and professional value.

My daughters perfected their English to an almost native level, and we all learned to function fluently in a multicultural environment made up of Hong Kongers, American expatriates, Europeans, and Asians.

We had the opportunity to live and experience the daily life of a super modern and globalized economy that represented a high-speed connection point between East and West, where the efficiency and coverage of public services and the availability of products and services did not leave anything to be desired.

We made a few friends, some for life and others we remember fondly from short-lived relationships.

Hong Kong taught us how a city can be in continuous movement and transformation, with frequent changes in its urban planning and roads, unlike many large European cities, where urban planning restrictions maintain a very stable face over time.

Hong Kong introduced us to a culture where most shops are open from Monday to Sunday and many companies work half a day on Saturdays. It is normal to go to the dentist, or if necessary to a private doctor during the weekends, this scheme makes the life of a working-class that has little free time on weekdays easier.

Hong Kong allowed us to live in a society where a very high percentage of the middle class has domestic help, who are generally women of Filipino or Indonesian origin. This is possible thanks to a system of employment contracts that establishes minimum wages, health insurance, and specific conditions of permanence in the territory.

Hong Kong taught us how society can adapt to living in spaces that are too small for western tastes and the majority of middle-class families live in apartments ranging between 500 and 900 square feet that, depending on the area, can easily cost more than a million. of American dollars.

The family trips from Hong Kong were not as varied as in Spain but included a few visits to Shenzhen, Stanley, or Macau.

Shenzhen is a city 30 kilometers from Hong Kong where in the early 90s tourists came to buy imitation items that looked like perfect originals such as watches, wallets, bags, shoes, phones, etc, but as the years went by, it grew exponentially and became one of the great technological centers of China.

Macau, a former Portuguese colony located 65 kilometers from Hong Kong, also visited several times to enjoy its cuisine and browse some of the many casinos that represent the basis of the city's economy.

Stanley is an old fishing village that over the years became a tourist market and a gastronomic center with countless restaurants where you could enjoy a day of recreation without leaving Hong Kong territory.

Another special and memorable experience was the trips on a small boat that the company had rented and was frequently used to organize trips with employees, friends, and business partners. The boat could easily accommodate between 20 and 30 people and the trips included visits to a nearby island and food in typical restaurants.

Hong Kong was a shorter experience with fewer trips than what we had experienced in Barcelona, but it had a much deeper impact on understanding cultural diversity and the challenges that globalization was beginning to show on the economic and geopolitical dependence on East and West.

China was not just a cheap factory; it was emerging as a strong competitor to lead the world economy.

DIFFICULTIES IN PREMATURE RETIREMENT

262

GOING THROUGH AN EXISTENTIAL CRISIS

It was 1998, I had just turned 42 and I was experiencing an existential crisis since early retirement life was not how I had imagined it.

I had finished furnishing the house, I had a study with a good library, a computer with a 26-inch screen, and I had even bought a second-hand sports Mercedes.

I had a comfortable and fairly quiet life enjoying with my family what at that time was the house of my dreams on the outskirts of Barcelona, right behind the American school where my daughters finished their high school education.

I had planned the family finances with a savings fund whose dividends would cover family expenses and there would be a surplus that would grow slowly over the years.

However, in practice, family expenses were beginning to exceed the income from my retirement fund and if this trend continued, I would have to look for other sources of income since reducing expenses at the moment was not the most advisable for the family life.

For many years, I had dreamed of retiring young to dedicate myself to writing, playing sports, and sharing life with my family, but when the time came things did not work out as I expected.

On the one hand, my daughters were in their teens and their interests did not combine much with the topics of conversation that a former retired executive who was beginning his forties could offer them.

On the other hand, my relationship had been losing chemistry and topics of conversation over the years, and as we had more time together, the differences in interests became more evident.

The plan had not gone very well, the loneliness of my study, the analysis of financial markets, and stock market operations, and the difficulties of writing my first book were leading me to chronic depression.

When I realized that I needed to give my life a new direction and accepted that early retirement was not what I wanted to do in the next few years, I decided to call my old contacts to explore the possibility of returning to the corporate world.

A PROJECT OF ONE HUNDRED MILLION POUNDS

Curiously, the first telephone call worked, as fate would have it, BIT Co. UK was looking for someone with business experience to lead the second phase of a Pan-European reengineering project that had begun in 1997 in Belgium and in early 1999 would move to the UK to finish in the year 2000.

In late September 1998, I flew to London for an interview with Tony the CIO of BIT Co. to learn the details of a project manager position that seemed to be a good opportunity for a former senior executive who had retired early.

The offer was to take over the management of the "FALCON" project in early 1999 when it moved from Belgium to the United Kingdom as the person acting as a project manager would return to his position as logistics manager of the Southampton cigarette factory.

The "FALCON" project was already halfway through development and aimed to optimize the production management of several BIT cigarette factories in Europe, standardizing processes and using a set of software packages that revolved around SAP/R3.

The implementation team consisted of around 100 consultants from Anderson Consulting and some technical staff drawn from BIT's factories in Belgium and the United Kingdom.

Working as a project manager in a reengineering process in the tobacco industry was not something that excited me too much, but it was the door to return to a multinational with operations in more than 140 countries and the opportunity to return to a senior management position in some country in Asia, Europe or America.

The job offer was an expatriate contract that included a good monthly salary, accommodation expenses, use of a company vehicle, and a few small, etc.

When discussing the proposal with the family, everyone liked the idea of me returning to work, and we decided that the most practical thing was for me to travel once or twice a month between London and Barcelona and the rest of the family would continue their routine, this would protect the stability of my teenage daughters to pursue university studies in Barcelona.

GETTING TO KNOW THE PROJECT IN BRUSSELS

To familiarize myself with the work that awaited me, it was proposed that I spend some time in the project's operations in Brussels before it moved to London where I would take over.

This proposal seemed like a good idea to me and the first week of October I arrived at the BIT Benelux Factory, an industrial complex of more than 30 thousand meters that housed more than 600 workers and all the processes necessary for the manufacturing and marketing of a long list of cigarette brands.

The director of the "FALCON" project in Brussels was Ian, a long-term executive at BIT who was preparing to return to logistics management at the South Hampton factory, his second in command was John, an industrial engineer with a lot of experience and an excellent sense of humor, John was a huge guy with a very friendly character who always looked for the positive side in everything.

When I met Ian, he was friendly and politically correct, but he limited himself to giving me an overview of the project and then handed over to John the task of introducing me to the team members who were putting the finishing touches on the implementation of the project at BIT Benelux.

Although I had nothing to object to Ian's behavior, I got the impression that my entry into the project for the UK phase was not something that suited him, he maintained a politically correct attitude but did not leave room for fraternization in the interaction, something that I would have appreciated as it would allow me to capitalize on his experience managing the project.

John, for his part, extended his hand to me with a friendly attitude that allowed us to develop a good personal and professional relationship.

John was the soul of the project with a very clear vision at both a conceptual and detailed level, he went out of his way to explain all the relevant aspects to me and to provide me with copies of any report or presentation that I found interesting.

However, there was a small problem, every time I asked about the business objectives of the project he told me that I had to talk to Ian and he always avoided going into details when touching on that topic.

At the end of my induction period in Brussels, I returned to Barcelona for a few days to spend Christmas with the family and reread the contents of a suitcase full of copies of reports and PowerPoint presentations that described the project in terms of general objectives, scope, organization, IT resources, work equipment, general schedule and a financial summary that estimated the total cost at around 100 million pounds.

The total cost of the project impressed me as it was a huge sum and I thought there was some error, but when I looked at the numbers on a spreadsheet I found the answer, if you pay an average of £1000 per day per consultant and you have 100 consultants working 3 years at 20 business days per month you already have the explanation of 70% of the cost, the rest goes between software licenses, new hardware components, hosting costs and absorbed cost of some additional heads.

In my experience, reengineering projects can be justified in many ways, using tangible or intangible factors with measurable economic impact or with strategic benefits of competitiveness, productivity, or even survival, but in general, something measurable and concrete is always preferred, especially when the cost represented such an important magnitude.

LANDING IN THE UK

The second week of January 1999 I landed in London for another induction period at BIT's corporate headquarters in Globe House, where there were many faces I didn't know and some contacts from my previous days when I worked as a regional IT advisor at the end of 80's years.

After signing the employment contract, settling into an office assigned to me in Globe House, and doing the same in another in the Southampton factory, I understood that I was expected to spend my time moving between the two locations. Following this principle, I ended up renting a small house in a small town called Pyrford that was 10 minutes from Woking train station, located an hour and a half from Southampton, and 35 minutes from London.

As a project manager, I had three lines of reporting, one to the CIO, another to the COO of the Southampton factory and another to the CFO of the corporation who was officially the "SPONSOR" of the

"FALCON" project at the level of the Executive Committee of BIT Co., this matrix structure was very common in multinationals and although it had some advantages, it was not free of drawbacks.

BETWEEN LONDON AND SOUTHAMPTON

To manage the project in Southampton and maintain the reporting lines in London I had to move between the two locations from my rented house in Pyrford, this meant getting up at 5:00 am on the days I went to Southampton and at 6:00 am on the days I went to London.

When I went to Southampton the train took an hour and a half to get to the station, after arrival I had to queue to take a taxi that in 10 minutes took me to the factory where a desk was waiting for me inside a container located on the periphery of the parking lot of the factory next to a long line of containers for the rest of the project team.

If I had to go to London, I also had to get up very early because, although the journey was shorter, I arrived at Waterloo station at rush hour and had to wait in line to take a taxi to go to my office in Globe. House.

The days began to pass quickly as I immersed myself in meetings and assimilated the content of the planned work program for the implementation team.

WELL ORGANIZED, BUT YOU CAN'T SEE THE BENEFIT

Everything was carefully planned and specified for each work group, but I could not find anywhere the benefits of the project beyond a technology change that replaced an old "BPCS" software package with a more modern one that does more or less the same thing.

On the Anderson Consulting side, the project liaison account manager was Michel, a person with a lot of experience in the area of consulting and development of large projects inside and outside the United Kingdom.

Michel was a very prepared person, with excellent interpersonal skills and he quickly offered to help me in whatever was necessary, however, when I brought up the topic of the benefits of the project I ran into the same problem, I did not have anything quantifiable that was more beyond a technological renewal and aspects linked to safety, efficiency and maintainability.

At this point, I imagined that everyone was aware of this situation and I thought that the corporation's top management had approved the project on these bases, so I decided not to look for any more legs for the cat and to dedicate myself to facilitating the normal development of the project in everything. that was within my reach.

THE CFO ASKS FOR THE BENEFITS OF THE PROJECT

A few days after the project team arrived on their move from Belgium to the UK, I received an invitation to attend a meeting with Keith, the corporation's CFO.

Keith was a middle-aged man, very bright with a lot of experience both at the operating company level and at the headquarters. I met him during my time as IT manager at BIT Venezuela when he was the CFO of BIT Chile.

When I entered his office, as usual, he greeted me in Spanish and after joking for a while about the old days in Latin America and my experiences at British International Financial Services. We began to talk about what interested him, which was nothing other than the benefits of the "FALCON" project.

I tried to be as diplomatic as I could, but I couldn't help but be the bearer of confirmation of a fact that he already knew, the project until now had no defined measurable business benefit beyond a technological renewal.

The day after I met with Keith, I received a memo signed by him, asking me to organize a meeting with the project management team and the Southampton factory to review the terms of reference of the project and especially the benefits expected from its implementation.

Armed with the memo signed by the CFO, I asked to meet with Southampton's COO to discuss the issue. During the meeting, he informed me that he would support me in defining specific objectives, but that the benefits of the project were something that had been established at a strategic level and that this project had been imposed from above.

Given the COO's reaction, I tried to contact Ian again. but he did not call me back, the next day I spoke with all the project team leaders to inform them of the CFO's requirement and I had a mixed response, some saw it favorably and contributed good ideas, and others told me that this It should have been done from the beginning, and some only showed concern and asked me to be careful not to damage the progress of the project.

On the other hand, Michel P. reminded me that the business objectives were the responsibility of BIT Co. and that there was a signed contract that included the billing levels of Anderson Consulting's resources.

With all the information I had available I prepared a presentation covering all aspects necessary to review the project including some potential benefits that could be assessed and agreed upon with the support of the Southampton management team.

THE LOGISTICS MANAGER LOSES CONTROL

When the day of the meeting arrived, the entire management team from the project, the factory, and from Anderson Consulting showed up.

From the beginning of the presentation, Ian began to criticize the content and to make interruptions out of context that reflected a high level of annoyance and aggression. This situation was repeated several times until John intervened, asking Ian to control himself.

At this point, my level of stress, surprise, and disbelief of what was happening was at stratospheric levels and I decided that it was best to abort the meeting at this point and resume it when things were calm.

The next day I headed to London to ask Tony the CIO's opinion on what was happening and found another surprise, Tony was in an emergency meeting with the CFO, the COO, Ian, and the account manager from Anderson Consulting.

An internal political crisis had exploded over a fire that I had set off by being used as a messenger in a power conflict between headquarters and the management of the Southampton factory.

ABANDON THE BOAT OR SINK WITH IT

Given the situation, I carefully reflected on what had happened and came to the conclusion that I should resign from project management and terminate my reunion with BIT Co.

Tony suggested that I take a few days of vacation and that the CFO had other positions in the group in mind for me, but I had already made my decision, the prevailing organizational culture was not compatible with what I would like to do in the coming years, so I formalize my resignation, handed over all the assets of the company, and took the first flight I could find to Barcelona.

This had been an experience full of lessons that I should analyze carefully and incorporate the positive part into my frame of reference.

REFLECTIONS ON THE FALCON PROJECT

When I was offered the management of the "FALCON" project, I assumed that Ian was eager to return to his permanent position in the management of logistics from where he could support the implementation of a project that would benefit the factory, however, in light of events I believe that my perception was not correct, but this is just speculation.

For me, defining objectives and measurable benefits of project implementation was necessary, healthy, viable, and desirable, however, other people saw it as an intrusion into their area of responsibility and possibly as an affront to the quality of their management.

In my opinion, business profit is a concept that, although flexible and subjective, must be carefully evaluated to protect the viability of the company.

I do not know if the "FALCON" project was implemented according to the original plan, but, in any case, there was no time to recover the investment.

When I looked for references to refresh my memory on this story, I discovered that the Southampton factory was closed in 2006 despite having been one of BIT's most advanced factories worldwide, as it could not compete in conversion cost with others. factories in Asia and Eastern Europe.

The decline of the cigarette market worldwide was a phenomenon known for a long time and a strategic planning error was made in the conception of the "FALCON" project that reminded me of my experience in the European single market project in my first year at BIT Co. headquarters in 1989.

Human beings tend to mix the personal with the professional at work, this causes the ego, emotions, and personal interests to compete with what is objectively viable or advisable. If the ego and personal interests had not affected the criteria and behavior of the protagonists of this story, the difference of opinion on the objectives of the project would possibly have been resolved and we would have formed a good team where each one contributed their grain of sand.

DESTINY OPENS ANOTHER DOOR

After my short and eventful experience at the BIT Co. headquarters in London, I returned to Barcelona with the idea of working as an independent consultant, and again fate crossed my path with a new project.

It was something totally different from what he had done before. A former co-worker had joined the Editorial Prensa Ibérica group as CFO in Barcelona and was looking for a company that would advise them on the development of an image digitization system.

AN EDITORIAL CONTROL SYSTEM

At that time, Editorial Prensa Ibérica was a group of companies that included several regional newspapers, and companies dedicated to the publication and marketing of books aimed at the general public, all focused on the Spanish market.

The first probing meeting of the project was held with the CFO, the personal assistant of the president of the group, and the head of the Editorial Control Unit in a house renovated for the presidency's office in the upper area of Pedralves in Barcelona.

The objective of the project was focused on developing a computer system that would facilitate the work of the newly created Editorial Control Unit so that it could present a daily report to the president of the group, the report would summarize the information flow published by both the group and by competition at the national level.

The information stream contains news on the economy, politics, events, extraordinary events, and other matters of interest covered in the group's and competitors' newspapers.

Monitoring these variables daily allowed the group to guide its coverage positioning and influence public opinion in an efficient manner that was coordinated with its editorial policy.

To achieve its objective, the Editorial Control Unit should read, summarize, and digitize the most important articles from about 30 newspapers every day, and based on this prepare a report that the group's president could see on a laptop.

I found the project interesting but obviously, I was not clear about the details beyond the digitization of images of the articles, and I suggested a second meeting with the head of the Editorial Control Unit to delve deeper into the requirements and possibilities of what they had in mind.

At the end of the meeting, my former BIT colleague invited me to have a coffee and suggested that I propose, something good, nice, and cheap since they were in a hurry to launch the Editorial Control Unit and a very complex solution or too sophisticated would probably not be very well received.

FINE-TUNING THE SYSTEM REQUIREMENTS

The next day I met with Javier, the head of the Editorial Control Unit, and two journalists who made up his team, in an office they shared with one of the group's publishing companies near Paseo de la Bonanova.

During the meeting, they explained to me the process they had in mind and showed me copies of the different newspapers of the group and the competition that they had to read and analyze every day.

Due to the nature of the work, it was evident that the key part was the identification and summary of the articles to be considered each day, while the digitization of the images represented an element of logistical support of great value. If you receive 30 newspapers every day and don't get rid of them, in a short time you will have a mountain of newsprint.

The rest of the week was spent conceptualizing a solution and researching costs for software licenses, servers, and scanning equipment large enough to accept the size of a newspaper page.

By the end of the week, I had enough information and had conceptualized a solution, so I set about putting it in writing in the form of a proposal.

The only problem was that I had to register a company to be able to propose legally, so that day "IMS Innovative Management Systems SL" was born.

PROPOSAL TO THE IBERIAN PRESS

The proposal included the design and implementation of a system in MS Access on a local network equipped with a server, a scanner, and three workstations where the summary of each article would be recorded in a database that could quantify the number of articles per day, by newspaper or by topic and also maintain a connection with the digitized image of the article to be viewed.

The system would also allow the generation of a CD each day with an executive summary of the editorial analysis, the summary of the day's articles, and the associated digitized images.

IMS DEVELOPS ITS FIRST PROJECT

The following week I submitted the project proposal and two days later they called me to inform me that the project had the green light.

At the moment, I had to work for more than 12 hours a day every day of the week, I converted my studio into the IMS headquarters and hired my nephew who was studying computer science as my assistant.

I started developing the system on my personal computer and as soon as I had the client's approval, I placed the order for the scanner, server, and workstations.

If the same person acts as an analyst, programmer, and test user, the development of a system in MS Access can be very fast, so by the third week I already had a prototype developed and I decided to invite Javier to my studio to test it.

Javier was surprised by how quickly the project was moving and the day after my call he came to my studio to test the prototype.

We did several article summary tests and tried scanning with my Oficejet printer which also had the scanner function.

The equipment I had ordered had not arrived yet, but Javier had an idea that was pretty close to reality with the configuration I had in my office.

Javier was delighted with the system and during the test the importance of the executive summary became evident and I convinced him that it should have his personal touch in addition to the titles and article counts.

The next week the equipment arrived and my studio became a war zone with cables and boxes everywhere.

My nephew Manyi and I dedicated ourselves to testing and configuring the entire system including the A3 size scanner and the tape drive to make daily backups of the database. The implementation was carried out in the second month after signing the contract and Javier began generating his daily report using the system.

Although the system was quite stable and required very little maintenance, Manyi came from time to time to resolve doubts, small configuration problems, and new functionality requirements, this encouraged Javier to hire a technical assistance service.

FAMILY LIFE IN BARCELONA

While I focused on my new company, each member of the family built their universe, my daughter Alejandra studied audiovisual communication, my daughter Tatiana began university studying photography and digital imaging, Manyi advanced in her computer studies, my wife and Isabel took care of the house, and my wife also occasionally assisted a doctor friend in surgical procedures.

The teenagers had become adults, we adults were quickly heading into the golden age, life continued under one roof, but in many directions.

On weekends we sometimes went to the movies, ate in a restaurant or prepared a barbecue in the garden, but it was not easy to coordinate the times so that everyone was present.

LOOKING FOR MORE PROJECTS FOR IMS

After finishing the project with Editorial Prensa Ibérica, I began to think about how to generate new clients and it occurred to me to send an email to my friends and old acquaintances in Spain, Venezuela, England, and Hong Kong telling them about my return to the world of work as an independent consultant. with my company "Innovative Management Systems".

A VERY ATTRACTIVE AND UNEXPECTED PROPOSAL

Then a very interesting door opened, my friend Kenny, who was now the business director of Zenith Life Insurance Hong Kong, replied to my email showing interest in my services to help them solve some problems with their information systems.

Kenny told me that they were developing a project to migrate insurance policies from the "Eagle Living" system to the "Harvest" system, but things had become complicated, and possibly I could help them.

Additionally, he told me that he had suggested my services to Amadeus the new CEO of Hong Kong and he had reacted positively and could offer me a one-year consulting contract to solve the problem of insurance policy migration and other priority issues for the sales force.

Kenny's quick positive response made me very happy, but the proposed contracting scheme surprised me since I was expecting a project for my company created in Barcelona, when analyzing the offer, I realized that it was better for both parties, since in a year I could collaborate on many things and we wouldn't have to be making contracts for each service.

Regarding fees, to make things easier, I suggested that they use my last annual package when I was director and COO of Hong Kong as a reference, since at the end of the day they were going to have my services full-time.

A few days later I received a proposal for a service contract as a consultant with an annual sum that I could divide into monthly payments and cover at my discretion, my expenses for accommodation, transportation, etc.

The contract was exclusive, had a 6-month termination clause, and gave Zenith the intellectual property of anything I developed during the contract period.

When I told my family about the Hong Kong offer, they were all excited about the idea, since my job in Hong Kong also included a vacation trip for everyone.

As Manyi knew well the systems he had developed for Editorial Prensa Ibérica, I left him in charge of providing customer support and transferred control of Innovative Management Systems to him.

When the trip was confirmed, I spoke to my friend Julia to tell her that I would be spending a year in Hong Kong and she very kindly invited me to stay at her apartment in Mid Levels while I rented something for myself.

REFLECTIONS OF A PREMATURE RETIREMENT

Spending half my life preparing to retire young, I think was not very wise, or at least for me, it was not a good path.

I am not attracted to the idea of spending my life doing nothing, although I appreciate the value of the freedom to choose how to use my time and my traveling companions to share the challenges and opportunities of being alive.

Experience has taught me that you have to enjoy life, take advantage of it and give it meaning whenever possible and not wait for the magical day of retirement to arrive to start living fully.

For most of us mortals who have had to work to live, finding a source of satisfaction in work is like winning the lottery; if you enjoy what you do and get paid for doing it, it is certainly a blessing.

Not all jobs are the same and the colleagues you have make a big difference, but above and beyond these two factors, the attitude we assume towards the activity we carry out, and the people we interact with also makes a huge difference, or at least this is what I have been able to verify in practice.

If you treat people with respect and consideration, they will often respond in kind, although there is no guarantee that this will happen. Each person is different and most humans have moments of weakness where we let ourselves be carried away by emotions.

If we feed our mind with optimistic and pleasant ideas about what we are doing, the brain is predisposed and prepares a scenario to perceive the positive side of what is happening and downplay the negative side.

In all the countries I have lived in there are kind and rude people, poor and rich, generous and selfish, wise and ignorant, what changes is the proportion of these attributes in the environment in which you operate.

If you live among honey, something sticks to you, so intelligently choosing the environment where you live, work and make friends has a very important impact on your quality of life.

277

UNEXPECTED RETURN TO HONG KONG

278

THE NEW HONG KONG AIRPORT

The first week of March 2000, when I was 43 years old, I returned to Hong Kong, this time I landed at Chek Lap Kok airport, which was inaugurated in 1998 after finishing my first stage with Eastern Star Hong Kong, so I didn't know it.

The Chek Lap Kok airport was beautiful, super modern, and efficient, it cost over 20 billion dollars, and was one of the largest and most complex construction projects of the modern era, as it required the formation of an artificial island of 13 square kilometers, the construction of passenger terminals, a fast train line, a new highway, and several auxiliary service complexes. All of this was done over six years using more than 250 contracting companies from around the world.

When I left immigration, Kenny's driver was waiting for me to take me to Julia and Steven's apartment in Mid Levels, this made me remember my previous stage and I felt like I was returning home.

REUNION WITH OLD FRIENDS

Julia and her husband have been excellent friends since my first stage in Hong Kong since we agreed on many of our values and we have shared a long list of unforgettable moments on a personal and professional level.

The next day I took a taxi and arrived early at the Zenith Insurance Group offices in Cityplaza III. The reception had some changes, but the rest of the offices were as I remembered them in 1997.

I met with Kenny in his 16th-floor office and while we were reminiscing about old times, Bobby joined the meeting.

I told them about my frustrated retirement in Barcelona and the adventures in the last two years in England and Spain.

They told me what had happened in Hong Kong since the return to China in '97 and then the absorption of Eastern Star by the Zenith group in 1999.

In general, the situation had not changed much, Hong Kong maintained a very open, dynamic, and competitive economy with low taxes, a legal system independent of China, its currency, many economic freedoms, low corruption, and high levels of security.

In general, things were much better than people had imagined, and many of those who had emigrated before 97 returned after a while since it was not easy to find jobs in Canada, the UK, or the USA like the ones they had. they had had in Hong Kong.

After the absorption by Zenith, the company maintained the integrated life and general insurance structure, but Amadeus was reorganizing the service units under a single management head.

Kenny had become head of the life insurance business and now had responsibilities that went beyond distribution channels, including underwriting, risk, customer service, claims management, and actuarial services.

Eastern Star's general insurance business had merged with that of Zenith and they were in the process of harmonizing rates, underwriting policies, standards, and procedures.

The support and service functions for the two business lines were integrated into a single structure and included areas such as personnel administration, office services, finance, legal, marketing, and IT, which made a lot of sense in my opinion.

A LONG LIST OF THINGS TO DO

After covering the general aspects of the company, we got into what Kenny and Bobby were interested in.

Although the list was long, there were three priority topics. One was the migration of the product portfolio from an old system called "Eagle Living" to another more modern system called "Harvest", this involved resolving functionality issues for over 280 different product codes or policy types.

The migration would allow a portfolio of nearly one hundred thousand life policies to be managed in a single system, which would increase the efficiency and productivity of the back office and reduce the cost of maintaining the systems.

On the other hand, they were developing a portable system to be used by agents during the sales process, but it was still somewhat crude and they had to find a way to accelerate development and make it effective.

The third area was the expansion of the functionality of the management information system "MIS" that I had promoted since 1994. After the meeting with Kenny and Bobby, I was assigned an office on the 15th floor near the IT area and there I saw many of my old friends such as Serena, Shing, Li, Tony, Tam, and many others who had met me. helped develop a few projects between 94 and 97.

GOOD CHEMISTRY WITH THE CEO OF HONG KONG

On the second day, I had a courtesy interview with Amadeus, the new CEO of Hong Kong. Amadeus was a tall, friendly, Swiss-born, middle-aged guy with a lot of experience in the industry who had been transferred to Hong Kong shortly after the takeover of Eastern Star. From the first meeting, we agreed on many ideas, there was good chemistry and we began to develop a good interpersonal relationship.

Amadeus was aware of my role in the integration of Hong Kong in the Eastern Star days and the push I had given to computer systems; I imagine this explained why he had readily supported Kenny's proposal to use my services as a consultant.

RECONNECTING WITH THE ORGANIZATION

The first week it was quite difficult for me to make progress on anything concrete, since, between phone calls, visits from former collaborators, and solving administrative issues, the hours and days went by in the blink of an eye.

My return to Hong Kong as a consultant generated curiosity and many of those who knew me paid me a courtesy visit or invited me to lunch.

Through one of these visits, I learned that the district managers of the sales force were somewhat upset with the access control to the management information system "MIS" since some of them had to memorize up to five security codes.

There were a few new faces that I got to know little by little.

A RENTED APARTMENT IN PARK VIEW

Although Julia was an excellent host, I could not overuse her hospitality, and in the second week, I decided to rent a suite in a complex called Park View located on the road to Repulse Bay.

Park View is a complex of several towers of single-family homes, an apartment hotel tower, a Park & Shop supermarket, a laundry, and ample parking for residents and visitors, which made it practical and attractive to satisfy my accommodation needs.

With Kenny's help, I located a second-hand Mercedes Benz E220 at a good price, and the company purchased it for my personal use, using part of my annual compensation package.

By the third week of March, I was settled in Park View, I had a car to get to the office, I had a mobile phone, I had reactivated my checking account at HSBC and the company had processed my work permit.

The efficiency of Hong Kong never ceased to impress me, especially when I compared it to other countries and cities that I prefer not to mention where it took months to rent a home and almost a year to process a work permit.

IMPROVING THE MIS

When I had the opportunity to speak with Serena, one of my old friends in the life IT area, I told her about the difficulties of access control for district managers, in the MIS, and after analyzing the causes and effects of the problem, she decided to give me a hand by creating a mechanism with a single password per district manager.

The rest of the pending improvements for the MIS would have to be handled by somebody else. Serena had just finished a master's degree and had decided to quit her job and dedicate herself to other activities.

I began to identify the rest of the MIS improvements in conversations with district managers and some back office users who knew the system well.

The list was long, but there were few critical elements so for the moment I left my list of improvements as new maintenance requests that should enter the user request work queue.

THE MELHI PROJECT

For the problem of migrating from Eagle Living to Harvest, I sought help from Li, another good friend who was the head of the living systems department and an expert in this matter.

After a long conversation with Li, I concluded that a good part of the problem was one of coordination between users and IT since there was a long list of change requests and development of functionality, but there was no overall vision that gave a time scale to everything that had to be resolved.

Everyone was working very hard renovating a multi-story building, but they had no idea when they were going to finish or how to optimize priorities to take advantage of the effort they were making in the short term.

Based on that information, it occurred to me to do an analysis of the portfolio to be transferred, calculating the number of policies and the premium volume by product code to see if Pareto's law could help me find a solution.

When I obtained the information, my horizon lit up, since more than 85% of the number of policies and 80% of the premiums were concentrated in only 42 of the 280 product codes, which would allow me to define a strategy with many benefits.

If the pending functionality was developed by product code starting with the highest volume of policies and maintenance transactions, and the policies were migrated by having their functionality in the new system, this would cause users to receive the benefits of the migration more quickly, they would not have to wait for all the functionality to be developed and all the policies to be migrated.

The effort per product code is independent of the number of policies it affected, and this was the key to the strategy.

When I had clear ideas about how to organize the project, I prepared a presentation explaining the strategy and proposing the formation of a work team with users and IT staff that would be coordinated by a project manager selected from among the users.

Kenny would be the project sponsor, I would act as project manager and meet weekly with the project manager to evaluate progress and make adjustments to the strategy if necessary.

As project manager, I proposed Karen T. since she had a lot of experience in projects and was a very hard-working, efficient person with good communication skills.

I have known Karen since 1994 in my first stage in Hong Kong when she was the head of a section that managed a pension product, and I always saw her working late, so I became interested in her area and by talking to her, I learned a few things about "MPF, ORSO and Employment Benefits".

I explained the idea of migrating the policies in waves based on the volume that each type of policy represented, and Kenny approved the plan, then the "MELHI" project was officially born, which meant something like "Migration Eagle Living Harvest Inforce".

Karen began managing the project meetings and within weeks the new strategy was launched, I met with Karen once a week to monitor progress, make changes if necessary, and update the overall project control schedule.

The MELHI project was successfully developed in five migration phases that finally allowed the disincorporation of the Eagle Living system and the administration of the entire life policy portfolio in a single system.

THE SALES AUTOMATION SYSTEM

Regarding the sales process support system, Kenny conceived the idea for the project after seeing a demonstration of a small system that Rex, a very intelligent and creative member of the sales force, had developed.

Rex had designed a series of tools using Excel and PowerPoint that facilitated the analysis of customer needs and allowed him to visualize how their needs changed throughout the life cycle.

For example, using an Excel sheet I could calculate how much money a person needed to retire depending on their age, spending level, and initial savings level.

What Rex had on his laptop was very good, but it was not a system prepared to be copied and distributed to hundreds of machines, it had to be refined, completed, generalized, and adapted to Zenith's corporate image.

To develop this project, I had to work as a team with two key people, one was my friend Shing, the sales channel support systems manager.

I had known Shing since 1994, as he had helped me develop several projects. Shing was a young guy, very responsible, intelligent, and dedicated, with a lot of experience and knowledge of both technology and processes related to the sales area. so your participation in this project was vital.

The other person was Regina, a young woman who had been part of Kenny's sales team when she was a district manager and who was currently a coordinator between the back office and the sales force.

Regina would be in charge of coordinating activities that required the participation of sales force agents and managers.

I had always been very interested in knowing in depth the sales and development processes of insurance agents since it was a critical area for the company and now I had the opportunity to delve deeper into this topic with the development of this system.

If an insurance company has a professional sales force, with high levels of efficiency, productivity, and quality of service, it will have a high chance of being a successful company. But unfortunately achieving this is not easy, it is necessary to align the client's needs, with a professional service from the agents and a good product portfolio.

With the copy of the system developed by Rex, I sat down with Shing and Regina to analyze how we could improve it, and what was needed to turn it into a corporate tool that could be distributed among all agents who were interested in using it.

After analyzing all these factors, we concluded that the project should be approached as an evolutionary process, starting with a relatively simple first version that would be progressively improved based on evaluations of utilization and impact on sales force management.

This approach would allow a first version to be released relatively quickly, evaluate the results, and use the lessons to prepare a second version, and so on.

LAUNCHING SAM

I put all this analysis into a PowerPoint that I presented to Kenny and he agreed with this approach, thus the project to develop SAM R0 was born, which stood for something like "Sales Automation Management Release 0".

The first version of SAM went into operation in July 2000 and had a good level of reception in the sales force, which we verified through surveys and analysis of statistics on how the system was used.

In terms of functionality, this version was similar to what Rex had done, but it had some additional elements, was organized from a main menu, used professional photos, had the Zenith corporate image, was bilingual, and generated usage statistics.

Responding to the requests of the agents, Shing and his team, in collaboration with the training and marketing departments, continued to develop, for a long period, new versions of SAM and other applications such as SAM lite for smartphone and SAMme for intranet.

For several years, Zenith led the life insurance industry in Hong Kong in using computer applications to facilitate the sales process.

TRAVEL BETWEEN HONG KONG AND BARCELONA

In the summer holidays of 2000, my wife and daughters came to visit me in Hong Kong for two weeks and in December I traveled to Barcelona to spend Christmas and New Year with the whole family.

We had all adapted to a new way of living on two continents, my wife and Isabel continued with their usual routines, my daughters Alejandra and Tatiana were advancing in their university studies and Manyi was doing the same.

We spoke on the phone frequently, but the time difference and each other's activities made it difficult to find suitable times for communication.

A NEW OFFICE NEXT TO KENNY

When I returned to Hong Kong in 2000 they assigned me an office that was not bad, but in my opinion, it had two problems, it was on another floor away from Kenny's and it did not have a meeting table, but almost at the end of 2000 an opportunity presented itself. A manager who had an office next to Kenny's had resigned and was not going to be replaced at the moment, so I saw the opportunity to merge two adjacent offices and create a new one next to Kenny's so it would be easier to keep in touch with him and hold my work meetings with the different teams with which I frequently interacted.

When I mentioned the issue to Amadeus, he understood my reasoning and supported the idea. A few days later the administrative services department contracted the remodeling and when I returned from spending Christmas with my family in Barcelona I found the office remodeled and I moved into the 16th floor.

Having my office next to Kenny's made it quite easy to interact with him since if I had something important to tell him and he was alone, I could do it immediately.

Something similar happened with other key people in the organization who were on the 16th floor, since now I frequently found them in the hallways not only during office hours but also at night and on some weekends.

I remember more than once when I was working late, Amadeus and other members of the management team made informal visits to me for the simple fact of working outside official hours.

Communication is a key aspect in the functioning of any organization, and sometimes small changes can make significant differences. If the organizational culture is open and facilitates personal interaction, you can move much faster and develop levels of trust, empathy, and credibility that are difficult to achieve through phone calls or email exchanges.

MYS ANYWHERE

In early 2001, one day talking to Tony, the computer services manager, about mobile phones, he showed me how to use my Nokia to connect my laptop to the IBM AS/400 and this experiment gave me an idea that could have many benefits on quality of service in the agent network.

At that time there were already many agents who used SAM on their laptops, everyone had a mobile phone and also an access code to the MIS, but they could only use it in the office.

If we made a few small adjustments to the remote access configuration of the IBM AS/400, we could allow agents who had a laptop to access the MIS almost at anytime and anywhere in Hong Kong, this would allow them to expand the range of services that they could provide to their clients since it gave them online access to the information on their policies, receipts, and applications in process.

For the agents, using MIS Anywhere had a small cost since they paid for the call, but this meant that they would only use the service if they needed it.

When I demoed it to Kenny, he immediately supported the idea and MIS Anywhere was born.

This was a small effort for the computer services department, but it created a significant benefit for the sales force and again put us at the forefront of computer services for the agent network.

A VENEZUELAN FRIEND IN HONG KONG

In 2001, one-day speaking with my sister Bárbara, she told me that an acquaintance of hers had been appointed as new Consul of Venezuela in Hong Kong and she encouraged me to contact him since my network of Spanish-speaking friends in Hong Kong was very limited.

Nelson was a very nice and friendly person, so we had great chemistry from the first time we met, and we established a relationship that evolved into a good friendship over the years.

The Latino community in Hong Kong is not large, so Nelson did not have many Spanish-speaking friends either.

Nelson and I met for lunch or drinks once or twice a month and in general we spent a good time talking about the political and economic situation worldwide. We didn't touch on the topic of Venezuela much, since it was a complicated area.

One place we frequented was an American restaurant in Pacific Place called Dan Ryan's, where they prepared some very appetizing pork ribs. One Friday night we met for dinner and while we were waiting at the bar, Nelson told me about a 40-year-old friend of his in Venezuela who had recently died of a heart attack. The story impressed me and I started sweating, then I felt like going to the bathroom and something worrying happened.

Suddenly I woke up lying on the floor and quite dizzy, I was alone and obviously no one had noticed my situation.

I left the bathroom and Nelson was waiting for me at the bar. When he saw me he told me I didn't look good. I told him what had happened, and we decided to cancel dinner, he drove my car to my apartment and accompanied me for a while until I felt okay.

It was the first and last time I had a faint of this type in my entire life, but it remains etched in my memory as did the kindness of that new Venezuelan friend in Hong Kong.

This type of fainting can happen to anyone due to low blood sugar, dehydration, or a drop in blood pressure. In my case, I don't know the origin, but it was something temporary that left no consequences to regret.

THE ZENITH LIFE GRAPHIC ANALYZER

In the first quarter of 2001, the second version of SAM had already been implemented, the MELHI project was progressing according to plan and several improvements had been made to the MIS, but, although all this was useful progress for the company, there were major problems who still did not have a clear solution strategy.

The profitability of the new production was not sufficient to guarantee the viability of the company, and this was a rather complex problem, which depended on many variables.

The key components of profitability could independently generate positive results, but when they interacted the result was not good enough.

The products were profitable, but the margin was not high enough, the salespeople were doing their job, but they were not selling the necessary volume or mix, and the fixed expenses were the usual, but when you add it all up, the numbers did not add up.

To further complicate things, the profitability of the products depends on actuarial assumptions that have a margin of error and fluctuations in the criteria with which they are formulated.

Sales force productivity depends on hundreds of people whose performance and turnover level are difficult to predict and control.

Fixed expenses depend on contracts that sometimes extend beyond years and room for maneuver is limited, especially in office space.

Competitors develop all types of strategies that range from very intelligent and profitable to some that only destroy the viability of the industry, complicating market conditions.

Knowing all these elements, I was very clear that I would not invest my money in creating a new life insurance company under these conditions, but that was not the case, the company already existed and although I did not have a single share, it was the source of work for many people he appreciated, in a city he admired and in an industry necessary for the prosperity of civilization where other companies survived and some gave good results.

In conclusion, I had to find a way to help improve the strategy with which we were operating in the market.

In my opinion, the origin of the problems we had was a lack of information and knowledge, they were not a lack of effort, dedication, or responsibility.

The problems and pressures of everyday life kept everyone super busy and often absent from the dangers that threatened survival.

That is why I began to develop a tool that would allow me to analyze the profitability of the new production mix and the productivity of the sales force. I thought that if I could make the problems and their possible solutions evident this would be a step in the right direction. operating expenses could be analyzed more easily in spreadsheets.

Since I heard the phrase "a graph says a thousand words", I incorporated it into my list of work habits since in my opinion, it works.

For this reason, my new analysis tool was based on the extensive use of graphs that allowed the company's production and portfolio to be visualized in a helicopter view that could go from the total level of the company to the level of a policy, an agent, a district, a distribution channel, a product or a line of products and all this in a chronological horizon that could range from a month, a quarter, a semester, a year or the life of the company since its founding in 1982.

Developing the graphical analyzer was relatively simple, thanks to the existence of a huge database available on the IBM AS/400 that could be interrogated with SQL to generate small summaries that could be represented graphically using the functionality of MS Access.

When I finished the first version of the graphical analyzer, I spent many hours studying how the productivity of the sales force originated and at first I didn't see anything new, I already knew that there were some star agents and many low-level agents, but when I visualized this phenomenon in several years, in several districts and related it to the rotation of agents and their monthly income, I saw a different reality.

There were consistently a few people who made millions every year selling life insurance policies while many other people barely survived a few months and quit or were fired.

Some group leaders combined a good personal production with their activity of guiding agents, if the agents did not survive, they took possession of the policies that they had generated, this made sense, but I wondered if it was the most suitable model.

In a network of hundreds of people, including managers, supervisors, and agents, there is a wide variety of personalities, skills, and performance levels, which could be classified as high, good, acceptable, and insufficient in practically all sales districts.

If a simplistic view of the problem was taken, one could consider:

- Eliminate all those who have "insufficient" performance.
- Give the "acceptable" a period of time to rise to "good".
- Recruit looking for people with "high" potential.
- Eliminate management positions that do not add value.

But implementing these measures was difficult, risky and unviable since each sales district is almost like an independent company.

Kenny did not have all the power to force each district manager to take extreme measures at once without risking losing the entire district. It was like expecting a person who is 30 kilos overweight to get on the line in a week.

Regarding the profitability margin of the product mix, in theory, a sufficiently profitable mix could be configured, but this would put the company outside the market line and produce a lower level of total sales volume.

In summary, the solution to the productivity and profitability of new production was a solvable but complex problem that could not be resolved with extreme measures unless high risks of decline were accepted for a period that was difficult to quantify.

Considering this scenario, I thought that the best way to help was to give this tool to Kenny and the entire management team so that little by little they could visualize in detail what they already knew at a conceptual level.

When I put the graph analyzer on the management team's personal computers, it began to be used frequently and some of the images it presented created a significant impact.

I could know the level of utilization, since every time someone used the system, the usage statistics were updated.

The analyzer had a summary image at the agent level where you could see in a single sheet, the entire productive history of the person year by year, the composition of the status of the policy portfolio, and the proportion of new clients in the sales of each year.

This image allowed us to visualize another important problem that the entire industry was suffering, which was the replacement of old policies with new policies, which further complicated the profitability outlook since it was a factor in the deterioration of the intrinsic value of the portfolio.

The use of the graphical analyzer spread and was also installed on the personal computers of the district managers, in this way the size and status of the composition of the portfolio of all the agents became evident, there were no secrets, everything was on the table.

TRAVEL, VISITS AND FAMILY AFFAIRS

My family in Barcelona continued with its usual activities, while I worked full-time for Zenith Seguros in Hong Kong, we spoke on the phone several times a week, but each member of the family lived their own set of priorities.

My daughters were progressing in their university studies, Manyi had started working and had become independent, my wife and my cousin were in charge of the day-to-day running of the house, and family life had become a routine spread across two continents.

The family visited me in Hong Kong once or twice a year and I traveled to Barcelona in December to spend Christmas and New Year.

My contract in Hong Kong had already been renewed twice and there were no indications that it would be ending anytime soon.

THE ESIS PROJECT

In early 2002, Amadeus asked me to help him resolve a problem that was getting out of control. There was a credibility crisis over the ability of the SIS general insurance system to meet the company's needs, and several members of the management team were pressuring him to return to the old system that Eastern Star used before it was absorbed by Zenith.

Following Amadeus's request, I began to collect information and interview key people involved in the problem until I was able to make a preliminary diagnosis and form a work team to carry out the "ESIS" project, which meant something like "Evaluation of SIS".

The problem had its roots in the early 2000s, in the absorption of Eastern Star by Zenith Insurance, when it was decided to use Zenith's computer system called SIS to concentrate the entire portfolio and policy processing of the two insurance companies. general.

Unfortunately, the native SIS functionality did not represent a friendly or efficient solution for the products and work methods that were used by Eastern Star and this resulted in a notable increase in staff work hours and a deterioration in efficiency and quality of work. service.

As the months passed, the pressure increased and temporary staff were hired to reduce the pressure, but this strategy, in addition to being costly, also generated problems due to the lack of knowledge of the temporary staff.

Additionally, the general insurance IT department had underestimated the seriousness of the situation by handling it as a continuous maintenance troubleshooting process instead of defining a functionality expansion project where all users had a clear view of the scope, cost, and time horizon.

By the time the pressure explodes and the problem reaches Amadeus as an emergency, the Eastern Star database had already been migrated to SIS, and all the company's administrative processes were done in this system, but there were many users dissatisfied, tempers were heated and the IT department of general insurance systems did not have much credibility.

Going back was possible, but it would imply a new range of risks, costs, and problems to solve, but people would not be satisfied if this possibility was seriously evaluated.

With the information he had gathered, he had the basis to form a work team that would carry out a formal evaluation of the situation and recommend a solution strategy.

The work required establishing the scope of the changes, and making an estimate of the cost and time necessary to solve the problem using two possible solutions:

Develop the functionality necessary to improve the efficiency, reliability, and productivity of SIS.

Return to the old I90 system, developing a reverse migration project and developing the functionality that SIS and I90 did not have.

With the help of Tam, Steve and Burni we developed a work program that included interviews and questionnaires with more than 200 users about functionality problems and the system's ability to perform the processes required by the business.

With all the information collected, it was relatively easy to make a summary and prepare cost and time estimates for the two possible solution scenarios.

The ESIS project report was presented to Amadeus and to other members of the management team who accepted the recommendations and implemented them. Over time, SIS was substantially improved and is currently still in operation.

TWO RESIGNATIONS AT THE MANAGEMENT LEVEL

In 2002, as a result of differences of opinion between several members of the management team, two resignations occurred that would end up affecting my level of activity in the coming years.

Some defended the idea that a new customer service system had to be installed to promote a "Customer Centricity" strategy and others thought it was an unnecessary expense.

As one of the parties involved in the matter told me, the system cost more than a million Hong Kong dollars and had a significant annual maintenance fee.

During the skirmishes for and against the project, the IT manager and the life back office operations manager ended up resigning from their positions.

When this incident occurred, I had little knowledge of the subject and since I had not participated in the project I limited myself to observing the development of events.

The theory of "Customer Centricity" seemed interesting to me, and potentially useful as a business strategy since it proposed the idea that if the customer is better known, and positive, frequent, and healthy interaction is facilitated, this allows in the long run to increase product density, retention and the degree of customer satisfaction.

The problem with this approach is that an organization is needed where products, distribution channels, and service standards are well aligned so that the expected benefits are generated.

In the case of Zenith Life, we probably did not have the necessary level of alignment at that time and profitability was not positive, so we had to be very prudent in the use of resources.

MANAGING IT AND LIFE OPERATIONS

A few weeks after the resignations, Amadeus asked me if I could collaborate temporarily to replace the two vacant positions, and I said yes. I had a good command of both areas and had very good relationships with the entire management team, so for me, it was not a problem and I could help establish a good organizational climate while replacements were developed through internal recruitment.

The Computer Division had four departments, Sales Systems, Life Systems, General Systems, and Computer Services, managed by Shing, Li, Berny, and Tony.

They were all very competent, responsible, very experienced people who I knew very well, so a weekly monitoring and coordination meeting was enough to keep the ship heading in the right direction.

In the Life Operations Division, there was also a very competent team covering the Underwriting, Policy Administration, Customer Service, and Claims departments.

Becky, headed Underwriting and Policy Administration while Customer Service and Claims were headed by Josephine.

Shortly after taking charge of the Operations Division, Josephine resigned due to maternity and this created the opportunity to make an internal promotion with a very experienced person.

It was someone I knew from my previous stage, K.C. was a mature, efficient, responsible man, with a personality tailor-made for customer service.

To optimize coordination and effectiveness in the Life Operations division, I established a weekly meeting where I guided them in the search for new mechanisms to optimize services and create competitive advantages.

From this effort came several strategies promoted by Becky that were very useful:
- Monthly operational statistics book
- Monthly review of service standards
- Month-end sales goal support process

The implementation of this type of strategies significantly raised the level of communication and coordination between the Operations Division and the sales channels, which made it a little easier to achieve the life insurance company's objectives.

Additionally, the development of the MELHI project depended on the effort and coordination between the Life Operations Division and the IT Division, so being in charge of both areas made things easier for me.

BUYING AN APARTMENT IN HONG KONG

With my new responsibilities, it was becoming clear that my stay in Hong Kong would be longer than I had initially thought, so I decided that it might be a good idea to buy a small apartment instead of continuing to pay a significant amount of rent each month.

Fortunately for me, due to the SARS1 crisis in 2003, the real estate market was in a negative cycle and I got a 900-foot apartment at a very good price in a complex called "Oscar by the Sea", in the Sai district. Kung.

The apartment had never been occupied, although the building had been completed in 2001, and had a nice view of a forest and a bay from the 31st floor of a 60-story tower.

This type of residential complex with several towers and many stories high is very common in Hong Kong, but when I told my friends in Spain and Venezuela about the 60 stories, they couldn't believe it.

When I bought the apartment at "Oscar by the Sea" I thought it was a way to improve the financial efficiency of my cost of living in Hong Kong, however, in the long run, it became a permanent life changer.

My apartment was about 15 minutes from the office if there was no traffic which was normal for me since I usually left very early and returned late.

Changing the apartment hotel for my apartment turned out to be a good decision since I had more space, it was decorated to my liking and it ended up being a good deal, but it had two small drawbacks.

The first was that I had to rent an expensive parking space and it seemed illogical to me that having my apartment in the same building did not include a parking space, but this was the reality of Hong Kong, where the majority of people do not have a car and travel by subway, bus and taxi.

The second detail I discovered over time, the real estate development in the area where I lived was advancing very quickly and the traffic to my office was becoming more and more annoying, so in the long run it might be better for me to sell this apartment and buy another one. in a quieter area.

VACATIONS AND FAMILY TRIPS

Spending Christmas and New Year with the family has always been important and therefore traveling to Barcelona in December is fixed on my calendar, but as time went by each member of the family began to have vacations or commitments on different dates thus the number of trips was extended to other times of the year.

In 2002 I made a special trip to Barcelona to take my daughter Alejandra to Montpellier where she would live for a year and a half to study French in an Erasmus program. She was always very interested in learning languages, this experience added to the credits of her university degree and would allow her to perfect her level of French. After making arrangements to rent her apartment, we wandered around Montpellier and then I learned that Michel de Nostradamus had studied there about 500 years earlier, but was expelled from medical school when it was discovered that he was a pharmacist, which was illegal at that time.

In 2003 my sister Bárbara visited me, but since she already knew Hong Kong, after the usual visit to Stanley and Shenzhen we organized a trip to Beijing to see the Palace Museum in the Forbidden City, Tiananmen Square, the Great Wall, the Queen's Palace and a few emblematic sites, such as a famous restaurant specializing in Peking Duck.

In the summer of 2004, my daughter Alejandra and Isabel visited me and on this occasion, we went to many tourist sites and shopping centers as this was Isabel's first trip to Hong Kong, so visits to Stanley and Shenzhen could not be missed.

In 2005, Manyi visited me during his vacation and we took a tour similar to the one I did with his mother and Alejandra, but including the nightlife in Lan Kwan Fong, an area full of bars and restaurants frequented by expatriates and tourists. During the fifteen days of his visit, Manyi went out to explore during the day by subway and bus, and at night I expanded his tour with more restaurants and shopping centers.

In 2005, my daughter Alejandra visited me to record a documentary about Hong Kong that she would submit as her final year project. On this occasion, we toured the city from top to bottom and visited several fishing areas to take the shots she needed. In just over two weeks she completed her work plan, and everything had gone very well, but on the day of her return, she lost her mobile phone in the airport waiting room. The following Monday I mentioned it to my secretary in the office and she told me that we could try to report it as lost and found, I gave her the identification information that my daughter had given me, but I had no hope that she would recover it, inside I thought. "How is a Nokia 5110 going to appear with a Hello Kitty sticker?" However, to my surprise, two days later they called from the airport indicating that they had found it and that I could pick it up, which was one of several occasions where Hong Kong's efficiency far exceeded my expectations.

In 2005, my daughter Tatiana also visited me during her vacation from university. On this occasion, in addition to visiting the usual sites in Hong Kong, we also went to Thailand on a four-day tour that included Bangkok and the surrounding area. The time passed very quickly as there were many things to see including temples, natural parks, boat tours, Tuk rides, and a wide variety of restaurants.

THE PROFILE OF THE STAR AGENTS

Returning to my professional activity, in mid-2003, the new computer tools for the sales force were being used by the majority of agents, but a substantial change in productivity levels was not observed.

There was a positive atmosphere in the sales force, as Kenny made a continuous effort to support them with new and better services as well as new products, but productivity had not taken off and this was a worrying factor.

The graphical analyzer allowed me to take an x-ray of any agent in the network, but analyzing the client portfolio and productivity did not explain why some had very good productivity and others very bad, there had to be demographic, psychological, physical, educational or social that will help explain the large differences in performance, and if he could identify them he would have a very useful tool for the recruitment and selection of new agents that would increase average productivity.

With these ideas in mind, I began to design a small research project that would allow me to establish the profile of different groups of agents and then compare them using qualitative variables of a social, demographic, and psychological nature to the extent possible.

Due to practical and privacy limitations, I could not do an exhaustive psychological analysis of each agent based on a long sequence of individual interviews; this was beyond my scope, and would also produce some discomfort and misgivings on the network.

Taking into account these limitations, I had to work with personal surveys that the agents selected to participate in the project would have to fill out voluntarily. I could also extract some physical feature information from individual photos that were easy to obtain; everyone in the sales force loves taking photos to remember almost any occasion.

The study design included a sample of 27 star agents, 27 low-producing agents, and 27 group supervisors, although I ultimately only obtained data from 21 supervisors.

The sample of 75 agents represented just over 12% of the entire agent network and if the management levels were excluded, the representativeness almost doubled.

The selection of participants required a seniority of at least two full years in the network and compliance with the minimum production levels established for each group.

With the help of Raymond from the Training department and Shing from the Sales Systems department, I prepared the questionnaires and obtained all the qualitative and quantitative information from the 75 people.

The questionnaires that the participants completed explored, on subjective scales, the degree of satisfaction, skill, and interest in variables that could potentially explain the differences in productivity.

The qualitative information was correlated with quantitative variables that measure the dedication, effort, and frequency of certain activities related to the sale of insurance, such as inviting clients to eat or calling them by phone to make appointments.

When I finished analyzing each group, I found some useful and interesting correlations, but I couldn't identify solid factors with enough predictive value to know who could be a star agent and who was going to fail.

However, the profile of star agents, although not highly predictive, had several indicators that could guide the selection process of new agents and shed some light on the effectiveness of having various levels of supervision.

After giving the conclusions of my little research project a few thoughts, I prepared a presentation and shared all the details of the project with Kenny, Bobby, and Kevin in a business meeting where I explained the research and shared the following profile with them. of the star agents.

1.   The majority are female.

2.   Over 27 years old.

3.   Good physical appearance.

4.   Formal university education is not a common factor.

5.   High degree of self-motivation.

6.   Invest many hours a day in their work.

7.   Eat almost every day with a client.

8.   Don't need to be pushed to work hard.

9.   Are very competitive.

10.   Enjoy personal interaction.

11.   Value economic independence.

12.   Get new clients every year.

13.   Do product replacement in their customer base.

THE NEW AGENTS DEVELOPMENT CENTER

In 2004, after studying the profile of star agents, the topic of recruiting agents as a key factor to improve productivity kept turning in my head, since, although we had identified some useful elements, we still did not have a concrete plan for how to take advantage of this information.

To maintain a sales force of hundreds of people, it is necessary to continually replace a good number of agents, since, even if things are going well, there is always a high level of turnover.

Some agents leave of their own accord when they discover that the job is not what they expected, or find another job offer more attractive, develop health problems, or simply reach retirement age, others are fired for performance problems or bad behavior.

The fact is that every year a good number of new agents have to be recruited, selected, and trained. Typically, most of this process was carried out by salesforce supervisors and managers.

On the other hand, the selection criteria, the recruitment effort, and the organizational culture of each sales district are different, some districts are more careful and professional than others, some put more emphasis on quality and others on quantity of the candidates to hire. new agents.

If not enough effort is put into recruiting, the size and production capacity of the sales force will decrease from one year to the next. Additionally, the development of the agent in terms of knowledge, skills, and attitudes is a complex process that requires covering a long list of subjects, which includes topics such as analysis of client needs, characteristics of different products, investment principles, and analysis. financial, legal aspects of insurance, preparation of presentations, interpersonal interaction techniques, etc.

In parallel with the training, each agent must be evaluated to establish if they have sufficient level to face the market and pass the tests that will allow them to have their insurance agent license.

When I considered all of these elements, with the profile of the star agents, it occurred to me that if we created a "New Agent Development Center" we could improve the quality of the selection, better control the volume of new agents, and ensure that the new blood who entered the sales force was closer to the profile of the star agents that interested us.

To put this idea into practice, I needed to design a recruitment, selection, and training process that fit with the contractual principles of the sales force, included the necessary training, and had sufficient resources to attract the necessary volume of candidates.

I developed a model of the outline of all the processes and discussed the feasibility of the idea with several of my frequent collaborators included for this project Raymond, Shing, and Steve.

When I had everything in black and white I presented the idea to Kenny and we analyzed the implications, advantages, and disadvantages of developing this initiative.

Kenny reflected for a few days and finally decided to put the project into practice, so we offered Steve P. the challenge of launching the New Agent Development Center.

Steve would report directly to Kenny and would have to turn the initial theoretical design that I had prepared into something practical and achievable in the short term.

Steve was a bright, dynamic young man with very good communication skills and quickly got the project moving, integrating efforts with the rest of the areas with which he should cooperate, which included all the sales districts, and the training, marketing, and administration departments. of the sales force.

The New Agent Development Center (NADC) began operating in the second half of 2004 and was key in the maintenance, growth, and quality of the sales force for several years.

The recruitment profile, duration, and content of the training program were modified from the original plan to adapt it to market conditions.

The idea of increasing the number of star agents, unfortunately, did not materialize in a statistically representative dimension, at least in the time in which I was able to follow up on the program.

MY LAST PROJECT FOR ZENITH LIFE

In the second half of 2005, a series of changes occurred in the organizational structure of the Zenith group that would substantially affect Hong Kong.

They had appointed a new chairman in the old continent and he had a vision for Asia that began with the appointment of a regional director of Chinese origin who came from a high position in an auditing company.

When Amadeus found out that he had not been chosen to lead the development of Asia, after all the effort he had made in recent years, he decided to resign, which negatively modified my organizational environment, since Amadeus and I had developed a good professional relationship over the last five years.

Xi-Che, the new regional director, began visiting Hong Kong in a transition period with Amadeus, and it then became clear that a change of direction was in the making.

On the one hand, Xi-Che's priority was not Hong Kong and on the other, Kenny, accompanied by several of the district managers, began traveling to China to participate in the development of the life insurance business from an established fledgling organization. in Shanghai.

The NADC had proven its usefulness, but the performance of the sales force still did not reach the level necessary to meet financial expectations, since the sales districts remained a heterogeneous space of organizational culture with different levels of productivity.

Under this scenario, I reflected for several days on the situation and decided that I would not renew my annual contract that would expire in March 2006 and I presented my resignation letter to Xi-Che, in October 2005 since it had a 6-month notice clause. months.

Until now I had worked in a climate of trust, where I had very good chemistry with the people with whom I interacted regularly, but in the new organization I did not feel comfortable and additionally, political pressure was dispersing the management effort of Kenny and a key part of the district managers on a project, which in my humble opinion had little chance of success.

To replace me in the CIO position, I suggested Tam K. and fortunately he and the organization reached a positive agreement, which facilitated the transition and gave continuity and security to the IT Division work team.

On the operations side of the life business, Becky was already very competent and had taken on the role as operations manager after gaining the support and trust of Kenny and the management team.

Regarding my role as Kenny's advisor, I decided to use my last months preparing a project on the transformation of the sales force into a new organizational model that proposed the creation of different groups of agents outside of traditional sales districts.

The project was based on the principle of specialization as a source of productivity and the idea that each person reaches a maximum level of competence.

When the maximum level of competition is reached, cost and added value must be aligned in a win-win balance for the organization to be viable in the long term, otherwise excess weight accumulates and ends up destroying the organization. This involved recognizing that a large number of agents were not going to go above a certain level and so instead of terminating their contract, they were allowed to operate part-time, maintain commission income, but without having an assigned personal office space or distraction. management capacity, which are costly structural elements. On the other hand, agents who qualified for the star level, and generated high added value, would have access to more comfortable office space and facilities to hold meetings with their clients.

By eliminating the presence of very unproductive agents from the sales districts, supervisors and managers can focus on productive activities that generate added value, they could no longer be distracted by a segment of agents that we knew from years of experience was not going to work.

In my opinion, the implementation of these changes was complex and involved extensive negotiation with district managers, but if carried out it could ensure the future of the sales force, since it would eliminate non-productive overweight and optimize the structure. of costs in a period of about 18 to 24 months.

I always mentally repeated to myself, if the competition is capable of having a profitable sales force of exclusive agents, because we cannot achieve it, it is a matter of time, patience and persistence in experimenting with changes. I presented this sales force segmentation project to Kenny in October 2005 in my last presentation titled "Conceptual framework for business strategy revitalization".

Little by little I disconnected from all the processes in which I participated, trying to transfer knowledge, files and presentations to all those people with whom I had had the privilege of sharing so many special moments in the last six years.

Finally, the company organized a farewell event attended by many people from all functions and levels of Zenith Hong Kong, thus ending this unexpectedly long period of return to Zenith Insurance Group Hong Kong.

REFLECTIONS ON A NEW CORPORATIVE END

When I returned to Hong Kong in 2000, with a one-year contract, I did not imagine it would be extended for six years.

Life had allowed me to do something that I liked, and enjoyed, and allowed me to be useful in an organization where I felt appreciated by many people. Money was important, but it was never my main motivator.

I can't say that all my days working with Zenith were a walk in paradise, but in general, my good relationship with people was a key ingredient to enjoying what I did, it was the central mechanism for feeling useful and appreciated by a group of people with whom I communicated well, respected, and sincerely appreciated.

For six years, I had the opportunity to research, experiment, and contribute as part of a team of extraordinary people, determined to do their jobs well.

We all have flaws and limitations, but we can always improve, learn, and grow, as was the case with most people I shared and collaborated.

But in life nothing is permanent, everything changes over time following cycles of replacement, ups, and downs in the objectives, values , and interests of organizations and people.

Cycle changes are related to the consequences of success or failure in achieving important goals. If we succeed, it will push us to another level, if we fail or stop adapting, the environment can become hostile.

Zenith had entered a cycle change where I was beginning to feel uncomfortable with the new dominant group, their strategies and values were not compatible with my way of seeing the world, so I needed a change of environment to find a new useful, meaningful and enjoyable paradigm.

SEARCHING FOR A NEW PARADIGM

AGAIN TO THE WORLD OF ENTREPRENEURSHIP

In 2006 I was approaching 50 years of age and began a stage of my life with many changes, since I had recently been divorced, my daughters had finished university and had become independent, as had my ex-wife, who had returned to practicing medicine and received the Barcelona house in the separation of assets.

For my part, I had decided to live permanently in Hong Kong, in my apartment at "Oscar by the Sea". I had built a small investment portfolio that served as a retirement fund and allowed me to live without working, although I had a certain level of leverage in a mortgage, but if everything worked well, my financial needs for a simple life were covered as long as a major financial crisis did not occur.

As the idea of retiring had lost its appeal, and my mind needed to be active, I wanted to explore new consulting sectors, especially in the area of international trade.

My main objective was to expand my experience by developing consulting projects that I found interesting when working with clients in Asia, Europe, or Latin America.

HONG KONG IS AN IDEAL OPERATIONS CENTER

For my objective, Hong Kong was the ideal place, since it remained one of the most open economies on the planet, with excellent services, a reliable legal system, and a level of security difficult to find in other cities.

In the last 40 years, the world has globalized into a gigantic network of exchange of goods and services where China played a fundamental role, Hong Kong was at the center of the exchange process between Asia and the rest of the world, and I had some ideas and knowledge that could be useful to entrepreneurs in other countries.

At that time, the communications infrastructure was already reliable, cheap, and efficient enough to work as a team, almost anywhere in the world through video calls and electronic documents.

The handover of Hong Kong to China had not deteriorated Hong Kong's advantages as a base of operations, as it maintained an attractive level of taxation, access to an excellent banking system, and a wide range of corporate services in legal, insurance, transportation, advertising, and marketing.

Considering all these advantages, I decided to offer my consulting services from Hong Kong, with a team of consultants who could do most of their work remotely.

The first step was to buy a "Shell Company" and change its name, thus "Golden Bright International Consulting" was born.

In those days, it was super easy to buy an empty company, open a bank account, and hire an accounting services company to prepare and file the necessary reports to comply with government regulations.

After registering the company, I dedicated myself to preparing a website and recruiting a virtual team of consultants who would form the staff to offer strategic planning, reengineering, internationalization, and project evaluation services, which were the areas of activity that most attracted me at that moment.

I also spent several weeks exploring the world of international trade using Hong Kong as the gateway to buying from China and exporting to Europe and Latin America.

Hong Kong is one of the most efficient ports in the world and has all the necessary services to structure import and export transactions at low cost and with a high level of efficiency and reliability.

Within the team of consultants was my sister Bárbara and some friends and acquaintances who were in the retirement stage, but could participate in projects in their areas of competence.

When I had the website and a presentation brochure ready for the company, I started making contacts to look for projects and the first opportunity appeared.

PROMOTE HONG KONG IN VENEZUELA

The Consul of Venezuela in Hong Kong gave me access to the general director of "Invest Hong Kong", a public organization dedicated to the promotion of Hong Kong internationally, which was preparing a tour to Latin America and needed a company to prepare the ground in Venezuela to present Hong Kong as the gateway to China.

This project would be an excellent opportunity to network and explore the world of internationalization, so I prepared a very attractive proposal to the director general of Invest Hong Kong and obtained the first contract for Golden Bright International Consulting.

The contract included the logistical preparation of the stay of the director of Invest Hong Kong in Caracas, the organization of a business conference lunch with a group of 50 businessmen belonging to the Venezuelan Chamber of Commerce, and the coverage of the visit in different media such as newspapers, magazines, and television news.

My sister Bárbara would be in charge of managing the logistics of the project in Venezuela and I would travel to Caracas with the material prepared for the seminar two weeks before the arrival of the director of Invest Hong Kong.

My sister Bárbara had good contacts at Fedecamaras and thanks to her it was possible to select a group of 50 high-level businessmen and invite them to the conference lunch in a room in one of the best hotels in the capital.

Bárbara was also responsible for coordinating media relations to write articles about the Invest Hong Kong director general's visit and the conference lunch at the hotel.

The Invest Hong Kong director general's visit went smoothly, with good press and TV news coverage.

SEMINAR ON HONG KONG AND CHINA

Since the visit of the director general of Invest Hong Kong to Venezuela would create some movement of news and interest about China, I thought it would be a good idea to organize a one-day seminar to present Hong Kong as the gateway to China, and China as the factory of the world.

The seminar would be developed under the corporate image of Fedecamaras, which is the organization that brings together the chambers of commerce in Venezuela, and Golden Bright International Consulting.

The following week the seminar took place in one of the Fedecamaras rooms, where I presented all the advantages of using Hong Kong to do business with China and explained the dimensions and characteristics of the Chinese industrial base that had emerged after the creation of special economic zones.

The seminar was attended by more than one hundred people from different sectors of the economy and also had good social media coverage, including a personal interview in a high-circulation newspaper in the capital, called "Tal Cual".

When we finished the project, my sister and I were very motivated since we had contacts with several companies that were interested in opening operations in Hong Kong, but unfortunately, a few weeks later, the political situation in Venezuela evolved negatively, with a high level of legal instability, inflation, and import taxes, thus destroying internationalization projects.

However, other opportunities appeared, a SAP consulting company owned by a client of my sister was interested in developing a strategic plan and thus the second project for Golden Bright International Consulting was born.

STRATEGIC PLANNING AT CSCORP

In 2007, CSCorp was a consulting company specializing in the implementation of SAP systems and had nearly 100 consultants active in different projects in some of the most important companies in Venezuela.

The systems consulting business can be very profitable, but also very unstable since downtime between projects is very difficult to control and can force the workforce of consultants to be reduced, which can significantly damage the company's operational capacity.

In the case of CSCorp Venezuela, they were specialized in the area of human resources, which in itself is a market niche with little competition which favored them strategically, however, they had a significant dependence on a large client and this made them vulnerable.

My sister Bárbara and I were a good team and we developed several management workshops to cover the objectives of the project, the first was aimed at making an organizational diagnosis of CSCorp and its project portfolio, and the second was designed to formulate the strategic plan using the methodology SWOT with the client's management team.

The project was completed to the client's satisfaction and I returned to Hong Kong to update my own strategic plan, since the Venezuelan market did not have much potential at that time due to all the problems of inflation and legal and political instability.

While studying the opportunities in the market for the internationalization of Chinese products to the rest of the world, the client, CSCorp Venezuela, was considering merging with another company to advance its internationalization plan, and asked us to evaluate the financial and strategic convenience of a possible merger, which involved estimating the market value of the two companies and an in-depth analysis of the client portfolio and sources of competitiveness of each company.

We could do this type of work remotely, and we quickly got going. The only slight inconvenience was the 12-hour time difference between Hong Kong and Venezuela, but we adapted quickly.

Evaluating CSCorp and establishing its market value was relatively simple since we knew the client and were familiar with its financial statements; the problem was the implications of inflation and the factors of legal and political instability in the country.

The other company was in the United States and we had to request and analyze all the information to do an analysis similar to that of CSCorp.

When we finished the analysis and evaluation, the client was slightly surprised since the conclusion was that the merger was not suitable for him in the terms in which it had been proposed.

The relationship with CSCorp was maintained despite the distance and the time difference, and became a good friendship that went beyond a business relationship.

THE WORLD OF INTERNATIONAL TRADE

I continued exploring the internationalization market, I investigated the development of companies such as Amazon and Alibaba, I made new contacts in Venezuela, Spain, Colombia, and visits to manufacturers in Shanghai, Beijing, Shenzhen, and Guangzhou.

I researched the cost and conditions of international transportation methods and discovered that there is a whole network of highly sophisticated services that allow moving goods of all types to almost any part of the planet. For example, shipping a 40-foot container from Hong Kong to Barcelona can take four to eight weeks and cost between $2,500 and $4,500 depending on conditions and time of year.

I also visited several product fairs, but little by little I lost enthusiasm in this type of business since the market had already reached a high level of development, it was very competitive, and unfortunately there was also a wide range of non-transparent activities.

There came a point where almost anyone could set up an online business offering products on Amazon, presenting themselves on a website as a solid company with thousands of customer reviews that had actually been artificially generated.

This type of activity was definitely not what I wanted to do in the coming years, so once again I began a search process to refocus my professional activity.

TRIP TO EGYPT WITH MY DAUGHTER ALEJANDRA

At the beginning of 2008, when I was in the middle of reflecting on my personal strategic plan, my eldest daughter changed jobs and I suggested that we take a trip to Egypt to learn about the wonders of its ancient culture, taking advantage of the time we had available.

My daughter booked a tour from a travel agency that included activities in Cairo, Giza, Luxor, Aswan, Alexandria, and Sharm el-Sheikh since she loves diving.

The tour also included a cruise on the Nile and it was an unforgettable experience, which in many ways exceeded expectations, although it also presented us with unexpected situations.

The visit to the Great Pyramid, the Sphinx, the Temple of Luxor, the Valley of the Kings, the Temple of Karnak was worth it and confirmed firsthand how special and mysterious these monuments are.

Most of the people who assisted us were very friendly and contributed to making the trip a pleasant and memorable experience.

On the less attractive side, the traffic in Cairo is very heavy and the driving style in general is very dangerous. I remember that on more than one occasion I had to ask the driver of the vehicle we had hired to slow down since they loved to run fast and did not keep a safe distance from other vehicles.

A FINANCIAL STORM ON A PERSONAL LEVEL

Upon returning from Egypt, the 2008 financial crisis exploded and took me by surprise, since I had underestimated the seriousness of the situation in the United States and unfortunately the Bank of America, General Electric and Fannie Mae had a very important weight in my portfolio, so in the blink of an eye an important source of dividends and the value of the portfolio that supported my retirement fund disappeared.

To make matters worse, at that time I had invested in several tourist apartments in Barcelona that had a mortgage attached and normally had positive cash flow, but the financial crisis also hit the tourist market and triggered a major drop in the Spanish real estate market.

I have always tried to be a cautious optimist, so I normally invest in companies or properties with high intrinsic value and maintain a good level of diversification of my assets, but the financial crisis had cornered me like a perfect storm with a very significant drop in value. of my portfolio and its cash flow generation capacity, so I had to take emergency measures.

My experience told me that if I waited long enough there was a high probability that the value of my shares would recover and if I bought more when the panic spread I could make a good capital gain, but I had to solve my cash flow problem and wait for the opportune moment.

Fortunately, my apartment in Hong Kong had appreciated and I was able to sell it with a good profit margin, I bought a cheaper one on the outskirts of the city and with the surplus cash I was able to meet my expenses and buy more shares in Bank of America, General Electric and Fannie Mae, these assets appreciated over time, and I sold them to accumulate some profit and offset the losses.

With the tourist apartments, the story was less happy, since, although the occupancy level improved over time and the cash flow became positive again, two additional problems arose.

Tourist rentals began to have problems due to the restrictions of the municipalities and the value of the properties recovered very slowly, so

I decided to sell them when they reached a reasonable price, I finished paying the mortgage, and I got rid of a bad investment that had become a headache.

A PERSONALIZED INVESTMENT SYSTEM

As a result of all these experiences with my investment portfolio, I decided to systematize its management as much as possible, which ended in the development of a small computerized system that helps me maintain a continually updated view of my financial situation and the risks and opportunities that appeared on the horizon.

With the help of my investment control system and a good dose of reading, market analysis, and stock market operations, I compensated for the losses I had accumulated and my portfolio was once again theoretically enough to support me, however, upon careful analysis as the value of my assets had risen and fallen over the years, I discovered that the most significant fluctuations had been the result of fortuitous events.

My investment decisions had helped, but the big moves had been the product of something I could call "the hand of fate".

For example, when I lived in Venezuela, between 1983 and 1987, I bought three properties with mortgage loans and a personal loan at fixed rates, all of this occurred before a period of hyperinflation, therefore, the debt protected my purchasing power and my savings capacity.

In 1996, I decided to sell all my properties in Venezuela and transferred all the money to Spain to buy a house in Barcelona. This decision made possible an accumulation of wealth that at its current value would be unthinkable, since the deterioration of the Venezuelan economy in the last 25 years destroyed the dollar value of most of the real estate assets of the middle class.

The sale of tourist apartments in Barcelona in 2018 unintentionally protected me from the depreciation of the Euro and the collapse of tourist rentals for three years due to Covid-19.

In summary, although the financial analysis of investment vehicles, the study of macroeconomic variables and market analysis is essential to manage an investment portfolio, there are invisible forces that no investor can anticipate, therefore, there is always a level of risk that cannot be eliminated.

From this experience in my financial situation, I decided that I should dedicate between two and four hours a week to study the markets and adjust positions in my portfolio, but I could not let money be the center of attention of my daily activity.

In my humble opinion, the purpose of life has to come from a useful, pleasant and enriching activity, where you can cognitively and emotionally enjoy what you fill your time with.

DIVING BAPTISM ON TOSSA BEACH

For a long time, I had been curious to live the experience of an underwater dive with oxygen tanks, so, in 2009, on one of my visits to Barcelona, my daughters Alejandra, Tatiana and Manyi organized a diving baptism for me on the beach of Tossa near Barcelona.

The experience was interesting and unforgettable, it was quite cold, but I really enjoyed it, especially all the explanations and stories they gave me before and after the dive.

The most difficult part was adjusting the ear pressure, which was a bit difficult for me, if you can't adjust it is quite uncomfortable and even painful.

We were underwater for about 20 minutes and we did not go deeper than 10 meters since it was my first dive, the time flew by and I wanted to do it again.

Coming out of the water, I felt that the diving equipment was much heavier, since the body had become accustomed to the effects of flotation and additionally it was wet.

Walking back to the dive center also became longer, I imagine it's because of the fatigue caused by all the effort of swimming underwater, but this is all part of the experience.

After cleaning the equipment and taking a shower with fresh water, we went to eat at a nearby restaurant to finish celebrating my first dive and we spent a good time talking and sharing stories of the landscapes and marine animals that each of us had seen.

AN EMOTIONAL INTELLIGENCE PROJECT

After my 53 birthday, at the end of 2009, while reorganizing my library, I reread several of the reports I had prepared over the past few years, and suddenly realized how important emotional intelligence had been in the way I had handled many conflict situations and the difference that existed between seeing things cold or seeing them hot when emotions override common sense.

With that spark of motivation, I dusted off all the books I had on emotional intelligence, neurolinguistics, psychology and interpersonal relationships and changed the direction of my activity, pausing the development of consulting to focus on deepening emotional intelligence.

Since the first time I heard about emotional intelligence, in 1995, the topic caught my attention and I thought it was an important area that I should cultivate, however, at that time beyond reading Daniel Coleman's book, I was unable to delve deeper in a practical way.

I think most people are aware of the importance of emotional control, but they also know that it is not something easy to achieve.

I have always been very curious about psychological topics, and over the years I have become familiar through readings and some research projects with some theories and models that help understand human behavior and have a certain predictive value. In this way I came into contact with behaviorism, psychoanalysis, transactional analysis, neurolinguistic programming, and recently with cognitive models.

This knowledge has helped me understand other people, avoid conflicts and obtain cooperation, but without always reaching an adequate level in personal interaction, most of the time it works, but sometimes it doesn't.

Psychology is not an exact science and I am not sure that the psychological models I use are completely valid, but in my opinion, they generally work in a high percentage of situations.

When conceptualizing my emotional intelligence project, I imagined a three-stage process, the first would be a market study to establish people's general perception and interest in the topic, the second would be a theoretical and bibliographic review of what was available, and the third is the development of emotional intelligence tools that could be useful to many people.

The project should help people improve their quality of life through the development of their emotional skills and should be self-financing in the long term, although the main objective was not financial benefit.

THE EMOTIONAL INTELLIGENCE MARKET

With the collaboration of my sister Bárbara, my daughters and some friends in Hong Kong, I got more than 100 people to complete the research instrument in three groups of volunteers at university study institutions in Hong Kong, Barcelona and Caracas.

The tabulation of the responses indicated that more than 90% of the people knew of the importance of emotional intelligence, they did not master the topic in depth, but they were interested in the use of tools that will help them develop their emotional intelligence.

The results of the research further stimulated my interest as they confirmed the existence of a market that went beyond the cultural differences between East and West.

THE THEORY OF EMOTIONAL INTELLIGENCE

I spent almost a year rereading and summarizing all the relevant books in my library, and researching recent works on the internet, that essentially translated into the following points:

Emotional intelligence is the ability to perceive, understand, manage and express emotions appropriately.

Human beings are emotional machines 100% of the time, since everything we think or perceive has an effect on how we feel.

Many of the emotions we feel are positive, useful, adaptive, they help us survive and succeed in what we do.

Positive emotions drive us to develop useful activities and healthy interpersonal relationships. They are also the source of energy to do things that may sometimes seem unattainable, but when we put in enough effort and persistence, they materialize into important achievements.

Unfortunately, we also frequently feel negative emotions, which are destructive, do not help us and generally make life more difficult.

Learning to control our emotions is not easy, it requires time, effort and persistence, it matters more to some people than others, but in general, whoever sets their mind to it can achieve it.

THE EMOTIONAL INTELLIGENCE TOOLS

Developing emotional intelligence is fundamentally a process of behavior modification based on the acquisition of knowledge and the development of skills, so the first step was the selection of the conceptual tools that should be considered.

Fortunately, I had at my disposal a wide range of tools available in operant conditioning, neurolinguistic programming, transactional analysis, cognitive models of thinking and physiological principles derived from endocrine functioning.

I just had to design, develop and verify a model that was sufficiently useful, secure and easy to use.

The model should consist of different types of tools, some would have to be focused on providing basic knowledge, others on stimulating the development of adaptive values and others on facilitating the development of specific skills, such as communication, empathy, self-control, assertiveness, self-acceptance, self-criticism, self-responsibility and self-development.

Helping people to recognize and manage their emotions appropriately is 50% of the problem. This implies that individuals must become familiar with the mechanisms that activate basic emotions and with possible strategies to redirect their negative aspects.

The other 50% is learning to recognize and interpret the emotions of others and react in an intelligent way.

To develop the model, I created a list of concepts, functional principles and beliefs that facilitate the recognition and interpretation of basic emotions and then linked it to typical scenarios and situation management strategies in the family, social and work environment.

As the months passed, I developed cases, examples, and tests for the different skills and interaction environments that I had identified, but the list became endless; every time I finished a case, immediately I saw the need to develop another one. At the end of 2011, I decided to stop the development of new cases and began to build a prototype computerized system with the content I had at that point.

TESTING THE EMOTIONAL INTELLIGENCE SYSTEM

By mid-2012, the first prototype was well developed and I began testing it with a small number of friends and then discovered several problems and difficulties that I had not anticipated.

People needed to have many sessions and spend hours interacting with the system to cover all the content.

Some cases had problems of subjectivity in choosing the intelligent way to handle the situation or solve the problem; it was not realistic to sell the same solution model to everyone.

The number of cases and examples was not sufficient to satisfy the expectations of different age groups, occupation and family responsibility; an enormous effort was needed to populate the system with enough cases for all tastes and user profiles.

Some volunteers were concerned about the amount of confidential information they were providing to the system as they interacted with its different sections.

Some users expressed concern about the legal problems that could arise if any recommendations included in the system did not work as intended in the real world.

By evaluating the observations and comments of the people who tested the prototype, I came to the conclusion that the project was not viable with the conceptual design that I had used, I had to find a more practical, simple and interesting way to encapsulate the helping tools. to develop emotional intelligence.

People expected to interact with a system that understood, listened to and responded to them in a free and unstructured conversation; they did not feel comfortable interacting with a menu system full of questionnaires and multiple response tests.

I also had to accept a new element that I had not anticipated, although many people express interest in improving their level of emotional intelligence, there are many people who are not prepared or willing to make the necessary effort.

It is like the case of physical exercises and health, almost all adults know the importance of doing exercises to be healthy, but a high percentage is unable to make the effort. Lack of willpower and persistence is a very common weakness in human beings that limits the development of many people and I had not taken this factor into account.

After digesting the results of the prototype testing, I reflected on the project and decided that I should give it a rest period until the AI technology was developed enough to try again.

I had learned a million new things and really enjoyed developing the project, but I was tired and needed a change of activity to something that was useful, valuable and enjoyable.

FROM MERCEDES TO PORSCHE AND THEN TO TESLA

In 2012, just after archiving my emotional intelligence project, my Mercedes CLK, which I had had for several years, began to fail. I don't ride much, but having the freedom and flexibility that a car gives is something I value in my daily life.

When the mechanic checked it, he warned me that the repair could be expensive and made me an interesting offer, it was a second-hand Porsche 911, with few kilometers and at a very good price.

I was encouraged to take it for a spin and fell in love with the damned car, so I handed in my Mercedes CLK and began to live the experience of owning a Porsche Carrera 911.

I don't regret buying the Porsche as it was an interesting experience, the acceleration, the interior design, the sound of the engine, it really is a special car.

However, my luck was short-lived, since at the end of 2014 it started to fail and when the mechanic checked it, he discovered that the engine block had broken.

A new engine cost a fortune and the only more or less reasonable solution for my pocket was to make a repair not approved by the manufacturer. The mechanic bought the Porsche from me after the repair and I ended up buying other second-hand Mercedes, which in principle was an excellent deal.

It was a Mercedes CLK 500 with 30 thousand kilometers in perfect condition and at a bargain price. The problem came later when I found out that the annual registration tax was very expensive.

In 2021, something very good and unexpected happened, the Hong Kong government started an incentive policy to replace gasoline cars with electric ones, which overnight exponentially increased the value of my old Mercedes CLK if I exchanged it for a new electric car.

This way I bought a Tesla M3, handed over the CLK for scrap and ended up making an excellent deal that has reduced my annual transportation expenses significantly with a car that accelerates better than any other car I've ever owned in my entire life.

VISITING SOUTH EAST ASIA

In search of my new paradigm, starting in 2012, in addition to my end-of-year trip to Barcelona, I began to dedicate one or two weeks each year to visiting special places that I did not know, or that were worth seeing again, Traveling is not my favorite activity, but with some motivation and curiosity I can enjoy it.

KUALA LUMPUR IN MALAYSIA

My friends Julia and Steven had invited me several times to spend a few days with them in the capital of Malaysia, since they had several businesses in that country and went several times a year to an apartment they had bought in the center of Kuala Lumpur. In 2012, I finally accepted the invitation and was delighted with a multicultural environment where Malays, Chinese Hindus and a small colony of Europeans and Americans coexist in harmony. Malaysia is a country of around 33 million inhabitants and 330 thousand square kilometers with a fairly diversified economy despite being a major producer and exporter of oil and natural gas.

BALI IN INDONESIA

Bali is an Indonesian island with a population of about 5 million inhabitants and an economy based on tourism. In 2013, I joined a group of friends in Hong Kong who had organized a trip to see it and it really exceeded my expectations, the people are super friendly, there are spectacular beaches, restaurants and hotels for all tastes and you can buy a great variety of handcrafted souvenirs at a very good price. Unfortunately, the island also has a semi-active volcano, which in 2017 created serious problems for the population and the economy.

GUAM IN MICRONESIA

Guam is an American island territory in Micronesia, in the western Pacific and it was another adventure with my group of friends from Hong Kong that was worth experiencing in 2014, for the beautiful beaches we visited and an unforgettable helicopter flight around the island. On the less pleasant side, I was left with the memory of a long wait in the immigration process at the airport that echoed the consequences of the terrorist attack in the USA in 2001.

HANOI AND HO CHI MINH IN VIETNAM

Vietnam is a Southeast Asian country of around 96 million inhabitants known for the war with the USA, its Buddhist pagodas and bustling cities with hundreds of thousands of motorcycles. In 2015 I had the opportunity to visit it with my sister Bárbara on a tour that crossed the country from Hanoi in the north to Ho Chi Minh in the south. The mountain landscapes, beaches and Halong Bay are spectacular, but the history and scars of war are the part that touches your heart the most and you pray to God it will never be repeated.

DUBAI AND ABU DHABI IN THE EMIRATES

In 2016 I decided to visit this territory since I was extremely curious to see the Burj Khalifa and take a look at the long list of skyscrapers in Dubai and Abu Dhabi. The United Arab Emirates is a country of about 83 thousand kilometers and nearly 9 million inhabitants, of which 90% are foreigners. For many years it has been presented as a development model to build a service economy and stop depending on oil.

The cities are spectacular and what they have achieved in architectural terms is worth seeing, however, when digging a little under the rug, a series of social and economic problems appear that call into question the sustainability of the development they have achieved.

ANKOR WAT IN CAMBODIA

Cambodia is a country of 180 thousand square kilometers and a population of about 16 million inhabitants located in the Gulf of Thailand. I visited it on a tour with my friends from Hong Kong in 2017 since I was very curious to see the Ankor Wat Temples, with its 160 hectares and 900 years old. The visit to the temple complex is impressive, especially when considering the level of detail and artistry of the thousands of figures carved in stone.

SHANGHAI IN CHINA

Shanghai is the largest city in China when considering its metropolitan area, which has about 40 million inhabitants, and in 2018 I decided to visit it again to explore its urban development in recent years. What I saw was really impressive, it is a gigantic city that of course you cannot gauge in a weekend since it extends for dozens of kilometers. Its heart is the Bund, a famous promenade lined with colonial-era buildings. Across the Huangpu River rises the futuristic skyline of the Pudong district, including the Shanghai Tower and the Oriental Pearl Television Tower, with distinctive pink spheres.

ALEJANDRA VISITS ME ON HER VACATIONS

My daughter Alejandra has visited me in Hong Kong on many occasions, the most recent visit was during her summer vacation in 2014, at that time I swam every morning and since my daughter likes to swim, she accompanied me to the pool, even though she had to get up at 6 in the morning.

During the day we went out to explore shopping malls and eat at our favorite places in Central and Stanley, and we never missed a visit to Shenzhen.

After 2014, my daughter got married, and later the pandemic hit, suspending trips to Hong Kong for several years.

TATIANA AND HER DIVING VACATION

My daughter Tatiana loves diving and has organized her annual vacation several times combining it with a few days in Hong Kong.

In 2014, before going diving in Palau, Micronesia, she came to Hong Kong with Jaume, and we had a great time visiting shopping malls, restaurants, and emblematic sites since it was Jaume's first time coming to Hong Kong. In 2016 her diving trip was to Okinawa, Japan, and she combined it with a week with me in Hong Kong. In 2017 she also organized her holiday with a diving trip, this time to Sipadam, an island east of Malaysia and then visited me in Hong Kong. In 2018 her diving destination was Puerto Galera in the Philippines, but first she spent a few days with me and some of her old classmates from the international school in Hong Kong.

Whenever my daughter visits me we have a great time touring Hong Kong and enjoying our favorite restaurants in Stanley, Central and the Gold Coast.

I remember that, on one of our outings in 2018, we went to a Japanese restaurant that I didn't know and I discovered that it was completely automated, orders were placed from a tablet and the food arrived in a small robotic cart that moved along a track to where we were sitting.

Another special experience was watching a marathon of episodes of a Netflix series with my daughter until dawn since we were hooked on the plot and couldn't stop.

As of 2020, travel to Hong Kong was suspended due to pandemic restrictions, but we have contact almost daily.

BACK TO THE UNIVERSITY

Since I was a child, I have always been very curious about the physical and cognitive functioning of the human being, but I had not had the opportunity to do it full time, and now at 56 years old at the beginning of 2014 it seemed like the right time.

Postponing the emotional intelligence project and visiting the south east of Asia, led me to identify the acquisition of knowledge as the vital energy of my life purpose. Learning something new is something that I have always enjoyed, especially if it involves topics that make my imagination fly.

I knew that the road would be long, but I was sure that I was going to enjoy it, I needed a purpose that would make my time a useful, pleasant and enriching experience, so I embarked on this new journey of exploration of the human being.

Understanding the phenomenon of life requires exploring an immense universe of knowledge where everything is interconnected, but humans have been forced to divide it into different sciences and specialties due to our cognitive limitations and chronology of scientific discoveries.

To have a comprehensive and systematic understanding of the human being, I had to become thoroughly familiar with different disciplines to put together a puzzle that integrated elements of physiology, neurology, anatomy, biochemistry, bacteriology, virology, genetics, and psychology.

Medical and biological knowledge would help satisfy my curiosity, but it would also be useful in my personal life, since the years were beginning to take their toll with prostate hyperplasia, hypertension, and type 2 diabetes in their early stages.

Through recommendations from friends and searching the internet, I had discovered four high-quality platforms that suited my needs, but I had to focus with a study plan, otherwise I could get lost in an incoherent ramble.

I analyzed the medical curriculum of several universities and prepared a study plan that focused on Coursera and was complemented with videos from the other three platforms, some books from my library, and consulting Google from time to time.

UNIVERSITY COURSES IN COURSERA

Coursera.org: It is a company created in 2012 by two Stanford University professors, which has become one of the best online learning platforms, currently offering more than 5000 courses and specializations, developed by teaching staff from more than 150 of the best universities. The cost per courses ranges between forty and one hundred dollars, but they have payment facilities and allow you to view the content for free. The courses contain a wide range of teaching aids and knowledge tests that, if you pass them, allow you to obtain a certificate.

ANATOMY WITH CORPSES

TheAnatomyLab: A YouTube channel specializing in human anatomy, using donated cadavers for medical teaching, has more than 5.7 million subscribers, and more than 400 videos available.

The videos do not replace the practical experience of working with a cadaver, but they give a very realistic feeling and totally different from what you learn from anatomy texts.

MEDICAL TOPICS IN DEPTH

NinjaNerdOfficial: It is a YouTube channel dedicated to the production of high-quality didactic videos to teach almost all the curricular content of the medical career. Each video covers a specific topic, developing it in a very didactic way that allows you to understand the content in depth.

MIT MASTER CLASSES

MITOpenCourseWare: It is a channel that contains more than 7 thousand videos that teach practically the entire MIT curriculum, from the introductory to the advanced level. I mainly used material related to neurology and psychiatry topics. The videos are recorded during master classes and are generally of very good quality.

THE EFFECT OF PASSING 41 COURSES IN 7 YEARS

Following the curriculum, I completed 41 courses and reviewed the content that interested me in another 27 between 2014 and 2020, these seven years passed so quickly that I almost lost track of time.

When you do something you love, the hours fly by and I often had to set alarms to force myself to take breaks that I used to exercise, go to the grocery store or clean the car.

When I talked to my friends and family about my study program, I often shared details of what I was studying at the time, but I think I abused their patience more than once, because when I get excited about a topic, I tend to talk more than necessary.

As I advanced in my search for knowledge about the structure and functioning of the human being, my degree of admiration for nature grew and it became increasingly difficult for me to accept the idea that human beings are just the product of millions. of years of evolution without the intervention of an intelligent entity.

There are too many things that have to fit together perfectly for an organism to stay alive, grow and function physically and cognitively, but many people are not aware of this, some due to ignorance and others due to an ideological conception that, in my opinion, overvalues theory. of natural selection.

I remember that in one of the courses I took on human anatomical development, I learned that when children are born, they have small structures within the jaw bones that will transform over time into the two systems of teeth that will emerge during growth.

When I saw the x-ray images, I thought it was obvious that the movement and growth of these small structures had to be carefully planned and controlled. Nature had anticipated a process that would take many years to complete in each human being; it did not occur simply because the child stimulated the gums when biting; the teeth are part of a plan that includes two sets of teeth and requires about 20 years to complete.

The case of teeth is like that of the fusion of vertebrae in the coccyx, the closure of the foramen ovale in the heart, the involution of the thymus, the growth of bones, sexual development and menopause.

The existence of a plan in the anatomical and physiological design of the human being is evident and undeniable; however, we still do not know in what language it is written, although it is believed that it is encoded in DNA.

In any case, these examples stimulated my imagination and made me reflect on how it was possible for so many things to happen in our bodies and we were not aware of them.

As a consequence of my exploration of the vast ocean of medical and scientific knowledge that I had the opportunity to see, I introduced changes in my lifestyle, my perception of scientific development, my attitude towards some industries and in my way of conceiving the human being.

On a personal level, I made substantial changes in my eating habits, my physical activity, and my attitude toward aging.

These changes have given me very good results and alone make all the time and effort made very profitable.

When it comes to the use of medicines and medical services, I also made important changes by reducing the frequency of their use, to give nature more opportunities to do its work.

Regarding the scope and depth of medical and scientific knowledge, I progressively developed a feeling of humility in understanding how little we still know.

Although civilization has made leaps and bounds in the advancement of medicine, we are still light years away from having the upper hand.

There is the problem of technology transfer and the massification of medical services, which continues to be a pending issue for the majority of the world's population, even in developed countries, many effective treatments are not within the reach of the majority of people and I am not sure of whether they will be.

If life expectancy rises too quickly and the problem of the low birth rate in developed countries is not corrected, there will be many old people and few young people everywhere and the economic systems will collapse. From this perspective, I wondered to what extent the Government leaders will be interested in substantially improving medical services, thus extending life expectancy.

The advancement of medicine is continuous, but it depends on the development of other sciences, interdisciplinary cooperation, and the continuous improvement of treatment protocols. I am sure that we will continue to move forward, but it is not an easy path.

There is a long list of experiments that would give us very useful information, but we cannot do them with living people, and finding the answer in other ways is not always feasible. The results of experiments with animals cannot always be extrapolated to the human species.

On the other hand, in the functioning of life, there are phenomena at the atomic and molecular level linked to quantum physics that we still have no idea how they work or the technology to study them.

I also suspect that there is a level of energy and matter that is not scientifically known and could explain well-documented cases by highly reputable doctors of near-death experiences and regressions to previous lives that point to the transfer of information through unknown mechanism.

THE THIRD GENERATION BEGINS

In July 2017, my daughter Alejandra began to experience the profound beauty of being a mother. My first granddaughter was born in Barcelona, a beautiful baby girl named Valentina, who marked the beginning of the third generation.

It was a normal birth and thank God everything went well. Valentina's birth was a momentous event for the entire family, for some of us, it was the first time they could call us grandfather, grandmother, or aunt and for others like Alejandra and her husband Joan the beginning of a path full of countless joys, scares, satisfactions and a long list of new responsibilities.

PHYSICAL EXERCISE CHANGED MY LIFE

After completing several physiology and pathology courses, I learned well about the details behind some cardiovascular diseases and how physical exercise contributes to good health.

By applying what I had learned about physiology and the adaptations the body makes depending on the exercise profile, I realized that, although my level of physical activity was apparently healthy, it was far from producing the effects I needed.

I must especially thank the creators of four excellent courses on this topic:

1. Exercise Physiology, The University of Melbourne.
2. Science of Exercise, University of Colorado Boulder.
3. Introductory Human Physiology, Duke University.
4. General Pathophysiology, Saint Petersburg State University.

In those years, I had the habit of swimming 30 minutes a day, but I did it at very low speed, almost without increasing my heart rate, or inducing an appreciable adaptation in my muscular strength, I consumed very little energy and only lightly exercised some of the muscles of the body. It was almost like walking through the park contemplating nature, it is healthy, it is pleasant but not enough.

To reduce the risks of my hypertension and the type 2 diabetes I was developing, I needed to make major changes to my swimming or I could experiment with different exercise routines at home.

After thinking about the issue, I decided that the most practical thing would be to experiment at home with different exercise routines since I could control the times, record the exercises on video, and keep records of the movements, heart rate and blood pressure.

I started with 15-minute routines that were progressively extended by incorporating new movements and more repetitions until after two years I reached 90 minutes, at which point I eliminated swimming.

The daily practice of the exercise routine has produced very good results for me, including the normalization of blood pressure, the disappearance of type 2 diabetes, substantial improvements in physical resistance, a significant improvement in the symptoms of benign prostatic hyperplasia and an excellent mood to start the day.

Ninety minutes of exercise a day may seem exaggerated, but we must keep in mind that each person is different, not the entire session is high intensity and for me it is an activity that I really enjoy since I combine it with music, and it fills me with energy.

High intensity exercise, even for a few minutes, causes blood with oxygen and nutrients to reach the entire body, including peripheral tissues, this activates cellular metabolism and facilitates the release of accumulated toxins.

If a person spends a lot of time sitting or lying down, there are many parts of their peripheral tissues that are not properly oxygenated and accumulate toxic waste that is harmful to health.

The capillaries where the gas exchange of oxygen and carbon dioxide takes place have a diameter ranging between 8 and 10 microns, while red blood cells have a diameter of 5 to 7 microns.

Considering these dimensions, red blood cells do not have an easy time passing through the capillaries if we are resting on that tissue.

Without physical activity, muscles begin to atrophy, the skin deteriorates and eventually bedsores occur in areas without movement or adequate oxygenation.

The human body was not designed to spend the entire day at rest, it needs physical and cognitive activity to maintain good health, it is like a mechanism that if not used rusts, and if used properly it becomes stronger and more powerful.

IMPROVEMENTS IN MY EATING HABITS

Learning to visualize food as a biochemical process was another benefit of my study program that helped me formulate and adopt a healthier and balanced diet, additionally it made me reflect on some cultural aspects of food.

In this matter I must especially thank the creators of four excellent courses that I am sure can be very useful to a large number of people:

1. Introduction to Food and Health, Stanford University.
2. Understanding Obesity, The University of Edinburgh.
3. Exploring Your Microbiome, University of Colorado.
4. Diabetes - a Global Challenge, University of Copenhagen.

Eating to satisfy our energy and nutrient requirements is a basic human need, but the development of civilization has turned eating into one of the pleasures we can experience most frequently, and also into a huge food industry that frequently manipulates us with incomplete information, which is a serious problem that especially affects developed countries.

Obesity, cardiovascular disease, type 2 diabetes and some types of cancer are associated with poor eating habits.

We have created a culture where the quality and quantity of the food we consume does not match what we really need, instead, it responds to values, customs, and incomplete information about what is healthy and what is not.

We tend to eat and drink excessively which leads the body to accumulate nutritional surplus, we consume an excessive and unnecessary amount of sugar, sodium, preservatives, sweeteners, saturated fats and alcohols that in high quantities harm the body.

Our body is a very efficient machine that is not programmed to waste nutrients or energy, therefore, if we consume more than we need, we simply accumulate it, a small part in the form of glucose and glycogen, in the liver and muscles, but most of it in the form of body fat.

The body fat in theory will be used when we need it, but in practice that day never comes for most people in the modern world.

When we lived by hunting and gathering, things were different, as we often did not have access to enough food and were forced to frequent fasting.

Our genetic programming drives us to consume certain types of foods through taste, but for several generations the industrialization of food and the transculturalization of food customs has distanced us from a natural diet adapted to our ecosystem, which we have to replace with a diet guided by marketing and purchasing power in a multicultural society.

In nature, each species has a diet adapted to its physiology and dependent on the ecosystem where it lives, which tends to maintain the balance of the species and the food chain.

But humans have broken with the basic rules of nature and by dint of technology and commercial ingenuity, we have created a universe of foods that exploit our genetic tendency to seek certain flavors and nutrients, but without the balance that nature normally maintains.

A cow or a mare can eat grass all day, be healthy, produce muscles, milk, bones and everything they need from a food that humans cannot digest. This is possible because their digestive system is "designed" to process efficiently fiber and extract nutrients.

In the case of humans, if we ingest fiber, we cannot digest it and therefore we cannot assimilate it as a nutrient, but in return it helps us with intestinal transit, feeds the bacteria of the intestinal flora and helps us feel satiated, which is relevant because we overeat and have pushed our digestive system to select bacteria that feed on fiber.

If we have a diet rich in sodium, either because we put a lot of salt in our food or because we consume a lot of processed foods, the body will be forced to retain more fluid to regulate the electrolyte level, the increase in fluid will raise blood pressure and if this becomes chronic it will lead to permanent damage to the cardiovascular system and hypertension.

If we consume alcohol, it will progressively cause damage to the liver and when metabolized it becomes fat, this means that for the short time we enjoy with a drink, we end up paying dearly.

In short, our diet is a pleasure, a danger, and a basic need that we must satisfy intelligently to avoid serious health problems, but we must fight a battle every day to eat healthily and overcome the negative influence of advertising, industrialization of food and the consumption distortions that our society has created.

THE THIRD GENERATION GROWS

In March 2019, my second granddaughter was born, a beautiful and very healthy blonde baby girl named Avril. We were expecting her the following month but the girl was a few days early.

Like her sister Valentina, she came into this world in a normal birth and once again filled the entire family with the joy and tenderness that only a new life can generate.

Avril was another gift from heaven to give a friend and companion to her sister Valentina and feed the existential purpose of her parents, grandparents and aunts.

MY ENCOUNTER WITH COVID-19

In 2020, when I began to understand that the COVID-19 pandemic was much more serious than I had initially imagined, I began to closely monitor the information that was published about the situation in the countries where my family was, and I ended up developing an information system to analyze the evolution of the pandemic worldwide, which gave me the opportunity to put into practice the knowledge about virology and epidemiology that I had acquired in my medical studies.

Johns Hopkins University maintained an online database with very complete information on new cases and deaths in more than 140 countries, but it did not show some important parameters such as the speed of spread or the number of cases and deaths per million inhabitants.

The first weeks I did the calculation in an Excel sheet, but after a while with the help of my friend Shing I began to copy the Johns Hopkins database every day to my computer and that way I could easily generate what interested me.

From these analyzes I was able to draw some conclusions that, beyond clarifying the issue from a scientific point of view, taught me the political and social side of the pandemic.

The figures per million inhabitants indicated that many countries did not report the data correctly, or manipulated the information for political reasons.

What the official figures indicated, what my family told me on the phone from the West and what I could observe personally in Hong Kong was very different from what appeared in the media.

Covid-19 officially infected more than 700 million people and caused more than 7 million deaths, worldwide. These figures in general are much lower than reality since I am sure that many cases were not reported even in the best organized countries.

On the other hand, the greatest impact of the pandemic was not the deaths caused by the infection, since during 2021 and 2022 global mortality increased by only 0.043%, however, the world economy did have a significant drop estimated at one 3.4%.

More than one hundred million people lost their jobs, hundreds of thousands of businesses closed, and millions of families experienced economic and social problems and a deterioration in their quality of life.

A SELF-HELP BOOK IS BORN

At the beginning of 2022, when the world was going through a difficult time in the COVID-19 pandemic, and I divided the day between my medical studies and the analysis of financial markets, a very important person in my family environment began to have self-esteem problems that affected her quality of life.

Every time we spoke, I tried to help her, sometimes by listening and other times with some advice or suggestion, but it was not easy to give effective help from a distance, so I began to write her supportive phrases, advice, book summaries, articles, and even questions I thought could it be useful.

As time went by, the material that I had sent her accumulated and one day I realized that it was over 100 pages long and then I thought that this material could be useful to other people who had similar problems and thus the idea to write a book about self-esteem and interpersonal relationships.

I began to organize the material I had prepared, I reread all my research projects on related topics, I analyzed several books already published on the subject, I developed new examples, I modified some tests from my time as a consultant and structured a first table of contents.

At this point, the initial hundred pages had turned into two hundred and I had a first draft of something that could be a self-help book.

My idea was to combine examples, cases, diagrams, questionnaires and some theoretical explanation in a sequence that would lead the reader in a process of self-assessment of their personal interaction skills, values and beliefs to help them identify areas of strength and areas of weakness with which to structure a plan for personal improvement of self-esteem and interpersonal relationships.

Then I decided to tell my sister Bárbara about the project and asked her to help me do a first review, since I had no idea if the material was clear and attractive enough.

My sister carried out a first review, suggested that I make some changes and proposed that we use the figure of the zero reader with a group of people she trusts to have a more representative opinion, which I thought was an excellent idea.

At this stage of the project, I was still moving forward with my medical study program, but I had long understood that I was traveling a path with no goal of arrival, since there was always some new course to review, or some research work to read, so I had to slow down my study schedule if I wanted to finish the book.

With the help of my sister I prepared a second manuscript and she distributed it among the zero readers who had about two months to read the text and send their comments.

Meanwhile I distributed my time between monitoring the markets, my study plan, refining some parts of the content and learning about how to publish a book.

On YouTube I discovered that there is an entire industry that allows the publication of texts on various platforms, among which Amazon stands out, which allows publishing in Kindle format and in printed version almost at no cost to the author.

Time passed and we began to receive comments from zero readers that were generally quite good, that motivated me even more to finish the book and I decided to add some additional chapters to it.

By now the book had grown to about 250 pages and then my sister and I discovered how hard it is to do a thorough spelling and editing check, since the MS Office spell checker does not cover the entire spectrum needed and I had to hire the services of an expert person to do this work since the one who writes the text does not see the errors and the editor is too contaminated with the material.

With a refined manuscript, the next step was to choose the physical size for the printed version, the images for the cover, the title, the subtitle, and the presentation summary of the book.

After spending a week looking for images and analyzing titles, it was finally time to upload the book to the Amazon platform for publication.

It had been over eight months since I had the idea to turn 100 pages of supportive messages into a self-help book, and I was finally about to hit the button on my computer to publish it on Amazon.com.

Once the book was published, I bought several author copies at cost to send to some friends and family and 10 days later I received the books at my apartment in Hong Kong in an Amazon box, it was a special experience to see the effort that had gone with the help of my sister from Venezuela, converted into a 6x9-inch, 250-page book, printed in "Moneé, IL, USA" on November 15, 2022.

Amazon has transformed the publishing industry, turning a long, complex process reserved for a minority into a system where anyone who has the imagination and the necessary discipline can publish a book, which does not necessarily improve the level of quality of what is published, but gives access to the majority to express their ideas and points of view.

Twenty years ago, to publish a book, a publishing company had to be convinced to assume the risk of a first edition, or the author had to make a risky investment assuming the costs of a small number of copies that should absorb the value of printing materials, printing machine time, operator time, layout designer, copy editor, illustrator, graphic designer, and legal advisor.

All of this has been replaced by a computer platform where the author, individually or with his team of collaborators, prepares an original in PDF or other compatible formats, uploads it to the platform, it performs some verifications and in less than 24 hours the book is available throughout the planet so that anyone can buy it online and receive it at their home in a few days.

In this publishing model, books are not kept in stock, they are printed to order if they are printed versions, or a download is authorized if it is the Kindle version, which allows immediate access on any compatible device.

WRITING IS AN ENRICHING EXPERIENCE

At 66 years old, at the end of 2022, I was able to personally see that writing a book is an extraordinary and very enriching experience, in which you learn a million things.

You have to learn how the new publishing world works, but the most important thing is the reflection process that generates the responsibility of writing something that in theory can be read by many people.

It doesn't matter if the book is a publishing success or not, as soon as you publish it, it is available worldwide and begins to appear in Google searches, this makes it a communication window that you have opened to the entire world, but only those who look inside will see its content.

Amazon is a platform that grows every year by just over 4 million titles, this is equivalent to more than 10 thousand new books every day available to a world that is losing the habit of reading and consumes information in concentrated pills on social networks, electronic games and internet search engines, but this did not discourage me, since I believe that in some way the universe will put my book in front of whoever needs it, it is like a small grain of rice that can appear in your food on the day that goes well for you.

After the launch of the Spanish version, I began the translation process into English, since my life takes place in this language and my circle of friends was curious to read it.

After finishing the translation, I repeated the process of asking for feedback from a zero group of readers, but this time they were friends in different countries at the south of China.

When I received the comments I was surprised, since the opinions were more varied than in the first group that reviewed the Spanish version.

A zero reader of Chinese origin commented that self-esteem was a very personal topic and that many people would not see it well if someone gave them a book on this topic.

Another zero reader of Chinese origin thought that it was a very useful and interesting topic and suggested exploring the applications in the work environment.

Another zero reader of Malaysian origin mentioned that he had never read a self-help book and that possibly many people had a certain predisposition towards this type of reading.

A zero reader of Anglo-Saxon origin did not look very favorably on the literary style and the cultural content contained in some examples.

Two young readers in Hong Kong found it very useful and interesting material, they also mentioned that reading the book had been useful to them in their personal lives.

By carefully analyzing the comments, I understood that I had to broaden my way of viewing self-help tools. I had entered this topic from a perspective in which self-esteem and interpersonal relationships were two factors of great importance in the life of any person, and that we all had some unfinished business in this matter, however, based on the response of some zero readers, not everyone thinks the same and this is important, since perception is more heavy that reality.

We think and behave based on what we know and what we perceive, not based on reality, which in practice is an approximate dimension and to a certain extent unknown to the mind.

After living the experience of conceiving, developing and publishing a book in a complete cycle, I came to the conclusion that writing to publish is an activity compatible with my purpose of searching for knowledge and that would help me in my evolutionary process as a human being.

REFLECTIONS ON THE LAST STAGE OF THE JOURNEY

Life has passed me by very quickly, without realizing it, I am in the last stage of the journey, I have no idea how much time I have left ahead of me, it could be more than 20 years, but I can also run out of time at any moment, no one is exempt from suffering an accident or a devastating illness, what changes over the years are the probabilities.

A few years ago I decided that the important thing is not how much time I have left, but how much I can get out of each day, to turn it into a useful, pleasant and enriching experience, which depends largely on factors that are under my control, for example:

- Physical exercise.
- Eating habits.
- Learning habits.
- Sleeping habits.
- Entertainment activities.
- Socialization activities.
- Adaptability.
- Planning horizon
- Purpose of life.
- Attitude towards life.

Each age has its advantages and disadvantages, in youth we are more agile, adventurous, impressionable and competitive, but that does not mean that things are easier, the lack of experience and knowledge makes us vulnerable to entering paths that sometimes do not have neither a good destination nor an easy return.

When we are older, we often have the luxury of looking at things calmly, reflecting, enjoying the moment, and finding meaning, value, and beauty in what a young mind doesn't have time or context to discover.

Understanding physical, mental, hormonal, cellular, genetic and cultural aging is super important since this way we can manage it, delay it and to a certain extent reverse it. It's like watching the weather forecast, if you know it's going to rain, you can take an umbrella with you.

In my opinion, age does not depend on the number of years we are, it is a consequence of how we feed and use the mind, the body, and the spirit that God has assigned to us.

Surrounding yourself with the right people is a super important element at any age, it is very difficult to enjoy life if you live totally isolated or if you live with the wrong people.

Humans need to socialize to give meaning and purpose to our existence, for which it is always useful to remember that we have the ability to build and destroy our interpersonal relationships.

If you learn to enjoy acquiring knowledge you become a lifelong student, as you have discovered an inexhaustible source of purpose and satisfaction.

There are so many things to learn and so little time available, that it is impossible to get bored or run out of important goals in life.

My intention is to continue learning and sharing part of what I have experienced and learned on my path through this beautiful but complicated planet, sometimes it will be about scientific topics that I am passionate about and other times it will be like in this book that I am about to finish, sharing stories with ideas and experiences that may be useful to some of my dear invisible readers.

If you are young, live your life with enthusiasm, enjoy and take advantage of your time, learn everything you can, if you are old I recommend that you do the same, only adapting to a level compatible with your physical and cognitive abilities.

Remember that the important thing in life is not what happens to you, it is how you handle it.

I wish you all the best in this world, see you in the next book.

ANNEXES AND BIBLIOGRAPHICAL REFERENCES

344

COURSES COMPLETED BY THE AUTHOR ON COURSERA BETWEEN 2014 AND 2020

The Science of Stem Cells	American Museum of Natural History	Grade Achieved: 98%
Dermatology: Trip to skin	Novosibirsk State University	Grade Achieved: 89.95%
An Introduction to Consumer Neuroscience & Neuromarketing	Copenhagen Business School	Grade Achieved: 100%
Advanced Neurobiology II	Peking University	Grade Achieved: 93.59%
Learning How to Learn: Powerful mental tools to help you master tough subjects	University of California San Diego	Grade Achieved: 92.83%
The Brain and Space	Duke University	Grade Achieved: 85.31% *with Distinction*
Introductory Human Physiology	Duke University	Grade Achieved: 85.44%
Stanford Introduction to Food and Health	Stanford University	Grade Achieved: 100%
Introduction to Clinical Neurology	University of California, San Francisco	Grade Achieved: 96.19%
Epigenetic Control of Gene Expression	The University of Melbourne	Grade Achieved: 93.04% *with Distinction*

Clinical Kidney, Pancreas and Islet Transplantation	Universiteit Leiden,Leiden University Medical Center	Grade Achieved: 87.16%
Introduction to Dental Medicine	University of Pennsylvania	Grade Achieved: 98.50%
Bacteria and Chronic Infections	University of Copenhagen	Grade Achieved: 81.66%
Thoracic Oncology	University of Michigan	Grade Achieved: 97.27%
The Addicted Brain	Emory University	Grade Achieved: 96.58%
Caries Management by Risk Assessment (CAMBRA)	University of California, San Francisco	Grade Achieved: 78%
Anatomy of the Chest, Neck, Abdomen, and Pelvis	Yale University	Grade Achieved: 99.21%
Introduction to Human Behavioral Genetics	University of Minnesota	Grade Achieved: 92.85%
Whole genome sequencing of bacterial genomes - tools and applications	Technical University of Denmark (DTU)	Grade Achieved: 96%
GPS: An Introduction to Satellite Navigation, with an interactive Worldwide Laboratory using Smartphones	Stanford University	Grade Achieved: 91.84%

Genes and the Human Condition (From Behavior to Biotechnology)	University of Maryland, College Park	Grade Achieved: 97.40%
Dog Emotion and Cognition	Duke University	Grade Achieved: 100%
Virology I: How Viruses Work	Columbia University	Grade Achieved: 90.60% with Distinction
Case Studies in Personalized Medicine	Vanderbilt University	Grade Achieved: 96.66%
Antimicrobial resistance - theory and methods	Technical University of Denmark (DTU)	Grade Achieved: 98%
Introduction to Genomic Technologies	Johns Hopkins University	Grade Achieved: 95.50%
Vital Signs: Understanding What the Body Is Telling Us	University of Pennsylvania	Grade Achieved: 86.90%
Schizophrenia	Wesleyan University	Grade Achieved: 85%
Understanding the Brain: The Neurobiology of Everyday Life	The University of Chicago	Grade Achieved: 89.05% with Distinction
Psychological First Aid	Johns Hopkins University	Grade Achieved: 90%

Philosophy and the Sciences	The University of Edinburgh	Grade Achieved: 68%
Understanding Memory: Explaining the Psychology of Memory through Movies	Wesleyan University	Grade Achieved: 94.28%
Introduction to Neuroeconomics: how the brain makes decisions	HSE University	Grade Achieved: 83.47% *with Distinction*
Astrobiology and the Search for Extraterrestrial Life	The University of Edinburgh	Grade Achieved: 88.30%
Diabetes - a Global Challenge	University of Copenhagen	Grade Achieved: 100% *with Distinction*
Stories of Infection	Stanford University	Grade Achieved: 100%
Synapses, Neurons and Brains	Hebrew University of Jerusalem	Grade Achieved: 83.75%
Circadian clocks: how rhythms structure life	Ludwig-Maximilians-Universität München (LMU)	Grade Achieved: 71.80%
Genomic and Precision Medicine	University of California, San Francisco	Grade Achieved: 75.65%
Exercise Physiology: Understanding the Athlete Within	The University of Melbourne	Grade Achieved: 67%

Programmed cell death	Ludwig-Maximilians-Universität München (LMU)	Grade Achieved: 72.80%
Nanotechnology: The Basics	Rice University	Grade Achieved: 96% *with Distinction*
Experimental Genome Science	University of Pennsylvania	Grade Achieved: 69.73%
Advanced Neurobiology I	Peking University	Grade Achieved: 95.76%
Acute and Chronic Rhinosinusitis: A Comprehensive Review	Icahn School of Medicine at Mount Sinai	Grade Achieved: 100%
How Viruses Cause Disease	Columbia University	Grade Achieved: 90.40% *with Distinction*

MACROECONOMIC DATA ABOUT VENEZUELA

View Venezuela's External Debt from Mar 1997 to Mar 2019 in the chart:

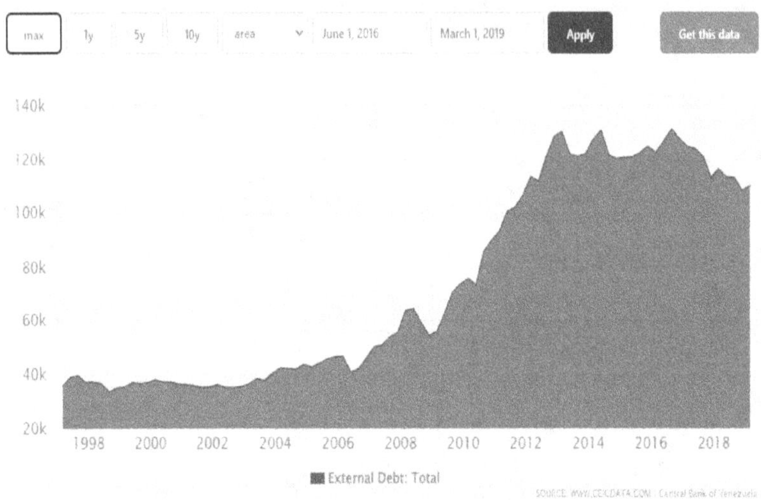

Below, we show how the price of oil has changed in response to various events over the last five decades.

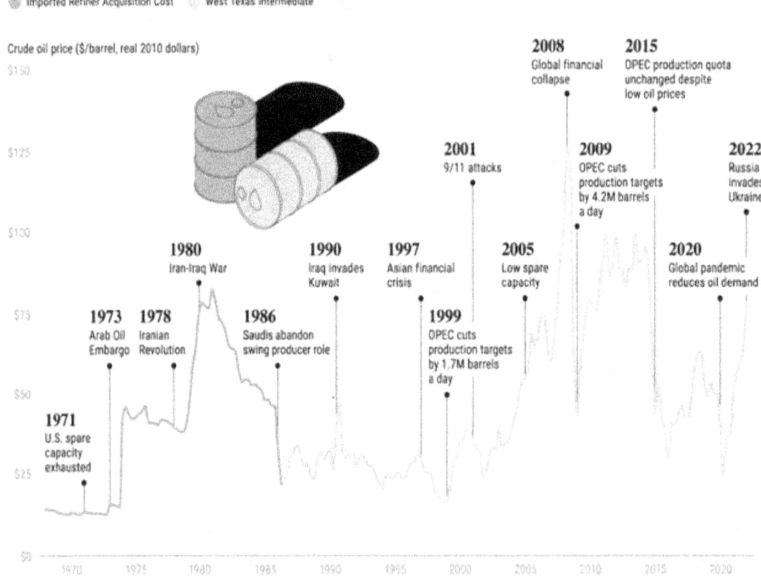

INTERNET WEB PAGES	
Coursera High-quality courses from more than 150 universities	
The Anatomy Lab YouTube channel with high-quality teaching anatomy videos.	
Ninja Nerd Official Canal de YouTube con clases de temas médicos con alta calidad didáctica.	
MIT YouTube channel with basic and advanced curriculum classes.	
IBM S/38 Intermediate range system, launched on the market in 1978 including advanced functions of large computers.	
IBM AS/400 Released in 1988, compatible with the S/38, it offers a wide range of intermediate range capabilities.	
IBM 4341 Processor compatible with the 370 series, released in 1979.	

IBM 4381 Processor compatible with the 370 series, released in 1986	
The Monetary and Fiscal History of Venezuela 1960–2016	
SAP/R3 Enterprise resource planning (ERP) software produced by the German corporation SAP SE.